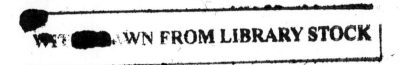
FOUNDATIONS IN CONTEXT

FOUNDATIONS IN CONTEXT

Editor

Scott Slorach

Contributors

George Daly, Susan Evans, Robert Foxall, Edward Jones,
Alex Morrice, Stuart Roberts and Trevor Tayleur

Published by
College of Law Publishing, Braboeuf Manor, Portsmouth Road, St Catherines, Guildford GU3 1HA

British Library Cataloguing-in-Publication Data

A catalogue record for this book is available from the British Library.

ISBN: 978 1 909176 10 2

Typeset and Designed by Style Photosetting Ltd, Mayfield, East Sussex
Printed in Great Britain by Ashford Colour Press Ltd, Gosport, Hampshire

Contents

Preface

This book is a 'foundation for the foundations', for law students to use before and during their study of the foundations of English Law – Contract, Tort, Criminal Law, Public Law, EU Law, Trusts and Land Law. It has been designed to be different. There are few references to legislation and even fewer to cases. However, there are many examples of the law in context. 'Context', in this context, means commonplace, readily understandable situations governed by the major principles and rules of English Law. Put another way, the prevalent situations which English Law has developed to govern.

This book, then, is designed to provide law students with clarity as to the purpose and practical effect of the foundations of English Law. It aims to provide answers to the questions 'why?' and 'how?' rather than simply 'what' the law is.

Many LLB and GDL students encounter English Law purely in the context of complex cases that deal with matters of interpretation, or complex fact patterns, or both. As a result, the purpose and principles of the foundations, and their common practical applications, become lost within the detail and complexities of a multitude of cases. By removing complexity, *Foundations in Context* is designed to provide a clear path to a proper understanding of the purpose and principles of English Law. With this understanding, students will be better placed to develop their knowledge of the more complex and academic areas of each foundation, and so make the most of their studies.

Professor J S Slorach
The College of Law

Abbreviations

CE	Conformité Européenne
CFSP	Common Foreign and Security Policy
CICA	Criminal Injuries Compensation Authority
CJEU	Court of Justice of the European Union
CMA	Competition and Markets Authority
CPS	Crown Prosecution Service
EC	European Community
ECHR	European Convention on Human Rights and Fundamental Freedoms
ECtHR	European Court of Human Rights
ECJ	European Court of Justice
ECSC	European Coal and Steel Community
EEC	European Economic Community
ETD	Equal Treatment Directive
EU	European Union
EURATOM	European Atomic Energy Community
HMRC	HM Revenue and Customs
JHA	Justice and Home Affairs
MEP	Member of the European Parliament
NCA	national competition authority
NHS	National Health Service
OFT	Office of Fair Trading
QMV	qualified majority voting
R	Regina or Rex (ie the reigning monarch)
RGM	relevant geographical market
RPM	relevant product market
s/ss	section/sections
SEA	Single European Act
SI	statutory instrument
TEU	Treaty on European Union
TFEU	Treaty on the Functioning of the European Union
v	versus (against)
VAT	value added tax
WTD	Working Time Directive

CONTRACT

CHAPTER 1

INTRODUCTION

Contracts are part of life. Unless you live on a desert island, far away from modern civilisation, you will come into contact with contracts from the moment you open your eyes in the morning.

You wake up in your flat (which you rent from your landlord under a tenancy agreement), make your bed (having recently paid for your duvet to be dry-cleaned), switch on your new television (bought on a monthly payment plan and for which you have purchased a television licence), turn on the bathroom light (which is powered by electricity that you buy from an energy provider) and jump into the shower (the water purchased by direct debit from your water company, and the shower gels and shampoo having been part of your weekly supermarket shop) – all before you grab a coffee (utilising your loyalty card points at a well-known coffee shop) on your way to catch a bus (the ticket for which you buy from a ticket machine beforehand) to your workplace (where you are paid for doing your job).

The previous paragraph contains many examples of everyday contracts and illustrates that contracts really are an integral part of modern society. While most people do not have a detailed understanding of their rights under 'contract law', many have enforced their rights by, for example, returning a defective product to the shop from which they bought it and being refunded the purchase price. Academics have their own favourite definitions of what is meant by the phrase 'contract law', but the theme that runs through all of them is a collection of rules regarding the enforceability of agreements made between individuals, consumers and businesses (or any combination of these parties).

While contract law is largely concerned with what happens when things go wrong, it is worth noting that the vast majority of contracts work out just fine. Clearly, though, when things do go wrong, knowledge of contract law becomes very useful. Who is liable? Does the contract itself cover what the parties should do? Are any legal rules imposed by the state that provide a solution? What is the likely outcome following legal proceedings?

As we shall see, some key ingredients are needed to make a contract. First, there must be an agreement (offer and acceptance) between the parties. However, since all contracts are agreements but not all agreements are contracts, other requirements must be met too, ie the intention of the parties to be legally bound by their promises to each other, and the presence of 'consideration'.

This, of course, presumes that each party has legal capacity to contract and, in certain situations, that some additional rules (referred to as 'formalities') have been complied with.

A contract contains terms – some of which are expressly stated and some of which are implied (even where the contract makes no mention of the point). We shall look at a few of these, including 'exemption clauses' which are used to limit one party's liability when the contract goes wrong.

A contract may be invalidated by a number of factors, such as illegality, mistake, where one party makes a misrepresentation, and duress or undue influence by one party upon the other. We shall look at these scenarios, as well at how contracts come to an end (referred to as being 'discharged') and the remedies available when things go wrong.

This work is not intended to be a definitive guide to contract law; there are many excellent academic texts already available. Instead, it has been written to cover some of the key aspects of contract law and provide contemporary examples, as well as to promote thought and discussion. It is hoped that, having read the following chapters, the reader will be keen to learn more about the issues discussed, by referring to their substantive studies and academic texts.

CHAPTER 2

FORMATION OF A CONTRACT

WHAT ARE THE KEY INGREDIENTS OF A CONTRACT?

A contract is much like a cake. Whilst they both come in many flavours, shapes and sizes, the key ingredients always remain the same. For a contract, these are offer, acceptance, consideration and intention to contract.

Before we look at each of these key ingredients in more detail, along with some additional issues, it should be noted that there are two main categories of contract which exist in society today: bilateral and unilateral.

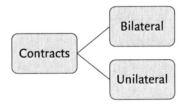

Figure 1: Categories of contract

The vast majority of contracts are bilateral, where each of the parties takes on an obligation.

> **EXAMPLE**
>
> Bob agrees to sell his smartphone to Julia for £300. He is promising to sell the phone (Obligation 1) and Julia is promising to buy it for the agreed price (Obligation 2).

Unilateral contracts are different, in that only one of the parties takes on an obligation – usually to pay if the other party attains the desired objective.

> **EXAMPLE**
>
> Tracey instructs a local recruitment agency to find her printing business a new receptionist. She signs an agreement stating that she will pay the agency £300 and 3% of the receptionist's first gross monthly pay should the agency find a suitable worker. In these circumstances, Tracey has clearly made a promise, but the agency has not promised to do anything in return, although it would clearly be in its own financial interests to find a suitable worker.

AGREEMENT

In a contract, one party must make an offer ('the offeror') and the other must accept it ('the offeree'). Once acceptance takes place, an agreement exists. Provided the other key ingredients – consideration and intention to contract – are also present, the agreement becomes a contract which is binding on both parties.

Figure 2: Elements of an agreement

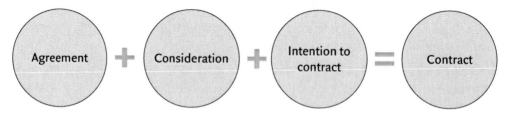

Figure 3: Elements of a contract

Let us look at some of these aspects in more detail.

OFFER

Normally, an offer will be made to a specified person, for example when Bob offered to sell his smartphone to Julia for £300 (above). However, an offer may be made to groups of individuals, or to even the whole country.

EXAMPLE

The course record for a marathon is 2 hours 15 minutes. On the entry forms, the organisers offer £1,000 to the first runner to beat this time. This year, the winner finishes in 2 hours 14 minutes. The entry form contained an offer to all runners, which became a (unilateral) contract when the winner beat the previous record. Acceptance is when the runner beats the course record. That runner is therefore entitled to the £1,000.

Whilst everyone envisages a contract being a formal document that contains writing or which is typed, there are very few rules requiring contracts to be in such form (see 'Which Contracts Must be in Writing?' below). The vast majority of contracts do not need to be in writing and may simply be made by words spoken between the parties. However, if a contract is written, the record of what was agreed can act as a reminder to the parties and act as evidence should anything go wrong and legal proceedings become necessary.

Invitations to treat

The formation of some contracts starts with just one party inviting others to make an offer.

EXAMPLE

Bob advertises his smartphone in the free local classified newspaper. He says he wants £300 for it but is open to offers. Bob has made an invitation to treat. Barbara contacts Bob with an offer of £250. Even though hers is the only offer that he has received, Bob is within his rights not to sell to Barbara since the £250 was merely an offer which Bob is not obliged to accept.

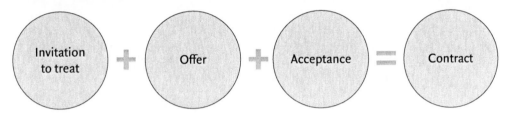

Figure 4: Invitation to treat becomes a contract

Price-marked goods on display at shops and supermarkets are also invitations to treat rather than offers to sell goods at that price.

EXAMPLE

Jenny visits her local supermarket and puts some bread (£1.15), a pack of eco-lightbulbs (£3.79), a fashion magazine (£1.95) and 2 litres of milk (97p) in her trolley. The sticker prices are invitations to treat placed on the items by the shop. When she presents the items at the checkout, Jenny has in effect made an offer, which is accepted only when everything is scanned at the checkout and payment is taken by the cashier.

This means that everyone is free to change their minds up to the point of acceptance, which from a shopper's perspective is a good thing. So, if Jenny had mistakenly picked up semi-skimmed milk, she is able to swap it for skimmed milk before the point of sale. In fact, the number of unwanted items placed to one side of many supermarket checkouts shows that this option is often utilised (perhaps without knowledge of the legal implications) by shoppers.

Another consequence of invitations to treat is that shops do not have to sell goods at the marked price, so if the eco-lightbulbs had mistakenly been priced at £1.50 but when scanned came up at the true price of £3.79, Jenny could not insist on buying them at the cheaper price. This does not mean that the retailer will refuse to allow the sale at the reduced price (usually thinking of goodwill and public relations), but legally it would be within its rights to decline the sale (Jenny's offer).

In addition, a shopper cannot insist on a shop selling a particular item to him (for example, a window display model of a heavily-discounted games console when it has sold out of its shop-floor stock). Displaying the goods is not an offer, merely an invitation to treat, so the shop may refuse to accept the shopper's offer to buy the goods.

What about self-service checkouts?

This method of paying for shopping seems to be on the increase due to the smaller size of supermarkets in built-up areas and the potential cost savings through needing to employ fewer members of staff. Nothing really changes from the standard invitation to treat scenario described above – there is simply a machine rather than a human cashier acting on behalf of the retailer.

> **EXAMPLE**
>
> Reggie goes to the express self-service checkout as the normal checkout queues are lengthy and his lunch break is almost over. When he self-scans the items, Reggie is making an offer for them. When the machine totals the items and asks for payment, it is accepting Reggie's offer.

What about auction sales?

In a traditional auction, the person who makes a bid is making an offer. If he is still the highest bidder at the end, when the auctioneer lets fall his hammer (the acceptance), the contract is made between the seller and the bidder.

It follows that the auctioneer may withdraw an item from auction at any time, provided a bid has not been accepted as part of the auction process. Earlier bids cease to be valid ('lapse') when a higher bid is made.

Online auction websites operate under similar principles. If the seller offers a 'buy it now' option, this is a standard offer which is accepted by a buyer using this method of purchase.

What about public transport?

Explaining this in a contractual sense is far from straightforward, since it is difficult to be sure where offer and acceptance fit into the process of buying a ticket.

Let us take travel by bus as an example:

(a) Is the timetable an offer by the bus company which is then accepted by the passenger boarding the bus, or is the offer accepted (once the passenger has boarded) when the passenger asks the conductor for a ticket?

(b) Is the offer made when the conductor issues the ticket, which is then accepted by the passenger paying for it?

Most people would say that the order in which these things occur really does not matter; the important point is that the passenger gets to his destination on time. That is certainly true, but there may be major consequences if the contract contains a clause, printed on the back of the ticket, limiting or excluding liability arising from the contract. In such a case, identifying what constitutes the offer and acceptance, and the point at which they become a contract, becomes very important. We shall look at exemption clauses further below.

Nowadays, with increasing installation of automated ticket machines along bus routes, matters are much simplified. These machines make an offer (subject to a whole array of conditions listed on screen) which is then accepted by the passenger pressing the on-screen 'confirm' button.

When does an offer end?

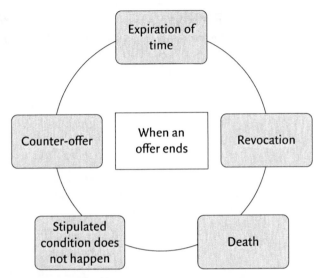

Figure 5: When an offer ends

The first way in which an offer may end before a contract is made is through expiration of time. If an offer is open for a fixed time, once that time has ended, the offer can no longer be accepted. If the offer is made without any mention of time, it lapses after a reasonable period of time. This is a question of fact depending upon the method used in communicating the offer and the subject matter of the proposed contract.

An offer to sell company shares (the price of which changes rapidly on the London Stock Exchange) or perishable foods (such as dairy products) would lapse after a very short period of time, whereas an offer to sell concrete blocks or aluminium cans would probably lapse much later.

An offer may always be made subject to conditions, as shown in **Example 1** below.

> **EXAMPLE 1**
>
> If Bob agrees to sell his smartphone to Tabatha for £300 next Wednesday lunchtime, provided she has a coffee with him beforehand, this would amount to a conditional offer, meaning that if Tabatha turned up at the coffee shop with the money, seconds before everyone was to return to work (and unable or unwilling to have that coffee), Bob would not be bound to sell the phone to her.

An offer may also end when the person to whom it has been made rejects it, as in **Example 2** below.

> **EXAMPLE 2**
>
> If Tabatha had simply said no to Bob's offer, that would be the end of it. Tabatha could not then meet Bob for a coffee on the following Wednesday and insist on accepting the offer.

A counter-offer will end the original offer, as seen in **Example 3.**

> **EXAMPLE 3**
>
> If Bob's offer had been met by Tabatha saying she would pay £290 for the smartphone but her sister Mary would meet him for coffee instead (a counter-offer), Tabatha could not later accept Bob's original offer as this is no longer available – Tabatha's counter-offer ended it.

Lastly, in the case of the death of a person who made an offer, provided the person to whom the offer was made does not know about the death, the offer remains open, so an acceptance will still be valid if the contract could be performed by the estate of the deceased. Much obviously depends upon the subject matter of the contract and whether it involved some form of personal service (which will now be impossible).

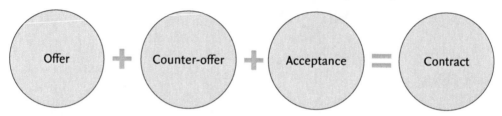

Figure 6: How a counter-offer situation becomes a contract

Can an offer be withdrawn?

The person making the offer may withdraw it prior to its acceptance, provided he or she takes reasonable steps to make prospective offerees aware of the change of circumstances. This will not be a problem in supermarket cases since these involve invitations to treat, but in situations such as the marathon (mentioned above), the organisers would have to notify entrants of the withdrawal of the offer prior to the event.

ACCEPTANCE

We have already seen that acceptance of an offer is a key ingredient of a contract. As stated in **Example 3** above, in respect of the Bob and Tabatha coffee scenario, a purported acceptance which does not accept all of the terms proposed by the seller but which actually introduces new terms can never be an acceptance since it is a counter-offer (which ends the original offer).

There are some additional rules governing an acceptance. The first is that it must (subject to acceptance by post, discussed below) be communicated properly to the offeror.

> **EXAMPLE**
>
> Desmond meets Farah in Kew Gardens and offers to sell his vintage Betamax video recorder to her for £100. Just as Farah begins to say she agrees to the terms, her voice is drowned out by an overflying aircraft heading to Heathrow. In these circumstances, there is no contract since Farah's acceptance was not validly communicated to Desmond. Farah would obviously have to repeat her acceptance once the plane had flown past (and before the next one flies overhead).

In a similar vein, an offer is valid only when it is communicated properly to the person to whom it is made. Needless to say, this is rarely a problem, but what if someone effectively accepts an offer which he or she never actually received?

> **EXAMPLE**
>
> Sangy offers £50 for the safe return of her missing cat and posts reward posters around the neighbourhood. Unaware of these, John finds the cat and is able to return it to Sangy. In such circumstances, John would not be entitled (legally rather than morally) to the £50, since to hold this to be a binding contract would be to say that John is subject to all obligations under the contract of which he would otherwise have been unaware. Acceptance must be in response to an offer.

Can silence amount to acceptance?

We have already seen that an offer may be made subject to conditions (**Example 1** above). Might one condition be that silence is to be the method of acceptance?

> **EXAMPLE**
>
> Vanessa is selling her car. She speaks to Paul, who offers to buy the car for £5,000. Paul asks Vanessa to think about his offer, but says that if he does not hear from her by the following Monday, he will consider the car to be his at that price. Vanessa does not contact Paul by the following Monday. In these circumstances, there will be no binding contract between Vanessa and Paul, since Paul has no right to impose a sale of a car unless Vanessa contacts him to accept his offer. Silence can never amount to an acceptance.

Acceptance by post

There are some circumstances in which acceptance may occur without being communicated to the person who made the offer. Where an offer is made by letter, it may (subject to anything stated to the contrary) be accepted by post. If an offer is not made by letter, it is a question of fact whether it would be reasonable to accept by post, so offers made in person, by phone, fax or e-mail are unlikely to allow acceptance by post.

Where the postal rule applies, acceptance will occur when it is posted rather than when it is received and read by the person making the offer. The reason behind the rule is historical, since a century ago sending a letter through the postal system generally took a lot longer than it does today and carried a high risk of delay or loss. The issue was whether it should be the offeror or the offeree who should bear this risk. It was decided that the offeree should be protected, since the alternative (of there being no valid contract until the offeror received the acceptance) might increase the risk of fraud by offerors (eg, a seller who claimed he never received the acceptance and who sold the item concerned for a higher price to another person) and impact upon the increasing speed of business transactions.

> **EXAMPLE**
>
> Raj writes to Sheila offering to sell her a 46" LCD TV for £1,000 and asks for an acceptance by return. He posts the letter on 10 June. Unfortunately, Raj's woeful handwriting confuses the Royal Mail's scanner and the letter does not arrive until 15 June. Having heard nothing from Sheila, Raj sells the TV to Frankie on 16 June. Sheila, on receiving Raj's offer, immediately posts her acceptance back to Raj on 15 June; Raj receives it on 17 June. In these circumstances, the contract between Raj and Sheila was made before the TV was sold to Frankie.

A timeline often helps in working out situations like this – see **Figure 7** below.

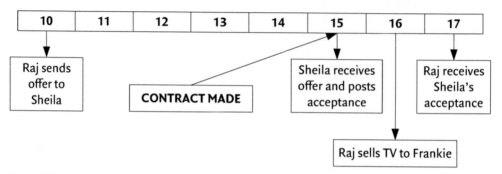

Figure 7: The postal rule

The contract between Raj and Sheila was binding on 15 June as soon as Sheila's acceptance was posted. Raj acted unlawfully by selling the TV to Frankie.

Proving when a letter was posted is relatively easy nowadays, with certificates of posting, 'signed-for' and special delivery options available at post offices. Proving when the letter was actually opened and read by the person making the offer would be practically impossible, so retention of the postal rule today makes sense.

INTENTION TO CONTRACT

This essential ingredient of a contract is sometimes referred to as an 'intention to create legal relations'. Irrespective of the wording, it simply means that agreements of a social or family nature are presumed not to be legally binding.

> **EXAMPLE**
>
> Karl notices his next-door neighbour, Joanne, having car problems one morning and offers her a lift to work. Joanne accepts and says she will contribute to the cost of the petrol, but in the event she does not. In these circumstances, there is no binding contract under which Joanne may be sued. As the arrangement was an informal, social one, Joanne's offer to pay for petrol probably was not made with the intention of being legally bound.

Whilst the presumption is against social or family arrangements having been intended as binding contracts, in the case of commercial or business arrangements, these are presumed to be intended as binding contracts. These presumptions may, of course, always be rebutted by producing evidence to the contrary.

CONSIDERATION

The final ingredient for a contract is consideration. This means either a benefit to the person receiving it, or a detriment to the person giving it or both. In other words, each party to the contract must give something in return for the other's promise.

> **EXAMPLE**
>
> David agrees to re-lay the lawn in Donald's back garden. Donald agrees to pay David £965 for doing this. In this contract, there are two promises: (a) David's promise to re-lay the lawn; and (b) Donald's promise to pay for the re-laying. Both are examples of consideration.

Many rules have evolved regarding consideration – see **Figure 8** below.

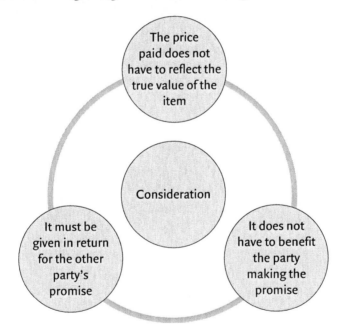

Figure 8: Rules concerning consideration

The price paid does not have to reflect the true value of the item

> **EXAMPLE**
>
> Jack sells his designer skateboard to Amy for £1. It does not matter that that is in no way close to being adequate when compared to the true value of the skateboard. It is still valid consideration.

The actual adequacy of consideration will not be called into question, provided there is some consideration. This is based upon the ideal of freedom of contract, whereby the parties themselves are allowed to make deals which suit them without state interference.

The consideration need not benefit the party making the promise

> **EXAMPLE**
>
> Henry promises to pay Reena £500 if she gives his son Tommy a course of 12 piano lessons. Henry refuses to pay after the last lesson. Reena will be able to enforce Henry's promise even though she has given no direct benefit to Henry. Reena has clearly suffered a detriment in that she has provided the music lessons.

The consideration must be given in return for the other party's promise

> **EXAMPLE**
>
> Jenny looks after Jane's chinchillas for two weeks while Jane is on holiday. Upon her return, Jane promises to pay Jenny £20 for her efforts, but no payment is ever made. In these circumstances, Jenny would not be able to enforce Jane's promise of payment since she had not agreed to look after the chinchillas in return for the money (she had agreed to do so out of friendship).

CAN EVERYONE BE A PARTY TO A CONTRACT?

It is often assumed that everyone has the ability (known as 'capacity') to enter into a contract, thereby binding themselves to the agreement reached. However, this is far from true. Society imposes rules in an effort to protect its most vulnerable members. In this regard, there are three main categories of person to consider (see **Figure 9** below).

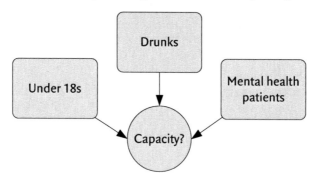

Figure 9: Capacity and categories of person

Under-18s

The rules imposed upon those aged under 18 are designed to protect them from their own lack of experience. In short, such persons will only be bound by a contract when it is, on the whole, for their benefit, taking into account their needs and age. These are legally known as 'contracts for necessaries' and relate not only to typical everyday consumer transactions, but can also concern the buying of clothes, private tuition and entering employment.

> **EXAMPLE**
>
> Jason, age 13, goes to the local newsagent to buy a bike magazine (£1.90) and a small bar of chocolate (79p). These items would be classed as 'necessaries'. However, if Jason then went to the local butcher's shop and placed an order for a joint of beef for Christmas (£45), it is unlikely that this order would be deemed a 'necessary' on the facts and it would not be binding upon Jason.

Many teenagers work part-time (and many 16- to 17-year-olds work full-time). A contract of employment is binding upon them if, when viewed as a whole, it is for their benefit.

> **EXAMPLE**
>
> Todd, age 16, works on Saturday at his local leisure centre. He has no contractual hours (so cannot be guaranteed work) but normally works from 10am to 2pm with an hour's lunch break. He is also entitled to discounted admission fees. When viewed as a whole, the contract is clearly beneficial to Todd and thus is binding upon him.

Mental health patients

Those individuals suffering from mental health issues and whose property is under the protection of the state are incapable of entering into a contract. In the case of other mental health patients (whose property is not under state protection), a contract is binding upon them unless the incapacity was known by the other party or should have been reasonably obvious.

Drunks

It sounds bizarre that society considers drunks as worthy of protection when they have clearly brought about their own 'incapacity'. However, fairness dictates that if someone enters into a contract but is so drunk that he or she does not know what he or she is doing, and this fact is known by the other party, the other party should not be able to benefit from the drunk person's impaired mental state. Hence, the contract will not be binding upon the drunk person. The same principle would also apply to people who were high on other drugs.

WHICH CONTRACTS MUST BE IN WRITING?

Most contracts are made from words spoken, although many are written or typed so that there is a record of what was agreed. There are, however, certain types of contract that must be in writing because society deems it necessary to maintain a written record of certain transactions. Reasons include consumer protection, confidence in the financial markets and also raising tax revenue (as it is the documents relating to certain transactions between parties that are liable to taxation rather than the transactions themselves).

Amongst the contracts that must be in writing are documents transferring the ownership of company shares from one person to another, certain consumer credit agreements (like the 'buy now, pay nothing for 12 months' type deals), guarantees (where one person promises to pay a debt owed by another if that person is unable to meet his or her payments), promissory notes (where one party promises to pay a certain amount of money to the other at some point in the future) and contracts relating to land (such as buying, selling or leasing a house). Some contracts, such as a power of attorney (whereby a person grants another the power to deal with his or her financial affairs), also have to be executed as a 'deed', which requires additional wording.

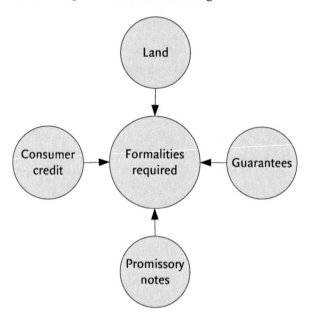

Figure 10: Contracts requiring formalities

WILL ALL THE TERMS OF THE CONTRACT BE STATED EXPRESSLY?

Sometimes a contract may not state every term expressly. The parties may omit terms that ideally should have been included to assist when things go wrong. The reasons for this may include insufficient time before the contract must be finalised, a lack of foresight or inexperience in writing (often referred to as 'drafting') a contract.

In certain situations, terms will be implied into a contract by custom, the courts and, most importantly, statutes (meaning Acts of Parliament) and their related statutory instruments (these being the rules that fill in the detail of the general provisions laid down in an Act of Parliament).

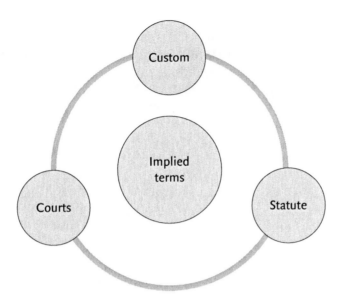

Figure 11: How terms are implied

Terms implied by custom

If the contract is silent on a matter, a term may be implied on the basis that it is so common in the market sector in which the parties' businesses operate, that they must have intended it to be a term of the contract.

Terms implied by the courts

The courts may be required to imply an otherwise unexpressed term into a contract to give effect to the presumed intention of the parties. In other words, the parties must have intended to include the term (even though it was never expressly stated) since having it was so obvious with hindsight.

Terms implied by statute

There are numerous statutes which imply terms into particular types of contract.

EXAMPLE 1

Dinah sells electrical appliances for a living. She agrees to sell a television to Bobbi and only expressly agrees the price and timing of delivery. The television does not turn on when plugged in. If there had not been a term relating to the product having to be fit for purpose (in short, here, to work as a television), Bobbi would be left without a remedy. The Sale of Goods Act 1979 implies such a term into every consumer contract.

EXAMPLE 2

Reena is a sales assistant for S Ltd. She has worked there for four years. Due to a downturn in business, the company sacks Reena with immediate effect. Her contract of employment states she should be given two weeks' notice of any dismissal. Reena wants to know whether she is able to claim two weeks' worth of pay. The employer has clearly breached her contract of employment. However, it is not just two weeks' worth of pay that Reena is due. The Employment Rights Act 1996 implies a term into all contracts of employment governing the length of notice an employer should give to employees when dismissing them. The implied term is a minimum term of notice based upon length of service – the parties can agree more, but never less. In Reena's case, she would be entitled to four weeks' notice despite her contract stating she was entitled to only two weeks' worth. She would be owed four weeks' worth of net pay.

Many statutory instruments also imply terms:

EXAMPLE 3

Greg decides to renew his holiday insurance by phone. He agrees to enter a new contract of insurance, but the sales representative forgets to inform him of a seven-day 'cooling-off' period within which Greg can change his mind and be refunded his premium (payment). Greg changes his mind about the new contract 10 days later. In this scenario, the Consumer Protection (Distance Selling) Regulations 2000 imply into Greg's contract a cooling-off period of (an extended) three months.

The state has increasingly intervened in contractual matters, and this does appear contrary to the concept of freedom of contract. That said, statutory implied terms have been justified as a way for the state to maintain minimum standards of behaviour and performance. Alternatively, they might be viewed as Parliament's attempt to consolidate and codify previous court decisions into one set of laws to make things simpler. However, its clear that, given the sheer volume of legislation now relating to contracts, the scope of freedom of contract has narrowed over the years. We shall look at another piece of legislation later, when discussing exemption clauses – the Unfair Contract Terms Act 1977 – which itself implies terms restricting the use and exclusion of terms implied by other statutes.

CHAPTER 3

ILLEGALITY

ARE THERE ILLEGAL CONTRACTS?

In this chapter we examine the concept of illegality, ie those contracts that may be illegal at the outset and those that may become illegal through the use to which they are put by one of the parties.

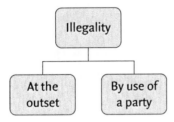

Figure 1: Illegal contracts

CONTRACTS ILLEGAL AT THE OUTSET

It will not come as a surprise to learn that such contracts include those involving the commission of a crime (including fraud and tax evasion) and those which are 'contrary to public policy'. Examples include the promotion of corruption in public office, those prejudicial to public safety and contracts that further anti-competitive practices (often referred to as acting in 'restraint of trade').

EXAMPLE

Dev hires Jeff to kill his business partner. Dev pays Jeff £500 up front, with the promise of another £500 after completion of the 'hit'. On the agreed day, Jeff refuses to do the job. Dev asks for the return of his £500, but Jeff says he has already spent the money.

If a contract is formed with an illegal intention, it is deemed to be void (meaning that it is treated as though it never existed) and so neither party will acquire rights under the contract or be able to sue for any breach. In the above scenario, this obviously rules out Dev suing Jeff for the return of his £500.

LAWFUL CONTRACTS THAT BECOME ILLEGAL

Some contracts are lawful at the outset but are then used by one party to achieve an illegal purpose. In this situation, an innocent party is entitled to be restored to the position he or she was in before the contract was made.

> **EXAMPLE**
>
> Gwen is a self-employed lorry driver. She enters a contract with a factory owner to deliver 10 tons of toxic material to a recycling plant by 9.00 am on Thursday. Gwen will be paid £500 plus expenses. Gwen is told the material must be delivered by that time, otherwise the factory owner will have to pay £2,000 under his contract with the recycling plant. Unknown to Gwen, but known to the factory owner, the legal limit on a lorry transporting toxic material is 9 tons. Gwen spends £200 on fuel. Gwen is late delivering the material. In these circumstances, the factory owner would be barred from suing Gwen for breach of contract, but Gwen would be able to recover the £200 expenses.

Whilst being unable to recover for loss of profit is far from perfect, restoring the innocent party to his or her pre-contractual position does illustrate how once absolute principles (here, that since all illegal contracts are void, the parties' losses fall where they lie) have evolved into general principles (with exceptions) in recognition of their potential unfairness and impact upon innocent parties to contracts.

Another example of a general principle with exceptions is contracts subject to competing public policy interests. In these circumstances, such contracts are said to be void unless they are reasonable in certain aspects. For example, the concept of free movement of workers and their skills may sometimes be at odds with the expectation that someone should be bound by their promise to another.

> **EXAMPLE**
>
> Bella works as a stylist at a top hairdressing salon based in London. Her contract of employment contains a clause which prohibits her from competing with her ex-employer within a 50-mile radius and for two years after Bella has left the salon.

Because of the competing public policies, rules have evolved so that such clauses will be upheld only if the employer has a real business need to protect and the restriction is no wider than is necessary to protect this business need. In other words, the actual terms of clause must be reasonable as to the breadth of any geographical limitation and the length of time for which the restriction will last.

Given that it is unlikely that all of Bella's ex-employer's clients will follow her to a new salon, meaning that it is doubtful that there is a legitimate business need requiring protection, it is unlikely that the geographical area in the clause will be justified. The 50-mile restriction is far too wide (it would effectively deny Bella the ability to work, since the whole of London would be prohibited, along with surrounding towns all the way to the south coast). As a general rule, a restriction for more than 6–12 months will also be difficult to justify, so the two-year restriction would be considered too long. The end result is that the clause in Bella's contract would be void as contrary to public policy.

CHAPTER 4

DURESS AND UNDUE INFLUENCE

WHAT IF I AM PRESSURED INTO MAKING A CONTRACT?

Much depends upon who has exerted the pressure and how much pressure there was or what it involved. If a party has truly been forced into a contract then this would run contrary to the idea of his or her agreement being given freely and would render the contract voidable (allowing the innocent party to choose to bring the contract to an end – see 'Rescission' in **Chapter 7** below). However, a party cannot rely upon the typical pressures associated with running a business or an inequality of bargaining position (eg, you in comparison with your favourite supermarket) as evidence of being 'forced'. As we shall see, for there to be a case of duress or undue influence, improper pressure must be at play.

DURESS

Duress means violence, or illegitimate threats or pressure which coerce a party into entering or varying a contract. The innocent party has to show that duress occurred.

EXAMPLE 1

Brian tells Derek that unless he awards him a valuable contract to supply computers to Derek's business, Brian will infect Derek's existing system with a virus. Derek agrees to award the contract to Brian's business.

EXAMPLE 2

Two companies are negotiating the terms of a deal when Company A informs Company B that unless it agrees to certain terms, Company A will do a deal with a rival business instead. Company B, worried about a loss of future revenue, accepts the terms offered.

The first scenario constitutes duress, since Derek is making the contract only because of a threat of damage to property. The second scenario is likely to constitute merely typical (and legitimate) commercial pressure and so will not amount to duress. There will also be cases where illegitimate pressure is placed upon one contracting party, who is left with no practical choice but to agree to the other party's demands. This will be a question of fact and degree, but will cover a situation where a family is forced to leave their home due to flood damage, only to discover that their insurance company will only pay for temporary accommodation if the family waive a valid claim for replacement carpets.

UNDUE INFLUENCE

Undue influence is not concerned with threats of violence or damage to property but with unacceptable influence over a person's decision whether to make a contract. In the same way that it is hard to be precise as to where legitimate commercial pressure ends and economic duress begins, the issue here is at what point influence becomes 'undue' in nature. The solution seems to be to list those relationships offering the potential for abuse (eg, doctor–patient and solicitor–client) and then to consider whether the contract that was made resulted from the dominant party abusing its position in the relationship. If the terms of the contract give rise to suspicions (perhaps by being too one-sided) then (unlike duress) the dominant party has responsibility for showing that the innocent party was not unduly influenced (eg, by showing the innocent party had an opportunity to seek independent financial or legal advice).

CHAPTER 5

MISTAKE

WHAT IF I ENTERED INTO A CONTRACT BY MISTAKE?

The old saying that mistakes often happen in life inevitably includes situations when contracts are made. The effect that a mistake has upon the contract depends on what the actual mistake was. Mistakes in some situations will result in the contract being non-binding because the parties had never, in fact, reached agreement.

Three types of mistake have been recognised over the years – see **Figure 1** below.

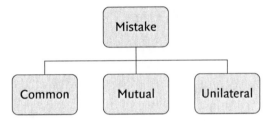

Figure 1: Types of mistake

COMMON MISTAKE

This is extremely rare, since it concerns a situation where both parties seem to be in agreement, but they have both entered into the contract under some misapprehension. Where this mistake goes to the very heart of the contract, the contract will be void.

EXAMPLE

Gabby remembers that she once bought a sunflower-shaped alarm clock but cannot find it anywhere. She decides to replace it and agrees to buy an identical second-hand one from Christine for £10. Christine cannot remember how she came to have the alarm clock but is happy to sell it since she has no need for it. Gabby then recalls that she had, in fact, lent Christine her alarm clock, so she would be buying something that she already owned. In this situation, the contract would not be binding.

MUTUAL MISTAKE

This occurs when there is a misunderstanding between the parties as to the other's intentions and everyone is at 'cross-purposes'. Here, no consensus was reached and so the contract is too ambiguous to enforce.

> **EXAMPLE**
>
> John is at an auction under the impression that he is bidding to buy paper, the auctioneer is under the impression that he is selling plastic, and the catalogue for the sale is far from clear. If John wins the auction, true consent to the terms cannot be said to have been given. The contract would be void for mistake.

UNILATERAL MISTAKE

This is similar to mutual mistake, except here only one party is operating under a misconception, and the other party is aware of that misunderstanding. Mistakes in this category may be divided into two categories, as follows.

Mistake as to the terms of the contract

In one party was to blame for the mistake, that party will generally not be released from the contract unless the mistake was so significant that the other party should have known it was a mistake. If the mistake results from an error in calculation rather than an error in business judgement, the mistaken party is more likely to be released.

> **EXAMPLE**
>
> Pat, a landlady, mistakenly offers to renew Susan's tenancy agreement at £650 per month, when she had meant to offer it at £850 per month. If Susan accepted the offer unaware of the mistake, the contract would be binding as the mistake had no effect upon it. However, had Susan been aware of the mistake, there would be no contract as Susan was aware of Pat's mistake.

Mistake as to identity

When we go shopping, for most of us, the identity of the seller is never really of great importance. We use the shop that is most convenient or has the best offers. This is why there is a presumption that a contract is valid even when one party has made a mistake as to the identity of the other. However, this is not the case where it is shown that the mistaken party had intended to deal with some person other than the person he or she did deal with, and where the identity of the other party was of great importance.

These days, mistakes as to identity are generally induced by fraud, in that one party is claiming to be someone else. There is obviously an overlap with misrepresentation, which we examine in **Chapter 8** below. However, a claim based in mistake is more favourable than one based in misrepresentation, as the effect of a finding of mistake is that the contract is void (treated as though it never existed) rather than voidable (where the contract is valid unless the innocent party decides to rescind it, thereby bringing the contract to an end). This is important when there is an ownership dispute.

EXAMPLE

Chardonnay portrays herself as Tabatha, a hard-working fundraiser, in order to gain entry to a heavily-discounted fashion sale by Wow Fashion for charity workers. Chardonnay buys a designer dress at the event and sells it on to Jessie. If the original contract is void (because Wow Fashion was prepared to sell at discounted prices only to certain, named charity workers, such as Tabatha), Chardonnay will never have received legal ownership (known as 'title') to the dress as the contract never existed. Accordingly, she will not be able to pass title to the dress on to Jessie by selling it to her. However, if the contract is voidable, the contract exists and title to the dress will pass upon the sale to Jessie. If the dress is sold to Jessie before Wow Fashion takes action to rescind the contract and thereby end it, Jessie will acquire good title to the dress.

CHAPTER 6

ALLOCATION OF RISK

HOW DO PARTIES ALLOCATE RISK IN A CONTRACT?

The main way in which risk is allocated between contracting parties is through the use of terms known as 'exemption clauses'.

These clauses are often viewed negatively, since they are typically used by businesses to limit their exposure to risk, often to the detriment of the consumer if the business breaches a contract or if the consumer has failed to read the relevant clause.

EXAMPLE

Desmond takes out a 12-month contract with a mobile phone network. He pays £20 per month and receives a free smartphone with 200 minutes of calls, 150 texts and unlimited data. He pays an extra £2.50 per month for the phone network's own insurance covering loss or theft of the phone. This policy (the terms of the insurance) contains an exemption clause (see below). There are other insurance providers but their policies are at least twice as expensive, although they are 'no quibble' policies containing no exemption clauses.

The following month, Desmond is mugged and his phone is stolen. His phone did not contain his simcard as he had been using it in his tablet pc due to its unlimited data benefit. Desmond makes an insurance claim for a new phone, but this is declined as the policy's exemption clause provides that the simcard must be inside the phone at all times (otherwise there is no obligation upon the phone company to replace a phone that is lost or stolen).

This exemption clause is likely to be valid, so Desmond would personally have to fund a replacement phone. While some may view this scenario as unfair, bear in mind that Desmond would have been given a copy of his policy terms before he entered into the contract, would have benefited from a cooling-off period during which he should have read the small print, and he did prefer to go for the cheapest deal. The phone network was able to offer a cheaper price because it knew it would not have to pay for replacements in such cases, while it could remotely disable stolen phones (and prevent future fraud) that contained the simcards.

If we have freedom of contract, consumers should not complain when their choice of contractual partner impacts negatively upon them (because, for example, their contracts contain exemption clauses). The reality is, though, that most businesses today use standardised forms (known as 'standard terms of business') which contain exemption clauses in the small print which most of us never read (let alone request copies beforehand to enable a detailed comparison to be made between the rival deals on offer and their respective terms). Businesses are very aware of this and may use their strong bargaining position to impose wide exemption clauses – thereby limiting their exposure to risk – knowing the consumer is unlikely to be aware of their existence. Such behaviour is clearly contrary to the spirit of freedom of contract, and the courts have developed rules of 'incorporation' and 'interpretation' in an attempt to protect the consumer.

INCORPORATION

There are three principal ways in which an exemption clause may be incorporated into a contract – see **Figure 1** below.

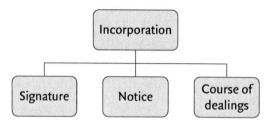

Figure 1: Incorporation of a clause

By signature

An exemption clause is a term and, like other terms, will be incorporated into a contract if that contract is signed by both parties. That you are bound by what you sign (in the absence of fraud or one party causing the other to think that the document he is signing contains terms different from those it really does contain) comes from the proposition that, by signing a document, you must have agreed to all of its terms even if you decided not to read it in full (or at all).

> **EXAMPLE**
>
> Jane takes her car in to her local garage for a MOT and service. At the reception desk, the garage assistant checks her details and asks her to sign a document containing pages of small print. Like many people (especially those with an early morning queue forming behind them and an assistant looking over their shoulder), Jane simply signs without reading the document. Jane would be bound by any exemption clauses contained within that contract.

However, not all contracts are signed, so the law allows terms (including exemption clauses) to be incorporated by notice.

By notice

The key issue here is whether the party seeking to rely upon the exemption clause has taken reasonable steps to draw it to the other party's attention. What constitutes reasonable notice is a question of fact and will change from case to case, depending upon the actual circumstances.

EXAMPLE

Tabatha goes to a local nightclub and pays to leave her expensive coat in the cloakroom, being given a ticket to present to the attendant when she wants to reclaim it. At closing time, the attendant cannot find Tabatha's coat. On the back of the cloakroom ticket are a number of terms, including one excluding liability for clothing worth more than £25. This was also clearly stated on a large sign next to the cloakroom desk. Tabatha had not read the back of the ticket, nor noticed the sign. Despite Tabatha's ignorance, in this case the exemption clause would have been incorporated as there was reasonable notice of the term, meaning the nightclub would not have to compensate Tabatha for the loss of her coat.

It is clear that reasonable notice of the exemption clause must be given before or at the time the contract is made. If there had been no sign at the cloakroom desk, Tabatha would have received the notice only after having entered into the contract, without the exemption clause being part of it.

Many tickets are issued by machines, such as in car parks and cinemas. This is why you will see signs displaying exemption clauses on the approach to car park entrance barriers, and an on-screen option to view 'all terms and conditions of sale' at the automated cinema ticket machine prior to purchase.

Course of dealings

A third way in which terms may be incorporated is where dealings between the parties have been regular. This is clearly a question of fact. In addition, the dealings must be consistent.

EXAMPLE

Vanessa had used a company's services on a monthly basis for the past two years. Harry used the same company, but only three times in the past five years. The document containing the exemption clause had always been signed by Harry, but Vanessa was often not asked to sign her contract containing the same clause.

The facts suggest that Vanessa had regular dealings with the company, but the lack of frequency of use by Harry is unlikely to amount to 'regular dealings'. This means that Harry's dealings cannot amount to a course of dealings, even though his dealings were consistent in that he always signed the document containing the exemption clause. As regards Vanessa, the fact that her document was signed only occasionally means that the exemption clause would not be incorporated due to lack of consistency.

INTERPRETATION OF THE CLAUSE

The exemption clause must cover any breach of contract and the loss or damage that has occurred. The party which included the exemption clause in the contract had the opportunity to make its wording clear and so should be the one that loses out if it is decided that there is ambiguity in its coverage and application. (The interpretation of a clause in a contract is also referred to as 'construction'.)

> **EXAMPLE**
>
> Ken has car insurance which excludes coverage if his car is carrying an excess 'load'. Ken is involved in an accident when driving himself and his four friends to a football match. His insurance company refuses to pay for any damage or liability arising from the accident, citing the policy exception. In this situation, the exemption clause would be interpreted as not applying in such circumstances. The term 'load' would be interpreted as being restricted to luggage and shopping rather than passengers.

THE UNFAIR CONTRACT TERMS ACT 1977

Unfortunately the rules governing incorporation and interpretation became largely procedural in nature and relatively simple to circumvent by businesses hiring lawyers to draft their standard terms of sale. It was therefore left to the state to legislate. Possibly the most important single piece of legislation in this area is the Unfair Contract Terms Act 1977, which aims to control the unreasonable use of exemption clauses and discourage businesses from dressing-up a denial of obligation as an exemption of liability.

This Act regulates the exclusion of liability by businesses in contracts with consumers and also in contracts with other businesses in some cases. The most morally objectionable exemption clauses, such as those seeking to exclude liability for negligently causing someone's death or personal injury, and those which seek to remove consumer rights implied by other legislation, eg the Sale of Goods Act 1979, are rendered void.

> **EXAMPLE**
>
> Denzel owns a scrap yard which is open to the public. There is a large and prominent sign at the entrance stating that everyone enters at their own risk and that the owner will not be liable for any injury whatsoever. Yvonne visits the scrap yard and is seriously hurt when a negligently stacked car topples over onto her. Denzel denies liability for Yvonne's injury as he claims that this had been excluded by notice. In this situation, Denzel's notice would be void, as the 1977 Act states that you cannot exclude or restrict liability for personal injury resulting from negligence.

Less morally objectionable situations, such as the exclusion of liability for other losses caused by negligence, and exemption clauses in standard written terms of business or with consumers in general are subject to a test of reasonableness. The test is whether the clause was a fair and reasonable one to have included in the contract, taking into account a list of factors including the strength of the parties' bargaining positions, whether alternative sources of the product or service were available, knowledge of the exemption clause and whether goods supplied were made especially for the party buying them.

CHAPTER 7

MISREPRESENTATION

WHAT IF I WAS MISLED INTO ENTERING A CONTRACT?

Some contracts are negotiated by the parties instead of the seller making an offer to the buyer on a 'take it or leave it' basis.

Statements that are made during the course of negotiations are either 'representations' or 'terms'. The distinction is important, as one will give rise to more legal remedies than the other.

A representation is a statement which persuades a party to enter into the contract but does not actually form part of it. If it later turns out to have been false, the innocent party's remedy lies in a claim for misrepresentation. Typical examples of representations include a seller of a smartphone describing it having 'a pristine screen', the seller of a laptop saying it 'holds its battery charge well', the seller of a television saying it has 'a great picture' and the seller of a moped commenting about it being 'a nice little runner'.

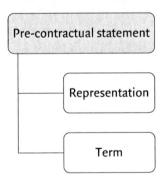

Figure 1: Forms of pre-contractual statement

A term is a promise or an undertaking that is part of the contract itself. If a term is broken, the remedy lies in a claim for breach of contract.

Whether a statement is a representation or a term is really a question of intention as between the parties. If they have indicated that a statement is to be regarded as a term, for example by putting it in writing along with other contractual terms, such as price and delivery, then it is likely to be viewed as such. Also, if one party has superior skill or knowledge relating to the subject matter of the contract, any statement in respect of it is likely to be a term. In other situations, the issue will be determined by considering additional factors, as follows.

The manner and timing of the statement

If the party making the statement asks the other party to check its validity (and that party declines), the statement is unlikely to be a term.

A noticeable delay between the statement being made and the actual contract being entered into may indicate that the parties never intended it to be a term. The longer the delay, the more likely that the parties never intended the statement to have contractual effect.

A promise regarding the future which is subsequently breached cannot be a misrepresentation as there is no statement as to existing fact. This aspect is not without limitation though: if you were to apply for a bank loan and state that it is intended to fund the installation of a new kitchen, but once lent the money you decide to fit a new bathroom instead, there is nothing wrong and no liability attaches to your representation; however, if you never intended the money to be used to install a new kitchen then this would be a clear misrepresentation.

The representation must have been communicated to the party concerned

> **EXAMPLE**
>
> Paul leaves voicemail for Penny in which he states that the watch he is selling to her later is guaranteed for two years. Penny does not access her voicemail before buying the watch. In this case, this uncommunicated representation would not have contractual effect.

There is generally no duty of disclosure in pre-contract negotiations

The phrase 'buyer beware' is key here, although there are circumstances in which silence may itself lead to a misrepresentation. For example, where there has been a change in circumstances following a previous representation that makes that representation incorrect.

> **EXAMPLE**
>
> Margaret seeks to take out a tenancy on a flat. She originally stated that she would not be bringing any pets with her, but after making that statement and before she goes to sign the contract and collect the keys she adopts a cat to live with her. This should be disclosed.

Some contracts require the 'utmost good faith' from the parties. The classic example is an insurance contract. In this situation, the client will have information which is not (and cannot be) known to the insurer. Here, the policy may be avoided if material facts are not disclosed by the client.

THE TYPES OF MISREPRESENTATION

Having decided that the representation concerned was a term of the contract, the next issue to resolve is which of the three types of misrepresentation is relevant. The remedies available depend upon which type is applicable. This is determined by the looking at the lack of care exercised by the party who made the representation – see **Figure 2** below.

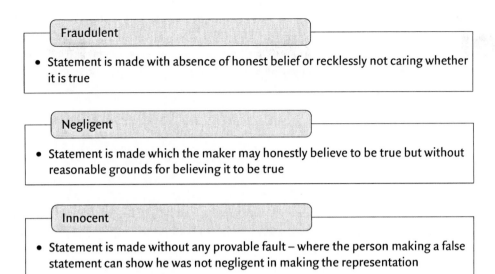

Fraudulent

- Statement is made with absence of honest belief or recklessly not caring whether it is true

Negligent

- Statement is made which the maker may honestly believe to be true but without reasonable grounds for believing it to be true

Innocent

- Statement is made without any provable fault – where the person making a false statement can show he was not negligent in making the representation

Figure 2: Types of misrepresentation

WHAT REMEDIES ARE AVAILABLE FOR MISREPRESENTATION?

Again, this depends upon which type of misrepresentation is applicable.

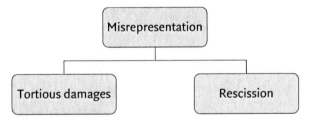

Figure 3: Remedies for misrepresentation

In the case of fraudulent misrepresentation, the innocent party is entitled to tortious damages and rescission. Damages for negligent misrepresentation are based upon similar tortious principles and rescission is also possible. The remedy for innocent misrepresentation is either damages or rescission, this being at the discretion of the court.

Tortious damages

Since fraudulent misrepresentation is based upon the legal concept of a 'tort' of fraud and deceit (a tort being a 'civil wrong'), the aim of 'tortious' damages is to restore the innocent party to the position he would have been in but for the tort (here, the representation), rather than to give him the benefit of the position he expected to be in if the contractual promise had been kept.

In other words, tortious damages are concerned only with what is known as 'reliance loss' (also seen in the second Example in **Chapter 3** following a lawful contract being performed illegally) as they do not take account of the profit which the innocent party was expecting to receive from the proper performance of the contract.

Why are tortious damages different from contractual damages? The reason stems from the different natures of the obligations concerned: in tort, it is the obligation not to commit a civil wrong against someone and thereby make them worse off; whereas in contract, it is an obligation to perform a promise, thereby fulfilling the expectations created.

Rescission

Since contracts induced by misrepresentation are voidable rather than void, the innocent party has the choice of whether to bring the contract to an end and have the parties put back in their pre-contractual positions, ie to rescind the contract. Rescission is generally available as of right (except in the case of innocent misrepresentation where it is available at the discretion of the court). It is not a remedy in the strict sense – in fact, many people will have rescinded contracts without legal proceedings or knowledge regarding the basis for their doing so.

> **EXAMPLE**
>
> Janet pays for a DAB radio from a local electrical shop by cheque. When she gets home, she discovers that the radio picks up only FM stations and not digital stations as implied by the description 'DAB'. In these circumstances, Janet could rescind the contract by returning the radio and cancelling her cheque.

Where circumstances are more complicated than those in the example above (where the party in breach objects to the contract being rescinded), a formal declaration by a court that the contract no longer exists is normally requested by the innocent party, and each party is obliged to return anything that passed under the contract.

Rescission may become unavailable in certain situations, as shown below.

Lapse of time

Fairness dictates that a party making an innocent misrepresentation should have the benefit of a time limit after which the contract is no longer at risk of being rescinded. The limitation periods imposed by statute are examined in the section 'Do legal proceedings have a time limit?' in **Chapter 9**.

The actual time limit depends upon the subject matter of the contract and how long a reasonable person would take to discover the truth from the date of the contract. For public policy reasons, in the case of fraudulent misrepresentation, the time limit starts to run from when the fraud has been or could reasonably have been discovered. Similar principles apply to cases of negligent misrepresentation.

> **EXAMPLE**
>
> Brenda buys a painting at auction which is described as being by a famous artist. Several years later, Brenda appears on a television antiques programme and is informed by an expert that her painting is a fake. The seller honestly believed it to be genuine and had originally purchased it himself on that basis. In this situation, too many years have passed (during which Brenda could have got the painting authenticated) for rescission to be allowed as a remedy for the misrepresentation.

Affirmation

Once the innocent party discovers that the representation concerned was false, he must take action to rescind the contract or be at risk of affirming it. Whilst there are no hard-and-fast rules governing how long the innocent party has before an inference of affirmation might be drawn, it is probably sooner than you think. This is to prevent the innocent party from speculating at the expense of the party who made the statement, with no risk to himself.

EXAMPLE

Emma agrees to buy 10 gold coins from Giles, a precious metal dealer, on Monday at 4.30 pm. Giles tells Emma that there is a worldwide shortage of gold and that the value of investment in gold will increase over the next 12 months. Emma is to collect her coins on Tuesday at 2.00 pm. That evening, Emma does some online research and discovers that she has been told a pack of lies; there is, in fact, currently a world surplus of gold. She decides to think about whether to rescind the contract to buy the coins overnight. The following morning, she is pleased to read a newspaper article saying that several gold mines will be closed for months due to strike action, which should see gold prices increase. On her way to collect her coins, she checks her smartphone and discovers that the planned strikes have been called off, resulting in the lowering of gold prices. Emma phones to rescind the contract at 1.30 pm. In these circumstances, the company could claim that Emma affirmed the contract (even though she waited less than a day to rescind) because she had speculated at its expense and wanted to rescind the contract only when she realised that her investment was going to lose money.

The example above illustrates how an innocent party is prevented from manipulating legal principles in the hope of making a profit, safe in the knowledge that she might rescind the contract at any time and get her money back.

Impossibility of returning the parties to their pre-contract position

This is often the result of the subject matter of the contract having been destroyed or its practical value rendered worthless.

EXAMPLE

Mona contracts to buy a working goldmine but the seller refuses to hand over ownership. By the time legal proceedings are heard, all the gold has been mined by the seller. In this case, rescission would be impossible. Mona would recover damages to compensate for her loss.

Someone else has acquired rights to the subject matter

> **EXAMPLE**
>
> Tony buys a motorbike from Dan, who lied to him regarding its history of ownership. Tony then sells the motorbike to Patrick without having rescinded his original contract with Dan. The motorbike now belongs to Patrick, and Tony cannot rescind the original contract as this would mean giving the motorbike back to Dan (which he cannot now do since it is lawfully owned by Patrick).

RELEVANCE OF EXEMPTION CLAUSES

Exemption clauses may cover innocent and negligent misrepresentation, but can never be used to exclude liability for fraud. Any such clause will be subject to the test of reasonableness (see **Chapter 6** above).

CHAPTER 8

How Do Contracts End?

Having looked at how contracts are created, we shall now look at how contracts come to an end. There are four ways in which a contract may be 'discharged' – see **Figure 1** below.

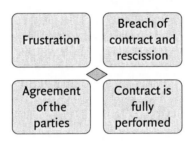

Figure 1: How contracts are discharged

FRUSTRATION

Examples of frustration of a contract

The term 'frustration' in this context has nothing to do with one party getting annoyed with the other! Frustration of a contract occurs automatically when something happens which is beyond the control of the parties who cannot prevent it from happening. Situations in which frustration has occurred include:

(a)   when performing the contract becomes impossible;

> **EXAMPLE**
>
> Brian agrees to buy Jane's garden shed for £50. The night before collection, the shed is destroyed by lightning. As the shed was destroyed by something beyond the control of either party, the contract would be discharged by frustration.

(b)   illegality;

> **EXAMPLE**
>
> Paul agrees to sell Melanie a hamster for £10. However, Parliament passes a law making it a crime to sell rodents. In this case, the contract would be frustrated due to illegality.

(c)   there is a major change in the circumstances surrounding the reason for the contract.

> **EXAMPLE**
>
> Brian hires a room overlooking Oxford Street in order to watch a cycle race, the final stretch of which will take place along that street. Jack also hires a room in the same building, mainly as a base for his shopping trip, but also in order to watch the cycle race. The race is cancelled. Brian's contract would be frustrated, as watching the race was the only reason for making the contract. However, in Jack's case, the contract will not be frustrated since the race was not the main reason for entering into the contract.

Relevance of exemption clauses

Exemption clauses often deal with the possibility of a frustrating event. If such an event actually occurred, the contract will not be discharged. The risks would instead be allocated in accordance with what had been agreed between the parties. See further **Chapter 6** above.

SERIOUS BREACH OF CONTRACT AND RESCISSION

We have seen in **Chapter 7** that one of the remedies for a breach of contract is rescission, where the innocent party chooses to end the contract.

AGREEMENT OF THE PARTIES

Parties to a contract may agree to change or vary any of its terms, and this includes its duration. In other words, provided all the parties agree, they may bring the contract to an end.

CONTRACT IS FULLY PERFORMED

Most contracts come to an end simply because both parties have performed their ends of the bargain.

> **EXAMPLE**
>
> Judy is hired as a nanny for two weeks. During that period, she performs her work and is paid in accordance with what had been agreed. At the end of the two weeks, both Judy and her employer have performed their respective ends of the bargain, which results in the contract having been discharged.

REMEDIES

WHAT HAPPENS WHEN THINGS GO WRONG?

As noted above, the vast majority of contracts come to an end by both parties successfully performing their end of the bargain. However, sometimes one party breaches an important term of the contract (known as a 'condition'), resulting in the other party suffering a loss. In this situation, the innocent party may be entitled to compensation (known as 'damages'), specific performance and/or an injunction. Breach of less important terms (known as 'warranties') entitles the innocent party to claim damages only.

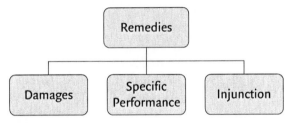

Figure 1: Remedies for breach of contract

DAMAGES

The purpose behind an award of damages is to compensate the innocent party for the loss suffered by the other party's breach of contract.

How are damages calculated?

Contractual damages are intended to put the innocent party (so far as this can be achieved by money) in the position he or she would have been had the contract been performed properly. This is known as 'loss of bargain' or 'expectation loss' damages and is by far the most common form of damages for breach of contract.

> **EXAMPLE 1**
>
> Terry, in breach of contract, fails to remove Maureen's old, dismantled shed from her driveway. An award of damages would reflect the cost Maureen has had to incur to get someone else to remove the shed.

Contractual damages may also be claimed for expenses incurred in reliance on the contract which have been wasted by the other party's breach of contract. Such compensation is known as 'reliance loss' damages.

EXAMPLE 2

Maureen hires a small skip for a day to coincide with the date Terry had agreed to remove her shed. The skip will be used to dispose of the shed's concrete foundation and its owner has been recommended by Terry. The cost of hiring the skip will have been wasted by Terry's breach and is recoverable by Maureen.

Another form of damages is based upon the benefit the other party gained from the breach of contract.

EXAMPLE 3

Had Maureen already paid Terry any money on account, this would also be recoverable since Terry would otherwise benefit following his breach.

Remoteness

The innocent party must show a strong causal connection between the breach of contract and the financial loss suffered; otherwise, the claim for damages is said to be too 'remote' a consequence of the breach and no compensation is payable.

An innocent party may claim damages only for:

(a)   loss arising naturally out of the breach (in the ordinary course of things); or

(b)   loss which did not arise naturally, but which might reasonably be supposed to have been within the contemplation of the parties, at the time the contract was made, as the probable result of the breach.

EXAMPLE 4

What if Maureen had told Terry that she needed the shed to be removed by the weekend as a new shed was being delivered and she was expecting visitors? Because of Terry's breach, the driveway was blocked, meaning that the new shed could not be delivered (costing Maureen a £30 redelivery charge), and the visitors decided not to come as they refused to use on-street parking. Maureen was due to sign a lucrative deal with the visitors to sell her home-made jewellery online. Because the visitors cancelled, the deal never happened, and Maureen lost £1,000 in potential profit.

It is likely that the redelivery charge would be recoverable, since this arose naturally out of the breach, but the lost profit would be too remote as Terry could not reasonably be supposed to have contemplated that Maureen would be signing a business deal with the visitors.

SPECIFIC PERFORMANCE AND INJUNCTIONS

Whilst damages are available as of right following a breach of contract, specific performance and injunctions are both discretionary remedies. They are both also quite drastic remedies, since they involve the state imposing personal constraints over the actions of the party in breach. Not surprisingly, the innocent party has a number of hurdles to overcome in order to be granted such remedies.

Specific performance

This compels a party to perform its end of the contract. Specific performance will be granted only if damages would be an inadequate remedy. For example, most contracts relate to the sale of goods, and if the seller were in breach of contract, the innocent party would be expected to buy an identical product elsewhere. If this resulted in his having to pay a higher price, damages would be awarded to cover the difference. Damages would therefore be an adequate remedy in most cases. However, when it comes to transactions where this is not possible, for example where simple substitution of one product for another is not possible, the remedy of specific performance would be granted.

When it comes to contracts involving personal services, such as a contract of employment, specific performance is rarely granted.

> **EXAMPLE**
>
> Jessica, in breach of contract, gives no notice to her employer that she is quitting her job. In this case, the employer would not be granted specific performance to compel Jessica to work her notice period, since he could recover damages for the cost of hiring someone to cover Jessica's work for the notice period, and to force someone to work against their will is tantamount to slavery.

Injunction

An injunction restrains a party from doing something that he or she promised not to do within the contract. An injunction will not be granted if it would force the party in breach to perform acts which could not be subject to a grant of specific performance (above).

This would seem to rule out contracts of employment, but where a contract contains a negative term (such as 'you agree not to work for a rival business in the same town for three months after you leave the company') it will be possible to grant an injunction to enforce this aspect without compelling positive performance of the whole contract.

> **EXAMPLE**
>
> Tara, a part-time singer, agrees in her record contract not to sing for another record company or work in any capacity for any other business without the prior permission of her employer. An injunction might be granted in respect of the first obligation but not in respect of the second, since this would, by implication, force Tara to work for her employer.

MITIGATION

Whilst damages are intended to put the innocent party in the same position as if the contract had been performed, that party is expected to take reasonable steps to put himself in that position, ie to mitigate (lessen) his loss.

> **EXAMPLE**
>
> Henry is sacked from his job in breach of contract. He claims 10 weeks of lost wages, but he had been offered an identical job after the ninth week of being unemployed, which offer he declined. Since Henry is under a duty to mitigate his loss, the fact that he turned down a suitable job will be taken into account and his damages will be reduced accordingly.

DO LEGAL PROCEEDINGS HAVE A TIME LIMIT?

Legal proceedings, like food products, have expiry dates. These are known as 'limitation periods'. The rules governing them come from statute. Where a claim is based upon a breach of contract, the general limitation period, after which legal proceedings are barred, is six years from the date on which the breach occurred. You will recall that some contracts have to be made by deed (see **Chapter 2** above), and the limitation period for these is 12 years. Where fraud or mistake is involved, the clock starts ticking for the limitation period only once the innocent party discovers the fraud or mistake, or should reasonably have discovered it.

> **EXAMPLE**
>
> Last week, Peter realises that he should have received a complimentary DVD player when he purchased his television from a national retailer in 2004. He has retained a copy of his invoice which clearly shows that he never received the DVD player. Despite having clear evidence of the seller's breach of contract, Peter would be barred from bringing a legal claim due to the period of time that has passed since the breach occurred.

CRIMINAL LAW

CHAPTER 1

WHAT IS A CRIME?

INTRODUCTION

What makes a person guilty of a criminal offence? A study of criminal law explores what has to be proved before someone may be convicted of a specific criminal offence. It also considers how someone may argue a defence to a criminal charge so that he avoids being found guilty of the crime. For example, if someone is accused of murder, what has to be proved to show that that person is guilty? What defence might the accused person be able to rely on – can he say, for instance, that although he killed someone, he did so only because he was defending himself from an attack?

It is important that the law relating to offences and defences is not considered in a vacuum. Students of criminal law need to understand the context in which those crimes and defences operate, so it is important to consider some preliminary issues:

- Why do we have criminal laws?
- What 'ingredients' generally are needed to establish a crime?
- How does the law operate in the courts?
- What are the roles of the prosecution and defence lawyers?
- What happens when someone is found guilty of a crime?

All of these questions will be considered here and will help in developing an understanding of the criminal justice system, which is crucial to understanding criminal law itself.

Unlike other areas of the law, crime is something to which all members of society are exposed. The police are a visible presence in the community, and most people know that they are the front line in the enforcement of the criminal law. If an individual is suspected of committing a criminal offence, he will be arrested by the police and taken to a police station, where he will be interviewed in order that he may give his account of an incident.

For example, if a woman (Jane Birtles) is accused of taking a dress from a shop (Mod Fashions Limited) without paying for it, this is, potentially, a crime of theft. She would be arrested and would have the opportunity of explaining to the police why she took the dress without paying for it. Imagine that she tells them that she just forgot to pay for the dress. If the police accept her account, they will release her from the police station and no further action will be taken. However, if they do not believe her story, they may decide to charge her with an offence of theft. This charge, at the police station, will be the beginning of Jane Birtles' journey through the criminal courts where, eventually, she will either admit the theft, by pleading guilty to the charge, or deny it, by pleading not guilty to the charge, in which case she will face a criminal trial and the court will consider whether she should be convicted (found guilty) of the crime.

CRIMINAL OFFENCES AND CIVIL PROCEEDINGS

Members of the public are familiar with the general process by which people are dealt with in the criminal courts. They read reports of crimes in newspapers and see fictional and non-fictional cases on television that are set in a criminal courtroom. Many people also know that there is a civil court system where people are sued for money. However, there is sometimes confusion as to the difference between criminal and civil cases. Which cases are dealt with in the magistrates' courts or Crown Courts (the criminal courts) and which go to the county court or High Court (the civil courts)? When do you 'sue' and when do you 'prosecute'?

In the theft scenario above, Jane Birtles could face prosecution through a criminal trial in the magistrates' court or Crown Court. What if the shop wanted to recover the cost of the dress that she took? It might decide to sue her in the civil courts to force her to pay the money it is owed.

There are many key differences between a criminal offence and civil proceedings. Some of the most important ones are summarised in **Table 1** below.

Criminal Offences	Civil Proceedings
The accused person ('the defendant'/'the accused') is *prosecuted* for the alleged crime.	The person allegedly at fault (the 'defendant') is *sued*, ie has a *claim* brought against him (for compensation).
Proceedings are usually brought, on behalf of the state, by the Crown Prosecution Service (CPS). It is not the victim (or the victim's family) who brings the prosecution against the defendant.	The court case is started by the victim (the 'claimant'), ie the person who claims to have suffered a loss.
Criminal cases may proceed to trial even if the victim does not want to take the matter any further.	A civil claim will be discontinued if the victim decides not to proceed or accepts a sum of money offered by the defendant to resolve the matter.
If a defendant is found guilty in a criminal case, the sanctions imposed are designed, primarily, to punish the defendant rather than to compensate the victim.	If a claim is proved against the defendant, any sanction will usually be of a financial nature, designed to compensate the victim.

Table 1: Key differences between criminal and civil proceedings

The title of a case also reflects the difference between civil and criminal cases:

- If Mod Fashions Limited decide to sue Jane Birtles for the cost of the dress, the title of the case will be Mod Fashions Limited v Birtles. The abbreviation 'v' stands for 'versus' or 'against'.
- If the police decide to charge Jane Birtles with a criminal offence of theft, the case name will be R v Birtles. The abbreviation 'R' stands for 'Regina' or 'Rex', as most criminal cases are prosecuted in the name of the monarch, reflecting the involvement of the state in a criminal action.

It is possible, therefore, to have criminal and civil proceedings arising out of the same incident. However, in some situations, the civil jurisdiction may be the only one available. For example, if a husband is unfaithful to his wife, she may have grounds for divorce in the civil courts, but being unfaithful is not a criminal offence, so the criminal justice system would have no part to play. Equally, if someone is killed in an attack, whilst there will usually be a criminal prosecution for murder, it is unusual for such an incident to generate a claim in the civil courts.

What criteria are used to decide whether the civil courts or the criminal courts (or both) are relevant to a particular situation?

- In a civil claim, the decision rests with the 'victim' as to whether to instigate proceedings. If the victim chooses to take no action, no court case will exist.
- The criminal justice system is likely to be involved when the state decides that a particular type of situation is too serious or too important to be left to the individual's right to choose whether to bring proceedings in the civil courts.

IDENTIFYING CRIMINAL BEHAVIOUR: THE AIMS OF CRIMINALISATION

For centuries, the state, in the form of Parliament and the courts, has decided what type of behaviour is 'against the law' and worthy of prosecution in the criminal courts. Many of the crimes created are well known to the public: many people would instantly recognise that deliberately killing someone without excuse is a crime of murder and that having sexual intercourse with someone who does not consent amounts to the offence of rape. Few people, however, will stop to consider why such behaviour is criminalised.

Most people would probably agree that there must be a justification for making certain behaviour criminal – there must be an aim to be achieved by criminalising certain conduct.

Often, the criminal law is described as a means of punishing people for doing something wrong. This description is accurate but gives rise to more questions. For example, who defines what is 'wrong'?

Crimes are committed against society – they amount to a public wrong. On the other hand, a claim arises in the civil courts when an individual has been wronged – it is a personal claim. In the context of the theft offence considered above, the offence has been committed against an individual – Mode Fashions Limited – but Jane Birtles' behaviour might be said to impact on society as a whole. Generally, society does not favour the idea of people taking an item that does not belong to them without paying for it. Such conduct causes economic loss to the retailer, increases the burden on the police, and has implications for honest consumers as the cost of goods increases to reflect the losses suffered by the retailer. As society does not condone such behaviour, it is a criminal offence to act in this way. Everyone can then see that there are consequences to behaving in an unacceptable manner – that the offender will be punished.

If punishment is at least one of the purposes of making certain conduct criminal, what is that punishment designed to achieve?

The criminal law is sometimes used to incapacitate the offender. In some cases, after deciding that a person is guilty of an offence, the court might decide that the offender needs to be removed from society. The offender might be dangerous and need to be imprisoned to protect the public, so convictions for crimes such as rape and robbery often attract long prison sentences. In a less serious case, but involving a persistent offender, the court might be aware that other forms of punishment have been tried and have not worked, so the ultimate sanction in our society – deprivation of liberty by sending the offender to prison – is used.

Even if prison is not seen as an appropriate sanction, criminalising certain behaviour ensures that other punishments may be imposed on the offender. Often, offenders are ordered to do unpaid work in the community. This type of punishment interferes with the offender's liberty – with his free time – and ensures that he puts something back into society.

Sometimes, the purpose of criminalisation is not just to punish but also to rehabilitate offenders, enabling them to become useful members of society. Once a person has been found guilty of an offence, the court may consider it appropriate to impose a requirement for that person to attend a drugs or alcohol rehabilitation programme if, for example, addiction to these substances has played a part in causing the criminal behaviour. So, for example, a defendant might be convicted of stealing from a local shop. If he is found guilty and the facts of the case suggest that he stole to fund his drug addiction, the court may order him to attend a drugs programme to tackle his addiction and therefore reduce the risk of his re-offending.

Conduct may also be made criminal in order to protect the public or certain vulnerable sections of society, such as young children. There are criminal laws in place to protect children from abuse by their parents and other people in authority, such as teachers. It is a crime, for instance, to use excessive force in the physical punishment of children, for example by smacking them. Similarly, offences of violence, ranging from causing a small bruise to killing or raping a victim, are criminalised to protect society from violent individuals.

Lastly, certain behaviour might be criminalised in order to serve as a deterrent. The majority of people will refrain from acting in a particular way if they know that such behaviour attracts criminal liability. For example, the public know that it is against the law to drive without wearing a seatbelt, or to fail to stop at a red traffic light. The sanction of the criminal law stops the majority from driving without the protection of a seatbelt and ensures that they do not present a danger to other road-users by driving through red lights. This deterrent effect also impacts on some of the other purposes of criminalisation, such as protection of the public.

Successful prosecution of some crimes might be said to achieve all the goals of criminalisation. For example, a conviction for the offence of murder might be said to incapacitate the offender by sending him to prison, to deter others from behaving in the same way and/or to provide the possibility of rehabilitating the offender. However, not all these goals will be achieved with every criminal prosecution. For example, it is a criminal offence to drive above the speed limit. Many motorists do exceed the speed limit, in spite of knowing it is a crime. If convicted, it is unlikely that the driver will be incapacitated, as the normal penalty for this offence is a fine, plus points on the driver's licence or a short driving disqualification. It is arguable whether speeding drivers are rehabilitated or educated as to the dangers of speeding, as many offend repeatedly; similarly, criminalising the behaviour does not seem to act as a deterrent as so many drivers do break the speed limit and, often, do not consider themselves to have committed a 'real' crime. Some car drivers might therefore argue that speeding should not be a crime as this does not achieve any of the purposes of criminalisation, but the parent of a child knocked down by a speeding car might have a very different view, arguing that the crime should exist to provide some punishment and to protect society.

Although the aims of criminalisation have been identified, they do not fully explain why certain behaviour is considered criminal. How does the state decide what forms of behaviour deserve incapacitation, deterrence and so on?

Attitudes on the criminalisation of certain forms of behaviour will often be influenced by one's own experiences and by one's moral, political and religious views. As society's views on what is right and wrong alter, it follows that criminal offences will change over a period of time.

There are two main schools of thought on why certain conduct should be criminalised:

(a) *The moralist view.* Those who subscribe to this view are of the opinion that conduct should be regarded as criminal if it is morally blameworthy. This school of thought is not concerned with whether any harm has been caused by the conduct. For example, it used to be an offence to engage in homosexual behaviour. Such behaviour was criminalised because, at the time, it was felt to be morally wrong.

Under the provisions of the Human Rights Act 1998, there is a (qualified) right to a private family life, but even before this Act was passed, the moralist view was criticised on the ground that it amounts to an invasion of privacy. Its opponents argue that if no harm is caused, the state should not be able to interfere in the private lives of its citizens and dictate the way in which they should behave.

Those who favour the moralist view argue that it promotes greater vigilance and enables the state to protect the vulnerable in society. For example, it might be argued that no harm is caused if a boy aged 18 has consensual sexual intercourse with his 15-year-old girlfriend on the eve of her 16th birthday. This is, however, a criminal offence (under the Sexual Offences Act 2003), because Parliament considers that it has a role to protect children under the age of 16 when dealing with sexual offences.

(b) *The utilitarian view.* Unlike those who support the moralist view, those who support the utilitarian view argue that conduct should be criminalised only if it is blameworthy and it causes identifiable harm. In recent years, there has been a growth in anti-terrorism legislation which has created new criminal offences. Undoubtedly this was due to public and political pressure following such incidents as the 7 July bombings in London, but it might also be said to be an illustration of the utilitarian view. Whilst various terrorist groups held views that were reprehensible and blameworthy in the eyes of many sections of society, freedom of expression prevented their views being criminalised. Once those views also caused identifiable harm, however, they became deserving of criminal sanction.

Many of the crimes with which people are most familiar – such as murder, rape, theft and criminal damage – fall within those covered by the utilitarian approach as they are blameworthy and involve obvious harm being caused, either to people (murder and rape) or to property (theft and criminal damage). There are, however, some crimes where the defendant could not be described as blameworthy and where no harm has been caused. In certain cases, therefore, neither the moralist approach nor the utilitarian approach seems to apply. Such crimes are known as offences of 'strict liability' and may be charged even if the defendant cannot be said to be at fault in any way, where he or she acted exactly as a responsible person would and where no harm has been suffered. For example, a landlord of a public house may be convicted of a criminal offence of serving alcohol outside licensing hours when he has a licence to serve until 11 pm and serves a customer at 11.05 pm, not having realised that his watch was slow. Many would argue that he is not blameworthy, so the moralist view is not satisfied, and that no harm has been caused, so the conduct does not fall within the utilitarian view, but the landlord would still be convicted because there is a criminal law that prohibits such conduct.

Strict liability offences often exist in areas where the state considers there to be an important need to regulate behaviour, and where the needs of regulation and risk management outweigh the need to establish blameworthy and harmful conduct. They are therefore often seen in areas of the criminal law dealing with environmental issues, such as pollution, and in health and safety offences, where the safety of the workforce is regarded as of such high importance that any failure to comply with the law is deserving of criminal punishment, irrespective of the fact that the failure might be slight and accidental, and irrespective of the fact that no harm has actually been suffered.

THE RULE OF LAW

How do people know whether their conduct might attract the attention of the police and the criminal justice system? The criminal law is set out in Acts of Parliament and in judgments of the senior courts, mainly the Court of Appeal and the Supreme Court (formerly the House of Lords sitting in its judicial capacity). Whilst most people will not know the detailed provisions of the law, as set out in these documents, ignorance of the criminal law is no defence. Therefore, if an individual strangles his friend, and is accused of murdering him, it is no defence to argue that he did not know that killing someone was a crime. The law is there for members of the public to discover, should they take the steps to do so.

However, the Rule of Law operates as a form of protection, to ensure that two fundamental principles must apply before anyone may be found guilty of a criminal offence:

1. *There can be no criminal liability except for conduct specifically prescribed by law.*

    This principle ensures that no one may be convicted of an offence unless there is an existing prohibition on such conduct at the time of the defendant's actions. For example, it is not an offence to eat ice-cream in public. A police officer could not lawfully approach a tourist eating an ice-cream and arrest him for 'eating an ice-cream in public'. There is no law that makes such conduct unlawful. Any arrest for this behaviour and any subsequent prosecution would be unlawful.

Until the late 20th century, there was no criminal offence designed to deal expressly with the issue of stalking. People whose lives were made difficult by unwanted advances from would-be boyfriends or girlfriends, found that the criminal law did not help them. Some high-profile cases in the 1990s led to the introduction of a specific criminal offence to deal with problems of harassment, under the Protection from Harassment Act 1997. Even when the Act was brought into force, it could not be used against those who had committed acts of harassment before the Act came into force. For these individuals, their conduct was not punishable by law at the time they committed their acts of harassment, and so the Rule of Law operated to ensure they could not be prosecuted. Obviously, if they engaged in further acts of harassment once the law was in force, they could (and did) face prosecution.

2. *There can be no criminal liability unless the offender is convicted following a proper trial according to the law.*

This second principle of the Rule of Law means that a person cannot be convicted of a crime unless there have been fair proceedings to determine whether he is guilty of the offence with which he is charged. It is not the police, for example, who decide whether someone is guilty. If they think there is information that suggests that a particular person has committed an offence, they refer the matter to the Crown Prosecution Service, which decides whether to prosecute the suspect for the crime he is accused of committing. Even if the decision to prosecute is made, it is for the court to decide upon the suspect's guilt, after listening to all the evidence that is relevant to the case and considering whether that evidence shows that the offence has been committed by that person. The procedures followed in court to arrive at this decision are considered further in **Chapter 3** below.

CHAPTER 2

ESTABLISHING GUILT – THE LAW

THE KEY INGREDIENTS OF A CRIMINAL OFFENCE

The Rule of Law (see **Chapter 1** above) is essential when considering criminal liability. Within our society, a person cannot be convicted by the courts unless his behaviour amounts to a defined criminal offence. Any party involved with the criminal justice system therefore needs to know what elements make up a crime. A lawyer acting for the prosecution will need to know what has to be proved in order to obtain a conviction. A defence lawyer has to consider whether a client's behaviour amounts to a criminal offence in order to decide whether or not that client should plead guilty or not guilty to the charge faced. In order to do this, they must identify the definition of the offence.

Criminal offences are defined either by statute or by case law. For example, if a person has stolen someone else's property, they will be accused of theft, which is defined under s 1 of the Theft Act 1968. Theft is therefore a statutory offence as its definition is found in an Act of Parliament. On the other hand, murder is a common law offence. Its definition cannot be found in a statute but comes instead from case law decided by the courts.

Generally, the definition of a crime, whether in statute or case law, will require the prosecution to prove:

(a)   that the defendant behaved in a particular way (guilty conduct or 'actus reus'); and

(b)   that the defendant had a particular state of mind at the time of that guilty conduct (guilty state of mind or 'mens rea').

If one or both of these elements cannot be proven, the defendant cannot be convicted of the offence.

Although Latin terminology has become much less important in the courts than it used to be, practitioners of criminal law will still use the terms 'actus reus' when describing guilty conduct and 'mens rea' when referring to the requirements of a guilty state of mind. Any attempt to abandon these terms causes difficulty, as no modern equivalents completely encapsulate the requirements of these elements of an offence.

Even if both actus reus and mens rea can be proved, the defendant may be able to rely on a defence which enables him to avoid conviction.

When considering criminal liability it is important to consider the necessary ingredients in the correct order, ie:

- actus reus
- mens rea
- any relevant defence.

ACTUS REUS

Unless the *actus reus* of a crime is proved, there can be no criminal liability. Identifying and understanding the *actus reus* of an offence is therefore the first essential step in considering whether a person might be guilty.

The *actus reus* of a crime is made up of one or more of the following elements (the '3 Cs'):

*   the *conduct* of the defendant
*   the surrounding *circumstances*
*   the *consequences* that follow from the defendant's conduct.

These elements are illustrated in **Table 1** below, which considers the *actus reus* elements of a statutory offence (rape) and a common law offence (murder).

Rape (Sexual Offences Act 2003, s 1)	*Murder*
Actus reus • The defendant had sexual intercourse with a person (V) = Conduct • At the time of the intercourse, V did not consent = Circumstance	Actus reus • Causing = Conduct • The death = Consequence • Of a human being = Circumstance

Table 1: The *actus reus* of offences

The offences of rape and murder demonstrate that the *actus reus* requirements of offences are not always the same. Offences are often categorised into 'conduct' and 'result' crimes. The difference between the two categories may be demonstrated by considering the offences of rape and murder in a little more detail.

Rape

In order to establish the *actus reus* of rape, the conduct or act needed is that the defendant has sexual intercourse with someone. But although intercourse is an essential element of rape, it is not the only one. The *actus reus* is not complete unless a particular *circumstance* also exists – here, lack of consent on the part of the victim. So the *actus reus* of rape consists of *conduct* by the defendant – the act of sexual intercourse – and the existence of certain *circumstances* – lack of consent by the victim.

No consequences need to follow from the defendant's conduct in order to establish the *actus reus* of rape. It is the behaviour of the defendant and the surrounding circumstances that are all important. Rape is therefore an example of a 'conduct' crime.

Murder

Contrast this with the crime of murder. The *actus reus* of murder is causing the death of a human being. For this offence to be made out, a consequence has to follow from the defendant's conduct. It is not enough to attack someone by hitting him over the head with a hammer – that person must die as a result of his injuries before the attacker may be charged with murder. So here, the *conduct* of the defendant is the attack on the victim, and the relevant *consequence* is that person's death as a result of the attack. Are there any essential *circumstances* to a charge of murder? The victim has to be a human being – this is a circumstance of the offence, although in the vast majority of cases, this element is uncontroversial and easily proved.

When considering liability for murder, a consequence must flow from the defendant's conduct – the victim must die. Murder is an example of a 'result' crime – unless the consequence is proven, the *actus reus* cannot be established.

Failing to act

Usually a person charged with a criminal offence has taken some positive steps in the commission of the crime. For example, a defendant accused of rape will have engaged in sexual intercourse. Many people accused of murder have taken positive steps to kill their victims, for example by beating or shooting them.

In some cases, however, the *actus reus* of an offence may be established even when the defendant has failed to act. This situation might arise, for example, when someone stands by and allows a person to drown or to die in a fire when he could have intervened to help the victim. In such circumstances, has the bystander committed the *actus reus* of murder? Might the prosecution argue that, by failing to intervene, the defendant has caused the death of a human being?

Under the law of England and Wales, there is generally no criminal liability for failing to act, and no general obligation to intervene to help someone in trouble. The starting point, then, is that, however morally reprehensible the bystander's behaviour might be, he commits no crime by allowing another person to die when he could have intervened to assist.

This general rule could cause difficulties if it was applied universally. Some people are paid to protect others and some have a legal obligation to do so. If such people faced no criminal liability for failing to act, this would undoubtedly cause a public outcry – if, for example, a child died as a result of their failure to act. There are therefore exceptions to the rule that there is no liability for failing to act. These exceptions are summarised in **Table 2** below.

1. Where there is a *special relationship* between the defendant and the victim (eg, if they are mother and daughter).
2. Where the defendant has a *contractual obligation* to act (eg, if the defendant is employed as a child minder and fails to intervene to save a child in her care).
3. Where there is a *statutory duty* to act (for instance, the Road Traffic Act 1988 imposes a duty to obey traffic signals, eg to stop at red traffic lights).
4. Where the defendant has created a *dangerous situation* (eg, if a person accidentally starts a fire in the kitchen, he is under a duty to take reasonable steps to remove or reduce the danger).

Table 2: Establishing the *actus reus* of an offence when the defendant fails to act

MENS REA

Although it is essential to prove the *actus reus* of a crime, doing so is often not enough to secure a conviction. A person might cause the death of another by accident – for example, a victim might step out in front of a car so that the driver has no opportunity to avoid a collision. If the victim dies as a result of the collision, few people would expect the driver to be convicted of murder, even though he committed the *actus reus* of that offence by causing the death of a human being. Society demands that those who are culpable should be convicted of a criminal offence. Culpability (or guilt) is generally established only if, when engaged in guilty conduct, the defendant also has a guilty state of mind – *mens rea*.

For the majority of offences, such as criminal damage, assault, theft, rape and murder, the prosecution will need to show that both the *actus reus* and the *mens rea* elements were present when the defendant committed the crime of which he is accused. The prosecution will also have to show that the guilty conduct and the guilty mind were present at the same time.

Although the precise *mens rea* required for an offence may be discovered only by analysing the definition of that particular crime, the prosecution usually have to show either:

(a)   that the defendant intended something to happen; or

(b)   that the defendant was reckless as to whether something might happen.

Intention

Some crimes may be proved only by showing that the defendant had a particular intention. For example, the crime of murder requires proof that the defendant intended either to kill or to cause really serious harm to the victim. In such cases, understanding what is meant by 'intention' is crucial to a consideration of whether a defendant has the necessary *mens rea* for the offence.

Most people would assume that they had an understanding of what is meant by 'intention'.

If a jury are considering the guilt of a defendant who shot his victim dead at point-blank rage, evidence that the defendant, on pulling the trigger, shouted 'I hate you. I want you dead' would make it easy for the jury to conclude that the defendant intended to kill his victim.

In such a case, the members of the jury will use their normal understanding of the word 'intention' to reach their verdict. They would conclude that the defendant had set out to kill his victim – he wanted him dead. The jury would not need any detailed guidance from the trial judge on what was meant by intention – they would use their common sense.

Where a defendant sets out to achieve a particular result, this is known as direct intent: the outcome achieved is the defendant's aim, purpose, goal or desire.

EXAMPLE

Karen has been arrested on suspicion of murder.

The allegation is that Karen killed her boyfriend, Jonah.

Karen admits that she pushed Jonah, who then banged his head on a stone fireplace. His head injury caused his death.

Karen's admission enables the prosecution to prove that she committed the *actus reus* of murder, but what about the *mens rea*?

Scenario 1
When interviewed by the police, Karen says she did not want to kill or cause serious injury to Jonah. She is devastated by what has happened. The police believe her. Direct intent to kill or cause serious harm cannot be proved – Jonah's death was not Karen's aim, purpose, goal or desire.

Scenario 2
Although the police accept that Karen had no direct intent to kill Jonah, they discover that the night before the tragedy, Karen and Jonah had argued and Karen had told a friend that she wanted to kill Jonah.

This information will not help the police to prove Karen had the *mens rea* of murder at the time she pushed Jonah:

- when Karen and Jonah had their argument, Karen may have intended to kill Jonah but she did not do so at that time;

- when Karen did commit the *actus reus* of murder (by pushing Jonah and causing his death), she did not intend that Jonah should either die or suffer serious injury.

In cases such as murder, few people would disagree with the conviction of a defendant who has set out to kill his victim, for example by stabbing the victim several times in the chest; but what if further facts come to light?

Would the situation be different if it was revealed to the jury that the only reason why the defendant stabbed his victim and wanted him dead, was because the victim had raped the defendant's young daughter a few weeks earlier?

The answer is 'No'. The motive behind a defendant's conduct is irrelevant to the issue of *mens rea*. Some may disagree with this and feel that someone who has a 'good reason' for committing a crime should not face criminal liability, but the important point to remember is that motive is not relevant to establishing *mens rea*. It may, however, in some cases, provide a defence to a criminal offence, and it may affect the sentence a defendant receives after he has been convicted. These are separate issues, however, which have no bearing on the *mens rea* of the crime.

In the vast majority of cases requiring proof of intention, the prosecution will seek to establish direct intent. However, the courts have had to consider whether intention may be established in any other circumstances.

Terrorist activities, such as the bombing of crowded places, often result in the death of victims. If those responsible for the killings were charged with murder, there would be little difficulty in establishing that their actions caused the deaths. However, such individuals will often argue that they carried out the bombings because they wanted to make a political statement. Their argument will be that they did not set out to kill (or seriously harm) anyone – that death was not their aim, purpose, goal or desire. This argument would cause difficulties for the prosecution, as they would not be able to establish a direct intent to kill or cause serious harm.

Much of society would be outraged if defendants could avoid a conviction for murder by advancing such an argument in circumstances where it was obvious that, in trying to achieve their purpose, they would kill or seriously injure people.

In order to address such situations, the courts have developed guidelines to assist the jury in deciding the question of intent in cases where direct intent cannot be proven. These guidelines deal with indirect intent. They are also sometimes referred to as guidelines on 'oblique intent'. Essentially, if the crime requires proof of intention, and if direct intent cannot be proved, the jury will be told that, even though a defendant lacked direct intent, they can still find that he intended to kill the victim if they conclude that:

(a)   the consequence was virtually certain to occur; and

(b)   the defendant foresaw that consequence as virtually certain to occur.

EXAMPLE

Trevor sets fire to Zack's house in the early hours of the morning. Zack dies in the fire and Trevor is charged with his murder.

Trevor admits that he knew Zack was inside the property, and assumed he would be alone and asleep. He also admits that he knew that Zack was disabled and that he could not move about without help.

However, Trevor tells police that he did not want Zack to die – he wanted to frighten Zack out of the neighbourhood because Trevor had heard rumours that Zack was a convicted rapist. Trevor had hoped that Zack would be able to escape from the fire. However, he accepted that he knew Zack had no phone and that it would be almost impossible for him to summon help.

Trevor has caused Zack's death, so the *actus reus* of murder is established.

If Trevor is believed, he had *no direct intent* to kill or cause serious harm. His aim was to frighten Zack out of the neighbourhood.

However, the court could decide that he had an *indirect intent* to kill if satisfied:

(a)   that death or serious injury was virtually certain to occur; and

(b)   that Trevor had foreseen death or serious harm as virtually certain to occur.

The admissions made by Trevor mean that it is likely that he did have an indirect intent to kill (or cause serious harm) and, if so, he has committed the *actus reus* of murder with the appropriate *mens rea*.

Recklessness

For many criminal offences, even if the prosecution cannot prove that the defendant intended a particular consequence, they can establish *mens rea* by showing that the defendant was reckless.

The layman's understanding of the word 'reckless' might include terms such as 'careless', 'foolish', 'thoughtless', 'heedless of danger' or 'crazy'. However, in criminal law the word has a specific legal meaning.

Recklessness involves foreseeing a risk and going on – without justification – to take that risk.

This definition raises a number of issues:

- When will taking a risk be *without justification?*
- *Who* must foresee the risk?
- *What* risk must be foreseen?

Without justification

It is impossible to decide whether a risk is justified or not in any abstract way. The *particular* circumstances in which the defendant acted need to be considered. Many assault offences involve proof of recklessness. The same injury might be caused to a victim by two people acting in very different circumstances (see **Examples 1** and **2** below).

EXAMPLE 1

A fire officer moves a victim from a car involved in a serious crash. He injures the victim by moving her. He recognised that he might hurt her by moving her but felt that he had to do so as the car was on fire.

EXAMPLE 2

A thief is trying to escape from the scene of his crime. In order to get away he pushes a police officer, causing him an injury. The thief admits that he realised he might hurt the officer, but says he had to do it in order to escape.

In **Example 1** the fire officer is trying to prevent greater harm by taking the risk of causing injury. If he does not take the risk, the victim might be killed as the car is on fire. The risk of causing injury by moving the victim is justified. Society would not expect this fire officer to face criminal liability for the injury caused – far from criticising the fire officer, the public would applaud his efforts.

However, in **Example 2**, there can be no justification for taking the risk of injuring the police officer. The thief's actions are entirely self-serving. Unlike the fire officer, he is not acting to prevent a greater harm.

Often, the issue of justification will be decided long before a case gets to court. The prosecutor will evaluate the social utility or benefit involved in taking that particular risk in those particular circumstances. It is an objective decision which is not concerned with whether the *defendant* thought he was justified in taking the risk. Instead the relevant question is whether a *reasonable person* would have considered there was any merit in taking the risk. Usually, a decision will be taken not to prosecute if there is clear justification for taking a risk. Consequently, if someone is charged with an offence involving proof of recklessness, that will appear before the court because the facts suggest the taking of a risk that would clearly be unjustified in the eyes of the reasonable person.

Usually, therefore, where a crime requires proof of the *mens rea* of recklessness, the main focus of the court will be on whether the defendant foresaw a risk and went on to take that risk.

Who must foresee the risk?

The prosecution have to prove that the *defendant* foresaw the risk. It is not enough that they prove the defendant *should* have foreseen the risk because a reasonable person would have done so. The test is therefore a subjective one.

An argument which is often raised against the subjective test of recklessness is whether it can be right that a defendant might 'get away with it' because he did not recognise a risk that most members of the public would have seen. This was a question considered by the criminal appeal courts over a period of many years. The final conclusion was that there should be liability for crimes requiring proof of recklessness only if the defendant had a *truly* culpable state of mind – if he did not foresee the risk, he should not face criminal liability. This may be of particular importance when dealing with potentially criminal actions committed by children – an 11-year-old child may not realise a risk that would be apparent to an adult. The current test of recklessness would prevent the prosecution from arguing that the child should have foreseen the risk, and so protect that child from liability.

What risk needs to be foreseen?

The risk that the defendant needs to foresee will always depend on the offence charged. It will be important, therefore, to scrutinise the definition of the particular crime being considered to identify the risk that needs to be foreseen to establish recklessness.

Sometimes the risk will relate to particular circumstances and sometimes to a particular consequence.

PRACTICAL EXAMPLE

The offence of criminal damage (Criminal Damage Act 1971, s 1(1))

Actus reus: destroying or damaging someone else's property.

Mens rea:

- Intent or recklessness as to damage or destruction (*consequence*).
- Knowledge or recklessness as to whether the property belongs to someone else (*circumstance*).

Situations requiring no proof of *mens rea*

The general principles considered above establish that, in order to be guilty of an offence, the defendant must have a guilty mind at the time of his guilty conduct. However, there are some situations when a defendant may commit a criminal offence even though he lacked a guilty state of mind.

Some crimes require proof only of *negligent* behaviour – the offence of careless driving is an everyday example. In such cases, it does not matter what the defendant was *thinking* at the time – if he drove below the standard expected of the reasonable driver, he will be guilty of careless driving. The absence of a 'guilty mind' means that negligent behaviour is usually a matter for the civil, rather than the criminal, courts. However, it is deemed appropriate to attach criminal liability, and to impose criminal punishment, to cases of negligent driving, presumably on the basis of the significant risk of harm posed by poor driving standards.

Other crimes are described as offences of *strict liability*, where a person is liable even though he is morally blameless. He might have acted exactly as a reasonable person would do, but if the crime is one of strict liability, he is guilty. This type of offence is even further removed from the general principles of criminal liability. Strict liability offences generally arise in situations where the need to protect the public from harm is considered paramount. They are most common in relation to environmental, licensing and many driving offences, so that accidentally polluting a river or driving with an excess blood alcohol level are examples of strict liability crimes.

CONSIDERING A RELEVANT DEFENCE

Even if the prosecution are able to establish that an individual committed the *actus reus* of a crime with the relevant *mens rea*, there cannot be a conviction if the defendant has a defence to the crime. There are many defences that might be raised by a defendant. Which defence (if any) may be relevant is dependent on the facts of the incident and the offence with which the defendant is charged.

Essentially, if a defendant raises a defence, he is generally arguing one of two things, either:

(a)   that he lacked capacity to commit the offence; or
(b)   that he had some justification for his behaviour.

It is sometimes possible, for instance, to argue a defence of intoxication. This involves the defendant arguing that he was too drunk to be able to form the *mens rea* of a crime. A defendant in this type of case would be arguing that he lacked the capacity to commit the crime. The existence of a defence of intoxication is controversial. Many would argue that it should not be possible for an individual to escape liability because he was drunk. The courts have endeavoured to establish principles on the defence of intoxication which acknowledge these concerns whilst also adhering to the general principle of criminal law that one should not be convicted if the *mens rea* of an offence cannot be established.

The defence of self-defence (using reasonable force to prevent harm to oneself or another) is an example of a justification defence. The defendant is arguing that although he committed the *actus reus* of the crime with the appropriate *mens rea*, he should not be convicted because he was justified in acting as he did. He committed the crime in order to protect himself or someone else from harm. This defence illustrates the point made above that, although motive is not relevant to the issue of *mens rea*, it may be significant in establishing a defence to a charge. Students of criminal law often query why this distinction is made – does it matter whether motive is looked at when considering *mens rea*, or when considering a defence? The consideration of criminal procedure in **Chapter 3** below will explain the significance of this distinction.

CHAPTER 3

ESTABLISHING GUILT – THE PROCEDURE

INTRODUCTION

When discussing criminal law, frequent references are made to the need for the prosecution 'to establish' certain points. The legal rules for establishing criminal liability were considered in **Chapter 2** above. In order to secure a conviction, the prosecution have to establish:

- *actus reus*
- *mens rea*
- the absence of a defence.

It is important for any practitioner of criminal law to understand the way in which this is done by considering the procedures that are followed in the criminal courts.

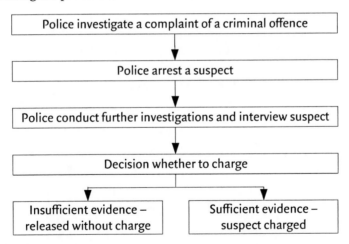

Figure 1: Getting a case to court

If a person is suspected of involvement in a criminal offence such as theft, assault or murder, he will be arrested by the police and taken to a local police station. One of the main purposes of detaining a suspect at the police station is to obtain evidence by questioning him. An interview will be conducted by police officers investigating an offence. The person arrested ('the suspect') will be asked questions about his alleged involvement in the crime which is under investigation.

Sometimes, the suspect confesses during the course of the interview, ie admits his involvement in the offence. In other cases, the suspect may choose not to answer the police's questions, or may give answers which involve a denial of any involvement in the crime.

In addition to conducting an interview with the suspect, the police will conduct other investigations into the offence. For example, if they know there were eye-witnesses to a crime such as a murder, they will speak to those witnesses and take statements from them, detailing what they saw. If a suspect is accused of theft, the police may search his home to try to find the stolen property, as this would be evidence that incriminates him.

Once the police investigations are concluded, a decision must be made as to whether to charge the suspect with a criminal offence. Charging a suspect involves a formal accusation that he has committed a particular crime. If a suspect is charged, his case will be dealt with in the criminal courts.

The decision whether to charge will usually be an easy one to make if the suspect has confessed. In other cases, the suspect will be charged only if there is believed to be enough evidence to prove the case against him.

Once a suspect is charged, the conduct of the case against him is handed over to the Crown Prosecution Service (CPS).

THE RELEVANT COURTS

When a person is charged, he will be required to appear in court. Once that person is in the criminal court system, he ceases to be referred to as a 'suspect' and is instead called a 'defendant'.

Everyone who is charged with a criminal offence, however serious, will make their first court appearance at the magistrates' court, and around 95% of criminal trials will take place in that court. The remaining 5% of cases (often, the more serious cases) will be transferred from the magistrates' court to the Crown Court.

In both the magistrates' court and the Crown Court, the case against the defendant will usually be presented by a CPS advocate, representing the Crown. The defendant will also have an advocate to represent him.

If a case is tried in the magistrates' court, it will be dealt with either by a panel of three magistrates or by one district judge. The magistrates will have no legal qualifications and they will be advised on the law by their clerk. A district judge will be a qualified solicitor or barrister.

The panel (or the district judge) decides all the issues in the case and then uses those decisions to determine whether the defendant should be found guilty (convicted) or not guilty (acquitted) of the charge brought against him.

In Crown Court trials, there will be a judge and a jury. Unlike in the magistrates' court, there is a division of functions in a Crown Court trial:

- The judge will decide all the issues of law. If, for example, there is a dispute between the prosecution and defence about whether a certain piece of evidence may be used at the trial, this will be a matter of law and the judge will decide on the admissibility of that evidence.

- The jury will decide the facts of the case. Members of the jury are drawn at random from members of the public. They are not required to have any legal knowledge. The jury are required to listen to the evidence presented at the trial and decide whether that evidence proves that the defendant is guilty of the offence with which he is charged. If the jury find that the evidence does not establish guilt, the defendant must be acquitted. If they are satisfied of his guilt, they will return a verdict of guilty and the defendant will be convicted.

THE CLASSIFICATION OF OFFENCES

The ultimate venue for trial is primarily determined by the classification of the offence with which the defendant is charged. There are three classifications of offence:

- summary only offences
- either-way offences
- indictable only offences.

Summary only offences

Summary only offences are those which are regarded as less serious crimes. Such offences must be tried in the magistrates' court and cannot be tried at the Crown Court. Many driving offences, such as driving without due care and attention, are summary only, as are the least serious forms of assault where no injury has been caused to the victim.

Either-way offences

Either-way offences are the middle range of offences which may be tried in the magistrates' court or in the Crown Court. These offences include theft, dangerous driving, burglary, and some types of assault and criminal damage. Many either-way offences cover a broad range of behaviour: for example, the offence of theft may cover anything from stealing a packet of sweets from a supermarket to stealing millions of pounds of money or property.

The venue for the trial of either-way offences will depend initially on whether the magistrates' court is prepared to deal with the case, ie whether the magistrates think that they can deal with the complexities of the case and specifically whether they feel, given the seriousness of the facts of the case, that their sentencing powers would be adequate to punish the defendant if he was found guilty.

If the magistrates decide that they are not able to deal with the matter, the defendant will be told that the trial must take place in the Crown Court. This will usually happen if the magistrates feel that the offence would merit a higher sentence than they could impose if the defendant was found guilty.

If the magistrates are prepared to deal with the matter, the final decision as to where the trial is held will rest with the defendant, who is able to decide whether he wants to be tried by the magistrates or go to the Crown Court for trial before a jury.

If a defendant is given the choice as to where his case will be tried, he will often opt for a Crown Court trial as there is a widely-held belief that members of a jury will be more sympathetic to a defendant's case than the magistrates might be.

Indictable only offences

The last group of offences, those which are classed as indictable only offences, are the most serious crimes, such as murder, manslaughter, rape and robbery. These have to be tried 'on indictment', ie in the Crown Court before a judge and jury.

It is often asked why everyone does not have the right to be tried by a jury. The cost of a Crown Court trial far exceeds that of the magistrates' court, and this is a key reason. Additionally, of course, if everyone was entitled to trial by jury, the system would be unable to cope with the increased number of Crown Court trials, resulting in considerable delays before a case came on to trial. Such delay would add to the stress of the defendant who is waiting for his trial to 'clear his name', and would impact particularly on those kept in custody whilst awaiting trial.

There appears little likelihood of Crown Court trials becoming increasingly available. Current political discussions are focusing on a planned reduction of the range of offences for which a defendant might be tried in the Crown Court, in order to save costs. For further information, see <http://www.lawgazette.co.uk/news/law-society-criticises-jury-trial-proposals-039entirely-wrong039>.

BURDENS OF PROOF

Regardless of whether the defendant is tried in the magistrates' court or in the Crown Court, his guilt or otherwise is determined by assessing the evidence put before the court. It is not possible for a person to be convicted of an offence he denies committing unless there is evidence to prove that he committed the criminal behaviour in question (the *actus reus*). As was seen in **Chapter 2**, in many cases there also needs to be proof that the defendant committed the criminal behaviour with a guilty state of mind (the *mens rea*).

The legal burden of proof

In criminal law, the defendant is protected by a presumption of innocence. This means that the legal burden of proving that a defendant is guilty of a criminal offence rests with the prosecution.

The legal burden of proof is a fundamental principle of criminal law. The allegation that someone has committed a criminal offence is a serious one that could have far-reaching consequences for that person's reputation and liberty. It is for this reason that the burden of proving criminal liability lies with the prosecution, rather than the defendant having to prove his innocence.

The burden extends to *proving*:

(a)   the guilty conduct of the defendant; and
(b)   any necessary state of mind required.

In addition, the prosecutor usually has to disprove any potential defences that might be available to the defendant.

PRACTICAL EXAMPLE 1

Carl is charged with an offence of murder. He is accused of killing his wife.

The legal burden of proof requires the CPS to prove:

(a)   that Carl killed his wife (*actus reus*); and

(b)   that he had intended to kill his wife (or at least that he had intended to cause her really serious harm (*mens rea*)).

If the prosecution can prove these two elements but Carl raises a defence, the prosecution would also have to disprove that defence.

If, for example, Carl said that he killed his wife only because she was attacking him with a carving knife and he was trying to defend himself, it is not for Carl to prove that he was acting in self-defence. The prosecution have to prove that he was *not* acting in self-defence.

The evidential burden

Even though the defendant rarely has a legal burden of proof to discharge, he may have an evidential burden imposed upon him in relation to the defence upon which he seeks to rely. Where such a burden exists, it simply means that the defence must raise some evidence of a particular matter so as to satisfy the court that the matter deserves consideration; it is then for the prosecution to disprove it.

One of the situations in which the defendant has an evidential burden is in relation to the defence of self-defence. **Practical Example 2** below revisits the example of Carl's liability for murder, but with a demonstration of the operation of the evidential burden.

PRACTICAL EXAMPLE 2

Carl is charged with an offence of murder. He is accused of killing his wife.

The *legal* burden of proof requires the CPS to prove:

(a)   that Carl killed his wife (*actus reus*); and

(b)   that he had intended to kill his wife (or at least that he had intended to cause her really serious harm (*mens rea*)).

Carl says he acted in self-defence. He must raise the issue of self-defence, as it is a defence that carries an evidential burden. Carl could discharge that evidential burden by going into the witness box and telling the court that, immediately before she died, he was being attacked by his wife, or by producing a medical report showing that on the day of the killing he sustained wounds to his back consistent with him being attacked.

Once that evidence is put before the court, the prosecution will have to disprove the defence: they will have to prove to the court that Carl was *not* acting in self-defence when he killed his wife. They could do this by producing other witnesses who contradicted Carl's story.

THE TRIAL PROCEDURE

The concept of the burdens of proof is often regarded as confusing. It helps if the operation of the burdens of proof is viewed in the context of the overall structure of a criminal trial. **Figure 2** below demonstrates the relevant procedure followed at a trial in the Crown Court. For the purpose of demonstrating the operation of the burdens of proof, the point would be the same in a magistrates' court.

Figure 2: Stages of trial in the Crown Court

The prosecution have to ensure that by the end of stage 4 they have discharged their legal burden of proof in establishing that the *actus reus* of the crime was committed by the defendant with the appropriate *mens rea*. They will seek to discharge this burden, primarily, with the evidence they put before the court at stage 2.

For example, assume a defendant is accused of murder, the allegation being that she shot her victim dead at point-blank range. The prosecution will call evidence from a witness who saw the defendant shoot the victim in order to prove:

(a)   that the defendant killed the victim (*actus reus*); and

(b)   that the defendant intended to kill the victim (*mens rea*).

If the defendant gave evidence at stage 4 that she had intended only to frighten her victim by shooting at him, the prosecution would need to challenge her evidence, by questioning her, in order to prove she had the *mens rea* necessary for the crime.

At stage 4, the defendant might argue instead that, although she intended to kill her victim (and so committed the *actus reus* with the appropriate *mens rea*), she did so only because he was about to shoot her. In such a case she would be raising the defence of self-defence.

This defence imposes an evidential burden on the defendant. The prosecution cannot anticipate every possible defence that might be raised by the defendant. She is therefore required to put some evidence of this defence before the court.

This might be done by questioning a prosecution witness at stage 2. The defence advocate could seek to obtain evidence from the prosecution witness that the victim was pointing a gun at the defendant just before the defendant shot him.

The defendant might also (or instead) discharge her evidential burden by giving evidence herself, at stage 4, that the victim was about to shoot her and that she was responding to that threat when she shot him.

If a defence has been raised by the defence at either stage 2 or stage 4, the prosecution also have to ensure that they have discharged the legal burden of disproving that defence. This might be done by questioning the defendant when she gives evidence at stage 4. The prosecution will ask her questions to challenge the truth of her story, and hope that by so doing they disprove the defence that is relied on.

At the end of stage 4 all the relevant evidence will have been given. The closing speeches by the prosecution and then the defence will review the legal elements of the offence with which the defendant is charged and the evidence heard.

The prosecution speech will review how the evidence heard establishes the guilt of the defendant.

The defence speech will focus on why the evidence heard does not establish the guilt of the defendant.

Inevitably, the closing speeches of each side are going to concentrate on the evidence that helps their argument. The purpose of the judge's summing-up is two-fold:

(a)   to direct the jury on the law; and

(b)   to summarise the evidence.

Once the jury have received the directions and the summary of the evidence, they will retire to consider whether the evidence establishes that the prosecution have discharged their legal burden of proof.

THE STANDARD OF PROOF

In discharging the legal burden of proof, the prosecution must satisfy the court beyond a reasonable doubt that the defendant should be convicted. This is a very high standard of proof – if the court is left with any reasonable doubt after hearing all the evidence in the case, about any of the issues in the case, it must acquit the defendant of the crime as the prosecution will not have discharged their burden.

EXAMPLE

Krista is charged with murder. The evidence has been heard and the jury have retired to consider their verdict.

The jury members are satisfied beyond reasonable doubt that Krista killed her victim.

Most of the jurors are unsure whether she intended to kill her victim, although they all think she 'probably' did.

The jury should return a verdict of 'not guilty'. They have not been satisfied *beyond a reasonable doubt* that Krista had the *mens rea* of murder.

The prosecution have therefore not discharged their legal burden of proof.

PROFESSIONAL ETHICS

If a defendant is charged with an offence, the prosecution have to prove the *actus reus* and *mens rea* of the crime. If the defendant raised a defence, the prosecution would have to disprove that defence in order to secure a conviction.

When considering issues of criminal liability, there is often a temptation to wonder why every defendant does not, for example, argue lack of *mens rea* or why every defendant does not put forward a defence.

The reality is that many suspects, when arrested, are unaware of the legal elements of the crime they are alleged to have committed. Similarly, they do not have the legal knowledge of relevant defences.

When arrested, every suspect has the right to access to (free) legal advice. When the suspect meets with his solicitor, the solicitor will advise the client on the law. However, the solicitor will not give that advice until she has heard the suspect's version of events.

If the client's story shows that he committed the *actus reus* and had the *mens rea* of the offence, and that he has no defence, the solicitor cannot help the defendant to 'invent' a defence. Solicitors are officers of the court and owe a duty to that court as well as to their clients. They are also bound by a Code of Conduct. This Code stipulates that a solicitor cannot assist a defendant to mislead the Court.

EXAMPLE

Lara is arrested by the police on suspicion of the murder of Mike. She tells her solicitor that she has admitted to the police that she deliberately killed Mike because she 'had had enough of him being miserable'.

Lara has therefore admitted that she has committed the *actus reus* of murder with the relevant *mens rea*.

The solicitor will then consider whether Lara's story reveals a possible defence to the charge.

Killing someone because you have 'had enough of him being miserable' is not a recognised defence to a criminal offence!

The solicitor will therefore advise Lara that the prosecution will be able to prove the *actus reus* and *mens rea* of the crime, and that she has no defence to the allegation. Lara should admit her guilt.

> It would not be possible for the solicitor to say to Lara: 'If you told the police that you killed him only because he was about to attack you with a carving knife, you would have a defence.' Only if those were indeed the facts of the case, would Lara have a defence of self-defence.
>
> However, the story she has given to the solicitor raises no suggestion that such a defence might be relevant. The solicitor would be encouraging Lara to lie about why she killed Mike, and the solicitor would therefore be in breach of the Code of Conduct.

One of the questions most commonly asked of criminal practitioners is how they are able to defend someone they know is guilty.

Often, a practitioner will not know that his client is guilty. A solicitor may recognise that there are gaps or inconsistencies in his client's version of events that reduce the credibility of his story, but if a client denies his involvement in a crime, the solicitor's obligation is to represent his client to the best of his ability and to act in his best interests by defending the charge against him.

The situation is different if the client tells the solicitor that he committed the crime. In the absence of any defence, in these circumstances the solicitor does know that his client is guilty. The solicitor's role here depends on the client's intentions:

(a)   If the client is prepared to admit his guilt to the police, there is no problem for the solicitor. The client will usually be charged and, in court, will plead guilty. The solicitor will then help his client by addressing the court on the relevant punishment to be imposed.

(b)   If the client chooses not to admit his involvement to the police but to conduct a 'no comment' interview, the solicitor can continue to represent his client. The reason for this is that the burden of proving a case against a defendant rests with the police (and the prosecution). The suspect has the right to choose not to answer questions at a police interview. It is not for him to help the police to prove their case against him by answering questions that might incriminate him. The solicitor is acting properly in this situation – his client is not lying (because he is saying nothing), so the solicitor cannot be accused of allowing his client to mislead the court.

(c)   If the client wants to lie to the police and deny his involvement in the crime, the solicitor cannot consent to this. He would be allowing his client to mislead the police and the court, and this is prohibited by the solicitor's Code of Conduct. If a client insisted on this course of action, the solicitor would have to stop representing him.

In scenarios (b) and (c), concern may be expressed about the fact that the solicitor knows his client is guilty. The solicitor cannot pass on the information given to him by the client. For example, if the client has admitted robbing a bank or killing his wife, the solicitor cannot tell the police about that admission, even if the solicitor is no longer acting for the client. This is because solicitors owe their clients a duty of confidentiality. They cannot, without the client's permission, share the information they have obtained through the solicitor–client relationship.

The points made above focus on the role of the solicitor at the police station. Similar issues may arise once a case is proceeding through the magistrates' court or Crown Court. The same principles apply, and they are as applicable to barristers representing a defendant as they are to solicitors.

CHAPTER 4

POST-CONVICTION CONSIDERATIONS

In many cases, a lawyer representing a client charged with a criminal offence initially will focus on the issues dealt with in **Chapters 2** and **3**. However, it is also necessary to be able to advise a client as to what might happen once the trial is over.

- If the defendant is acquitted, that is generally the end of the matter.
- If the defendant is convicted, the court will move on to deal with the punishment of the defendant by passing sentence.
- The defendant may also need advice on whether any right of appeal exists.

SENTENCING THE DEFENDANT

If Jane Birtles (see **Chapter 1**) is convicted of an offence of theft, she could be sent to prison for up to seven years. In deciding what sentence to impose, the law requires the court to have regard to the following purposes of sentencing:

(a)   the punishment of offenders;

(b)   the reduction of crime (including its reduction by deterrence);

(c)   the reform and rehabilitation of offenders;

(d)   the protection of the public; and

(e)   the making of reparation by offenders to persons affected by their offences.

These purposes of sentencing reflect the aims or goals of criminalisation considered in **Chapter 1**.

THE SENTENCING LADDER

There are four basic types of sentence which a court may impose. The range of options is often referred to as the 'sentencing ladder', with the particular rung of the ladder upon which a defendant finds himself being determined by the seriousness of the offence. **Figure 1** below sets out the types of sentence in descending order of severity.

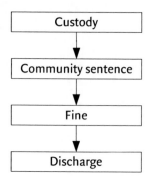

Figure 1: The sentencing ladder

Custody

Custodial sentences involve the defendant being deprived of his physical liberty by being sent to prison for a specified period of time. This is the most obvious illustration of the incapacitation goal of criminalisation (see **Chapter 1**). The sentence removes the defendant from society for a period of time: this punishes the offender and may serve to reduce crime if the sentence passed is regarded as a deterrent to other potential offenders. In some cases, a custodial sentence may have the added effect of protecting the public. If, therefore, a defendant is convicted of an offence of rape and sent to prison for five years, the sentence:

(a)   punishes;

(b)   deters others from committing the same type of offence;

(c)   protects the public from further attacks.

If a judge is sentencing a defendant following a conviction for murder, he must impose a sentence of life imprisonment. No other sentence is available to the court, although the judge is permitted to indicate the minimum term of imprisonment which the defendant should serve.

For all other offences, the court is not permitted to send someone to prison unless the offence is considered so serious that no other form of punishment can be justified. This is known as the 'custody threshold'.

Community sentence

In many cases, the court will decide, on the facts of the case, that the custody threshold has not been passed. In these circumstances, the next consideration will be whether the offence is sufficiently serious to justify a community sentence. This type of sentence involves the defendant being required to take part in one or more activities within the community. The defendant therefore keeps his liberty by avoiding custody, but that liberty is restricted – he may, for example, have to do unpaid work in the community for a specified period of time. Such a sentence will punish the defendant, but it might also enable the defendant to make reparation to people affected by his offence.

A community sentence may also involve the supervision of the defendant, which may help to reform and rehabilitate him so that he is less likely to commit further offences.

Fine

If the offence is not sufficiently serious to impose a community sentence, the court will usually impose a financial penalty on the defendant as a punishment for his offending.

In the magistrates' court, the maximum fine that can usually be imposed is £5,000, whereas the Crown Court has no upper limit on the level of fine that might be ordered. The court will take into account the financial circumstances of the defendant before deciding on the level of fine and, often, the fine amounts to no more than a few hundred pounds.

Some high profile reports of Crown Court cases reveal fines which run into millions of pounds. These are often related to health and safety cases brought against companies. A company, such as Network Rail, is a separate legal entity to the individuals which run it. It is not possible to send a company to prison or to order a company to do unpaid work in the community. In cases involving corporate liability, it is common to see the seriousness of the crime reflected in the heavy fine which is imposed.

Discharge

In rare cases, the court will decide that no immediate penalty should be imposed on the defendant. If the court's view is that the defendant should receive no punishment at all, it will impose an absolute discharge. This is rare, because it appears to achieve none of the goals of criminalisation or the purposes of sentencing. It might, however, be ordered if a person has committed a technical breach of the law but attracts no moral blameworthiness.

For example, an absolute discharge was given to a man who was convicted of an offence after evading payment of his bus fare in London. The facts were that the defendant was guilty because he had no credit left on his travel card when he tried to use it to travel on London transport. The court accepted that the defendant had not realised his card had no credit and so imposed an absolute discharge upon him.

However, it is important to bear in mind that the defendant has still been punished – he has been convicted of a criminal offence. This carries a stigma and could cause difficulties to the defendant in the future, for example in obtaining employment.

Alternatively, the court might impose a conditional discharge. This means that no immediate punishment is imposed for the crime; it is a 'second chance' for the defendant, in that the absence of any punishment is conditional upon him not committing any further offences within a specified period of time. This might be used to give the defendant the opportunity to reform, while retaining the power to punish at a later date if the defendant reoffends.

This 'threat' is intended to keep the offender out of trouble as he will know that, if he commits another offence within a specific period of time, he will be punished, not only for the new offence, but also for the original crime for which he received a conditional discharge.

DETERMINING SERIOUSNESS

The concept of seriousness is at the heart of the principles of sentencing. The law states that, in determining seriousness, the court must have regard to two matters:

(a)   the culpability of the defendant; and

(b)   the level of harm caused.

Culpability involves a consideration of the defendant's state of mind when committing an offence. The highest culpability will be when a defendant has intended to cause harm; where a crime is planned.

Many crimes, assault for example, have a *mens rea* element that may be established by proof of either intention or recklessness. Either state of mind will suffice to establish guilt. However, when the defendant comes to be sentenced, the defendant who intended to harm his victim will be regarded as more culpable (and so the offence will be more serious) than the defendant who was reckless as to whether his victim might be harmed.

In considering the second issue of the level of harm caused, the court can look at harm caused to individuals or to the community at large. 'Harm' does not mean just physical injury, but also, for example, psychological distress and financial loss.

DETERMINING SENTENCE

Once the court has considered the seriousness of the offence, it still needs to make a decision about the actual sentence to be passed.

•   If a judge has decided that the facts of an offence have passed the custody threshold, how is the length of any prison term calculated?

•   If a defendant is to do unpaid work as part of a community sentence, how does the court decide on the relevant number of hours of unpaid work?

•   How does the court calculate the amount of a financial penalty?

The court answers these questions by having regard to sentencing guidelines which are available to help the magistrates or judge make a decision on the appropriate level of sentence.

In the same way that the Rule of Law requires the specific proscription of criminal conduct in order to enable a defendant to be convicted of a crime, it is important that when the court sentences a defendant, that sentence should be proportionate to the offence and that sentences should be consistent. In order to ensure proportionality and consistency, a sentencing court will have regard to any sentencing guidelines prepared by the Sentencing Council for England and Wales. The Council has the power to prepare sentencing guidelines in relation to any sentencing matter. In drawing up the guidelines the Council must have regard to:

•   the need to promote consistency in sentencing;

•   the impact of sentencing decisions on victims of crime;

•   the need to promote public confidence in the criminal justice system;

•   the cost of different sentences; and

•   their effectiveness in reducing reoffending.

Every court has a duty to follow any relevant guidelines, unless it is satisfied that it would be contrary to the interests of justice to do so.

ADVISING ON APPEAL

Many principles of criminal law are decided not by Parliament in legislation but by judges sitting in the criminal appeal courts. Although criminal trials take place in the magistrates' court or Crown Court, if there is an appeal against the decision of the court, the matter could be referred to a number of different appeal courts such as the Court of Appeal and the Supreme Court.

The main routes of appeal which are available in a criminal case differ depending on two things:

- whether the appeal is made by the prosecution or the defence; and
- whether the original trial took place in the magistrates' court or in the Crown Court.

For an overview of the appeals process, see **Figure 2** below.

Practitioners of criminal law will need to understand these routes of appeal for two reasons. First, they may need to advise on whether there is a right of appeal in a particular case. Secondly, the decisions made in the criminal appeal courts often have considerable significance to the conduct of future cases.

Defence appeals

If a defendant wishes to appeal against the decision to convict him and/or against the sentence imposed by the court, his options will differ depending on whether he was convicted by the magistrates' court or by the Crown Court.

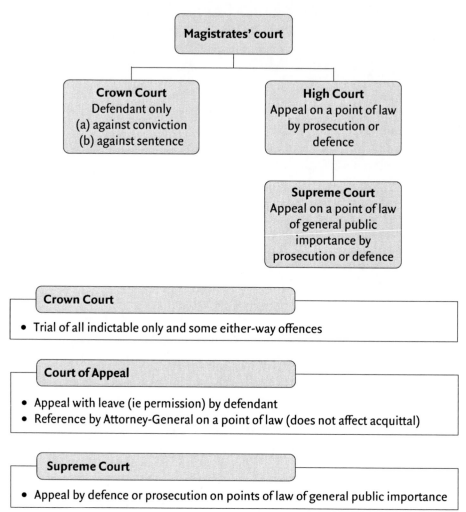

Figure 2: Overview of the appeals process

Conviction by a magistrates' court

A defendant may appeal to the Crown Court against conviction and/or sentence if he pleaded not guilty to the charge against him. If the defendant pleaded guilty, he can usually appeal only against the sentence imposed. If a defendant chooses to appeal against his conviction there will be a further hearing of all the evidence in the case.

If a Crown Court appeal fails, the defence may appeal to the High Court by way of case stated. This means that the appeal must be based on a point of law, and will often be argued on the basis that the magistrates misread, misunderstood or misapplied the law.

Any further appeal will be to the Supreme Court (the highest court of law in England and Wales).

Conviction by the Crown Court

A defendant convicted in the Crown Court may appeal against that conviction (and/or sentence) to the Court of Appeal. Permission to appeal has to be obtained from the Court of Appeal, and it will usually be given if the Court feels that the conviction may be 'unsafe'. This might happen, for instance, if it is felt that the trial judge gave wrong advice when summing up to the jury on the matters they should consider in deciding the defendant's guilt or otherwise.

Appeals to the Court of Appeal are quite different from appeals from the magistrates' court to the Crown Court. In the Court of Appeal there is no re-hearing of the case. The arguments are usually based on points of law, although the Court of Appeal does have the power to consider the evidence given at the trial and/or new evidence which has come to light in the case.

Appeals to the Supreme Court

Until 2009, the highest court in England and Wales was the House of Lords. In October 2009, the judicial functions of the House of Lords were passed to the newly-created Supreme Court.

A defendant may have a right of appeal to the Supreme Court against conviction whether he was convicted by the magistrates' court or by the Crown Court.

Any appeal to the Supreme Court will require leave (ie permission) and must involve a point of law of general public importance. For example, the guidelines for determining the mens rea issue of indirect intent (considered in **Chapter 2**) were developed by the House of Lords.

Many of the cases considered in the study of criminal law, and used as precedent authorities in practice, involve House of Lords (now Supreme Court) decisions. Appeals are often made to the Supreme Court where there is confusion or uncertainty in relation to a particular area of the law which requires clarification.

Key points of law which have been decided by the House of Lords or the Supreme Court include:

- whether a husband could be convicted of raping his wife
- whether a defendant should escape criminal liability because he was drunk when he committed a crime
- what mens rea needs to be proved to convict a person of criminal damage
- whether there is a defence to a charge of assault if the victim consented (or even asked) to be harmed.

Prosecution appeals

The prosecution have far fewer rights of appeal than are available to a defendant. The prosecution's options on appeal are limited where a defendant has been found not guilty of a charge against him.

Appeals following a magistrates' court trial

Usually the acquittal of a defendant by the magistrates' court is conclusive. There is no opportunity for the prosecution to appeal to the Crown Court for the facts of the case to be retried (as the defendant may if he is convicted). If the prosecution wish to appeal against the acquittal of the defendant, the only avenue available is to appeal to the High Court.

Any appeal to the High Court will be by way of 'case stated'. This means that no evidence is given on the appeal; the High Court will simply hear legal arguments on points of law put forward by the prosecution and defence.

The High Court may confirm, reverse or vary the decision of the magistrates' court, or send the case back to the magistrates with its opinion on how the case should proceed.

This is the only appeal route that might result in an acquittal of a defendant in the magistrates' court being reversed so that a defendant is convicted.

If the prosecution appeal to the High Court as above, any further appeal lies to the Supreme Court.

Appeals following a Crown Court trial

The prosecution have no right of appeal against an acquittal of the defendant in the Crown Court: once a defendant has been found to be not guilty by a jury, he or she can never be convicted of that offence on appeal. The jury are entrusted with the task of assessing the evidence in the case and deciding, on that evidence, whether the defendant is guilty. If they conclude that the prosecution have not discharged the burden of proving the defendant's guilt beyond a reasonable doubt, that decision is not capable of challenge.

The prosecution's position here is different, therefore, from that of the defendant if he is convicted. In the latter circumstance, the defendant is able to appeal against the jury's verdict, as discussed above.

There may be circumstances in which the prosecution believe that the jury acquitted the defendant because of an error made by the judge in explaining the law to the jury, or because there is uncertainty about the law in a particular area. Straightforward errors made by the trial judge will not enable the prosecution to take any further action by way of appeal. However, the prosecution may ask the Attorney-General to refer a case to the Court of Appeal where there is a point of law that needs to be clarified.

PRACTICAL EXAMPLE

This procedure involving referral by the Attorney-General was used following the acquittal in the Crown Court of a defendant facing a charge of burglary.

The case against the defendant had been that he entered a property intending to steal from it.

The defendant's evidence had been that he was planning to steal only if there was anything worth stealing at the property, that is, that he had no definite intent to steal but rather a conditional intent – if there was anything worth taking.

The jury acquitted the defendant. The prosecution successfully requested a referral to the Court of Appeal by the Attorney-General.

The question of law referred was whether a conditional intent to steal was sufficient to establish a charge of burglary.

> The Court of Appeal ruled that it was. However, this made no difference to the defendant who had been acquitted by the jury. His acquittal stood.

It is important, therefore, to recognise that references to the Court of Appeal by the Attorney-General are of considerable importance, but only in relation to future cases. The ruling of the Court of Appeal has no impact on the particular defendant in the case that was referred.

Most Court of Appeal decisions are reported in the name of the Crown and the defendant, eg as 'R v Hughes'. It is easy to recognise cases referred by the Attorney-General as they are cited in a completely different way, ie to show the referral was made by the Attorney-General, and to indicate the year of referral and the number of the referral, eg 'Attorney-General's Reference (No 1 of 1997)'.

Prosecution appeals to the Supreme Court

The prosecution may appeal to the Supreme Court on the same grounds as discussed above in relation to a defendant.

The prosecution are likely to want to refer a matter to the Supreme Court where a defendant has been convicted and has then succeeded on appeal to the High Court (from the magistrates' court) or Court of Appeal (from the Crown Court). Once the appeals process has been started by the defendant, therefore, if the prosecution are not satisfied with the outcome of an appeal, they may seek leave to have the matter considered by the Supreme Court.

THE RULE AGAINST 'DOUBLE JEOPARDY'

Historically, the acquittal of a defendant by a jury was always the end of the matter. A defendant could never face prosecution again for a crime for which he had been tried already. This is still true for the majority of offences, but the situation in relation to some serious crimes changed in 2003, when the absolute prohibition on re-prosecution was removed.

This change in the law resulted from the report of the Macpherson Inquiry in 1999. This was an inquiry into the police investigation of the death of Stephen Lawrence in London in 1993. A number of men were brought to trial in 1996 charged with the murder of Stephen Lawrence. They were acquitted of the charge after the judge directed the jury that there was not enough evidence to convict them.

A recommendation made by the Macpherson Inquiry prompted the law to be reformed, so that now an application may be made to the Court of Appeal in certain circumstances, for permission to prosecute for an offence of which the defendant has already been acquitted.

The law states that the Court of Appeal must order a retrial if there is new and compelling evidence and it is in the interests of justice for such an order to be made. In 2011, the Court of Appeal made such an order in respect of one of the original defendants prosecuted unsuccessfully in 1996 for the murder of Stephen Lawrence.

It is important to recognise that the partial removal of the rule against double jeopardy does not alter the points about the options of appeal made above. If a jury acquit a defendant of a charge, that acquittal cannot be reversed on appeal within those proceedings.

THE CRIMINAL CASES REVIEW COMMISSION

The majority of criminal appeal court decisions are the result of proceedings instigated either by the defence or by the prosecution, or by the Attorney-General as described above.

However, some cases are referred to the Court of Appeal by the Criminal Cases Review Commission. The Commission was established in 1997 to take on a role previously undertaken by the Home Secretary, ie to enquire into and possibly refer a case to the appeal courts, usually once all normal avenues have been exhausted by a defendant.

A defendant who has been unsuccessful in his appeal against a conviction in the Crown Court, may ask the Commission to investigate his case. If the Commission feels that the conviction may be unsafe, it can refer the matter back to the Court of Appeal for reconsideration.

Once the case has been referred to the Court of Appeal, that Court has exactly the same powers as it would have on appeal made directly by the defendant.

The Commission may perform a similar function following a conviction by a magistrates' court, but here it would refer the matter to the Crown Court.

The Commission describes its function as follows:

> Our purpose is to review possible miscarriages of justice in the criminal courts of England, Wales and Northern Ireland and refer appropriate cases to the appeal courts ...
>
> We are completely independent and impartial and do not represent the prosecution or the defence.

(See <http://www.justice.gov.uk/about/criminal-cases-review-commission>.)

Between 1997 and 31 March 2012, the Commission referred 498 cases to the Court of Appeal. Of those cases, 460 were heard by the Court of Appeal; and in 321 of those cases, the conviction of the defendant was quashed. This included the case of Sally Clarke, who had been convicted of murdering her baby sons, primarily on the basis of expert evidence relating to sudden infant death syndrome. This evidence was eventually found by the Court of Appeal to be unreliable and led to the quashing of Ms Clarke's conviction and a review of many other cases involving sudden infant deaths.

EUROPEAN UNION LAW

CHAPTER 1

INTRODUCTION TO THE EUROPEAN UNION AND EU LAW

'The future isn't what it used to be.' These words were spoken in the 1920s by Paul Valéry, a French poet, and were a sign of the pessimism that many people felt as they reflected on the carnage inflicted on Europe by World War I. The optimism of the early 20th century had drained away in the face of slaughter on an unimaginable scale. These words could also describe the present-day European Union (EU). The optimism that accompanied the birth of the euro (€) has also drained away as the financial crisis has swept across Europe. At the time of writing it is impossible to predict what will have happened to the Eurozone by the time you read this. Greece may have abandoned the euro and the economies of Italy, Ireland, Spain and Portugal may be under huge pressure. Alternatively the worst may be over, with the euro surviving the crisis. No one knows what the outcome will be.

In the midst of all this uncertainty, is studying European Union law (EU law) worthwhile? While the future is indeed unpredictable, most of the principles of EU law you will read about in this book pre-date the euro. The single currency is actually just one of many aspects of the EU, and the EU can exist without it. Whatever happens in the Eurozone, the core principles of EU law are likely to remain intact. As long as the UK is part of the EU, knowledge of EU law is essential for anyone practising English law.

THE ORIGINS OF THE EUROPEAN UNION

Before looking at why and how EU law has become so significant for English lawyers, a brief look at the origins of the EU will help to provide some context. To understand what the EU is, we need to understand its background and objectives.

Its genesis goes back to the aftermath of World War II. Europe had been torn apart by a deadly conflict and much of its infrastructure lay in ruins. Factories and homes had been devastated by bombing, and agricultural production had plummeted. Europe needed rebuilding on a massive scale, and there was also huge yearning for peace and stability.

The European Coal and Steel Community

There is a lot of debate about how the original idea came about, but Jean Monnet, a senior French civil servant, is generally credited with being the original architect of the European project. Robert Schuman, the French Foreign Minister, announced in a declaration on 9 May 1950 the proposed formation of the European Coal and Steel Community (ECSC). The coal and steel industries formed the core of the French and German economies at that time, and integrating their industries within a European framework promised considerable benefits. Coal and steel were essential resources for any war effort.

Accordingly, pooling coal and steel production would not only boost industrial output and economic growth, it would also make it difficult for Germany to rebuild its military machine. Schuman proposed that Franco-German coal and steel production should be placed under a common High Authority within an organisational framework in which other European countries could participate.

Schuman's proposals led to the setting up of the ECSC in 1952 under the terms of the European Coal and Steel Community Treaty 1951 (ECSC Treaty/Treaty of Paris). France and Germany were joined in the ECSC by Italy, Belgium, The Netherlands and Luxembourg. The UK decided not to participate as it was unwilling to put the recently nationalised coal and steel industries under a supra-national authority.

The European Economic Community

The setting up of the ECSC was an important development, but the really vital step was the next one, the setting up of the European Economic Community (EEC) in 1958. This was done by the European Economic Community Treaty 1957 (EEC Treaty/Treaty of Rome 1957). It is the EEC Treaty which ultimately resulted in the creation of the EU. At the same time the European Atomic Energy Community (EURATOM) was also established to provide a forum for cooperation in the peaceful development of nuclear energy.

The EEC's objectives were mainly economic. Its primary aim was to create a common or single market. The fundamental economic idea was that if there was one big market instead of six separate national ones, everyone would benefit. How? The main advantages that the EEC promised to achieve were:

• economies of scale
• increased choice for the consumer
• greater competition
• cheaper goods.

Also, Europe as a whole would become a bigger player on the world stage and so would be better able to compete with the economic might of the USA and the increasing economic power of Japan. However, the UK remained sceptical, and it was not until 1973 that the UK joined these three Communities under the Treaty of Accession 1972. (As described below, there are currently 27 Member States of the EU.)

Despite its name the EEC was always more than just a free trade zone with purely economic goals. Even the original EEC Treaty contained a number of important social goals, in particular the principles of non-discrimination on grounds of nationality and equal pay for men and women. The preamble to the Treaty also referred to achieving 'an ever closer union among the peoples of Europe', but this had little detailed expression in the Treaty.

How did the EEC hope to achieve its aims of creating a common market? It planned to do so in two key ways:

(a)   by eliminating customs duties and quotas on imports and exports between Member States; and

(b)   by promoting the 'four freedoms', ie the free movement of goods, persons, services and capital between Member States.

To prevent governments and businesses impeding the four freedoms, the Treaty outlawed:

(a)   anti-competitive practices by businesses; and

(b)   discrimination against nationals from other Member States.

It also provided for equal pay for men and women doing equal work to prevent 'social dumping', ie businesses moving from high-wage economies to countries where they could pay low wages to female employees.

The EEC Treaty also provided for the adoption of a Common Agricultural Policy (CAP), which has proved very controversial, and a Common Transport Policy (CTP). However, the CAP and CTP are outside the scope of this book.

The Treaty also set up machinery to oversee its provisions – to ensure that Member States performed their Treaty obligations and permitted the free flow of goods and people. We shall be looking at that machinery later in this chapter and in **Chapter 2**, but first we shall have a brief look at subsequent developments.

The Single European Act 1986

Despite its name, the Single European Act (SEA) 1986 was not an Act of Parliament but another Treaty. Its main purpose was to ensure the completion of the single market by 31 December 1992. The term 'single market' has supplanted the term that was originally used, the 'common market', and means a market in which there are no internal frontiers and in which there is complete free movement of goods, persons, services and capital.

Despite the abolition of customs duties, many barriers to free movement remained, for example different technical standards and administrative hurdles (red tape). The aim of the SEA 1986 was to sweep away the remaining barriers.

EXAMPLE OF TECHNICAL BARRIER

If a company made square widgets in the UK, the abolition of customs duties would not help it very much if French law banned square widgets and permitted only round widgets.

The SEA 1986 made it easier to harmonise technical standards across the Member States, making it possible for square British widgets to be sold in France and round French widgets to be sold in the UK.

The EEC's competence was extended to cover new areas, in particular environmental protection and health and safety in the workplace. This was part of a continuing process in the course of which Member States have given the EEC, and subsequently the EU, more and more powers.

The SEA 1986 also changed procedures to speed up decision-making, particularly measures concerning the single market.

The Treaty on European Union 1992

The Treaty on European Union 1992 (TEU 1992/Maastricht Treaty) was also a very significant – and controversial – treaty. The SEA 1986 had gone a long way towards creating a single market by 1992, but wider objectives were on the political agenda. The heads of state or government of the Member States met in Maastricht in The Netherlands and signed the Treaty in February 1992. However, it did not come into force until November 1993 as a result of a lot of wrangling and opposition within several Member States. It caused a major crisis for John Major, the then British Prime Minister, a referendum in France only narrowly voted in favour of it and Germany had to delay ratification until the German Constitutional Court had approved it.

The TEU 1992:

- created the European Union (the EU);
- introduced EU citizenship;
- made substantial amendments to the EEC Treaty, renaming it the European Community Treaty (EC Treaty);
- extended the aims of the Community to include new areas such as consumer protection; and
- increased the powers of the European Parliament.

However, its main aim was the establishment of economic and monetary union, as it paved the way for the introduction of the single European currency. The single currency, the euro, came into being on 1 January 1999, and the actual coins and notes entered circulation on 1 January 2002. At the time of writing, there are 17 members of the Eurozone. Most Member States are committed to joining the euro when they satisfy the criteria for membership, but the UK and Denmark secured opt-outs. However, the future of the Eurozone is currently clouded by huge uncertainty.

The European Community (EC) still continued to exist as part of the EU, as did the ECSC and EURATOM, though subsequently the ECSC was absorbed into the EC. It was said at the time the EU consisted of three pillars:

- the European Communities pillar
- the Common Foreign and Security Policy (CFSP) pillar
- the Justice and Home Affairs (JHA) pillar.

See **Figure 1** below.

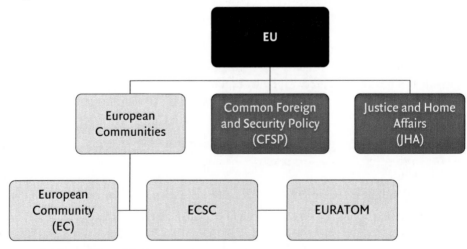

Figure 1: The three pillars of the EU

Technically there were three Communities; however, the EC was by far and away the most important, and the ECSC and EURATOM in practice functioned as part of the EC. The EC had a very developed institutional structure, with the power to make laws that had binding effect in the Member States, sometimes against the wishes of individual Member States. The EC was a 'supra-national' entity to which the Member States had handed over considerable power in certain areas. The Member States also agreed to cooperate in other areas:

- foreign affairs (CFSP)
- immigration and visa policy for people travelling from outside the EU (JHA)
- combating serious crime and terrorism (JHA).

However, in these areas the Member States did not transfer to the EU the extensive law-making powers that they had given to the EC. The CFSP and JHA pillars simply provided a framework for cooperation between governments.

Just in case you are becoming confused by all the initials, the good news is that we can now simply refer to the EU! The next section explains why.

Subsequent Treaties – the Treaty of Lisbon

Two more treaties followed in a relatively short time, the Treaty of Amsterdam 1997 and the Treaty of Nice 2000. In 2004 the Member States agreed the terms of a Treaty establishing a Constitution for Europe (the Constitutional Treaty). Following referendums in The Netherlands and France in which the voters rejected the Constitutional Treaty, the Member States agreed to abandon it and instead in December 2007 agreed the terms of the Treaty of Lisbon to replace it. The Treaty of Lisbon contained many of the provisions that the abortive Constitutional Treaty had contained, but did so by amending the existing treaties rather than supplanting them with an EU constitution. The EC Treaty was renamed the Treaty on the Functioning of the European Union (TFEU). The EU is therefore now based on two main Treaties, the Treaty on European Union (TEU) and the TFEU. The TEU sets out the EU's aims and general institutional framework, while the TFEU adds detail and contains the core provisions relating to the four freedoms, competition law, the CAP and CTP, and other activities of the EU.

For the purposes of this book the most notable feature of the Treaty of Lisbon was to absorb the EC into the EU. The EC therefore no longer exists as a separate entity and so we now simply refer to the EU. EURATOM still continues, but in practice we can disregard it as it has a very low profile. A common supra-national structure now governs most aspects of the EU's activities, including the areas originally covered by the CFSP and JHA pillars. We shall now refer to the EU and EU law, except where the context requires the use of the old terminology.

The combined effect of the Treaties of Amsterdam, Nice and Lisbon was to transfer further powers to the EU, and to make some changes to the institutional structure and decision-making procedures. For example, the EU was given powers to legislate in the field of employment protection and to combat discrimination on the grounds of age, race, disability and sexual orientation. The institutional changes are discussed below.

To deal with the current economic crisis, in March 2012, 25 of the 27 Member States signed the Treaty on Stability, Coordination and Governance in the Economic and Monetary Union (the Fiscal Compact). The Czech Republic and the UK are the two Member States that did not sign. The Fiscal Compact is due to enter into force on 1 January 2013. Although it may prove very significant in economic and political terms, it does not affect the core principles of EU law covered in this book. We therefore do not need to consider it any further.

Between 1957 and the present day, the European Economic Community has transformed into the European Union. The EU has become a body with wider political and social aims, in addition to the original economic ones. The membership of the EU has also increased from six to 27 States, as follows:

The 27 Member States

1957 – France, Germany, Italy, Belgium, The Netherlands, Luxembourg

1973 – United Kingdom, Denmark, Ireland

1981 – Greece

1986 – Portugal, Spain

1995 – Austria, Finland, Sweden

2004 – Czech Republic, Cyprus, Estonia, Hungary, Latvia, Lithuania, Malta, Poland, Slovakia, Slovenia

2007 – Bulgaria, Romania

Croatia is due to join on 1 July 2013. In addition, Turkey, Iceland, Macedonia, Montenegro and Serbia are officially recognised candidate countries. Despite all its current woes, the EU still looks likely to expand.

THE INSTITUTIONAL FRAMEWORK

As students of EU law, you need to know who makes EU legislation and how. You may have heard a lot on the news about the European Commission, the European Parliament and directives from Brussels. In this section we clarify some of the terms that are bandied about and explain briefly how the EU functions.

In developing an institutional framework, it is necessary to consider whose interests the institutions should represent. Even from the early days, the EU (or EEC as it originally was) was a supra-national body to which the Member States had given considerable power in certain areas which have expanded considerably over the years. It was therefore regarded as essential that there should be a body that promoted the aims of the EU and ensured that Member States complied with the obligations to which they had agreed when signing up as members.

On the other hand the Member States did not intend to give up their independence as the price of membership. Although undoubtedly they have transferred some of their powers to the EU, it was certainly not the plan that they should lose their status as sovereign States. Accordingly, there also had to be a body that represented the interests of the Member States.

Further, to ensure that the EEC, and subsequently the EU, had democratic legitimacy, it was vital to have regard to the interests of the citizens of the Member States. After all, the European project is intended to be for their benefit. Consequently, three political institutions were set up to run the EU. They are:

- the Council of the European Union, which represents the interests of the Member States
- the European Commission, which promotes the interests of the EU
- the European Parliament, which represents the people of the EU.

The Council of the European Union

Its composition

The Council of the European Union (often simply referred to as 'the Council' or the 'Council of Ministers') consists of one ministerial representative from each Member State. Its composition is not fixed, as the identity of the national minister attending depends on the subject matter of the meeting. For example, if the meeting relates to EU agricultural issues, the Agriculture Ministers from each Member State attend.

Its functions

The Council's main functions include responsibility for coordinating the general economic policies of the Member States and developing common foreign and defence policies for the EU. However, the function which is most relevant for our purposes is its decision-making role, as the Council plays a very significant role in passing EU legislation.

Voting procedure

Until the early 1980s the Council operated by consensus, so any agreement it reached had to be unanimous. However as the EEC/EU grew larger and larger, and extended its reach into new areas, voting by unanimity became increasingly cumbersome. A single recalcitrant Member State could frustrate the will of the overwhelming majority through its national veto.

Accordingly, since the SEA 1986, a system of weighted voting known as qualified majority voting (QMV) has been used more and more, making it possible for the Council to pass certain measures despite the opposition of a minority of Member States. Under QMV, each Member State is allocated a certain number of votes, chiefly dependent on its size. The number of votes for each State ranges from 29 (Germany, France, Italy and the UK) to 3 (Malta).

To reach a qualified majority, a minimum of 255 out of 345 votes must be cast in favour of the measure (73.9% of the total), and also a majority of Member States must vote in favour. Further, a Member State may ask for confirmation that the Member States constituting the qualified majority represent at least 62% of the total population of the EU. If not, the measure will not be approved.

Qualified majority voting is now the norm for Council voting, but there are a few crucial areas in which Member States retain their veto, for example taxation, social security and foreign policy.

The European Council

Before moving on to the Commission we should briefly mention the European Council, not to be confused with the Council! The European Council consists of the Heads of States or Government of the Member States, plus the President of the Commission, who meet together at summits about five or six times a year.

Originally the European Council was an informal body, but the Treaty of Lisbon made it an institution in its own right. It also created the post of President of the European Council, currently Herman Van Rompuy. The task of the European Council is to provide the EU 'with the necessary impetus for its development' and to 'define [its] general political directions and priorities . . .'. Although it is now a formal institution of the EU, its role is mainly political rather than legal. It formulates policy, and then instructs either the Council or Commission to implement the policy. Many important developments in the EU were preceded by European Council meetings which reached agreement in principle on the issue concerned; for example, enlargement of the EU, the agreement to adopt the euro and the Fiscal Compact.

The European Commission

Currently the European Commission consists of 27 members, one from each Member State. Its main functions are:

- initiating EU policies and legislation
- ensuring Member States keep to their Treaty obligations in its capacity as 'guardian of the Treaties'
- drafting the EU's budget
- implementing EU policies
- administering and enforcing competition law.

The Commission has real power, especially as initiator of most policies and legislation. Its base is in Brussels and it also functions as the EU's civil service; but unlike the UK's civil service it plays a politically active role in EU affairs. Each Commissioner has his or her own portfolio, for example agriculture and rural development, internal market and services, competition and health. To facilitate the Commission's civil service functions, it is divided into departments labelled Directorates-General or Services. For lawyers, one of the most important Directorates-General is that which administers and enforces EU competition law.

The European Council appoints the President of the Commission, subject to approval by the European Parliament. Theoretically the European Council, together with the President-designate, also appoints the other Commissioners, but in practice each Member State nominates its own Commissioner and the other Member States rubber-stamp the nomination. However, once appointed, Commissioners must act independently of their national interests. Indeed most Commissioners jealously guard their autonomy.

The European Parliament must also approve the new Commission as a whole, ie it can reject the whole slate but not individual nominees. Some critics have argued that the Parliament's inability to veto individual Commissioners makes the power of veto meaningless; it would be a brave Parliament that would be willing to veto the whole Commission. However, in 2004 the Parliament was so vehemently opposed to the proposed Italian Commissioner, Rocco Buttiglione, who had made homophobic and sexist comments, that it was ready to vote down the whole slate to prevent his appointment! Consequently, the Italian Government agreed to the withdrawal of his nomination to prevent a crisis.

The Parliament may also require the whole of the Commission to resign by a vote of censure adopted by a two-thirds majority. Although the Parliament has never done this, in 1999 the Commission resigned, as it realised that the Parliament was on the point of passing a vote of censure.

The European Parliament

Its composition

There are now 754 Members of the European Parliament (MEPs). The number will fall to 751 in 2014, when the next elections take place. The number of MEPs for each Member State is roughly in proportion to the size of their respective populations: the UK has 73 MEPs; Germany has the largest contingent with 99 (96 from 2014); and Malta has the smallest contingent with 6 MEPs.

The European Parliament was originally a consultative assembly, with its members drawn from the legislatures of the Member States. This changed in 1979 when the first direct elections took place. Each Member State decides for itself what electoral system it wants to use, though all States use some form of proportional representation, even those such as the UK which use a different system for domestic elections. Most MEPs sit according to their political affiliations, rather than along national lines.

The Parliament's official seat is in Strasbourg where it holds most of its plenary sessions. It also has offices in Luxembourg and Brussels. Committee meetings (which often tackle important issue) take place in Brussels, as well as some further plenary sessions.

Its functions

In the UK and in many other countries, most people probably think that one of the main functions of a parliament is to make laws. This is very much the case in the UK, where the UK Parliament is the supreme law-making body. Although the executive does pass a lot of delegated legislation, Acts of Parliament trump all other sources of law.

Perhaps surprisingly, the European Parliament's functions were for some time chiefly consultative and supervisory. However, the SEA 1986 and subsequent treaties have increased its legislative powers significantly; it has also become more assertive. Nevertheless, it is still arguably the case that the Council is the EU's foremost law-making institution, even though the Parliament remains the EU's only directly-elected body.

Supervisory powers

Apart from passing legislation, another key role for most parliaments is holding the government to account, and this is a role that the European Parliament does fulfil. It does have considerable supervisory powers. As you saw above, the Parliament can veto the appointment of the European Commission and may force the Commission to resign by carrying a vote of censure.

The Parliament can also:

- set up committees of inquiry to investigate violations of EU law by Member States
- appoint a European Ombudsman to investigate alleged maladministration
- table oral and written questions to the Commission and the Council
- ask the Commission to submit new proposals for legislation
- debate the Commission's annual report on the EU's activities.

Budgetary powers

The Parliament also has major role in approving the EU's budget. The Commission presents a draft budget to the Council. The Council (by QMV) submits the budget to the Parliament. The Parliament may propose amendments; and post-Lisbon the Parliament and Council now jointly agree the entire EU budget. In 2011 the EU budget amounted to €140 billion (about £112 billion). This compares to a forecast budget of £722 billion for the UK in 2013.

Legislative powers

The EU's legislative procedures reflect the need to balance the various interests that the institutions represent. It is the Commission's function to draft and submit proposals for legislation, so it plays a key part in setting the EU's legislative agenda. Indeed the Council and Parliament cannot themselves put forward their own proposals for legislation; they have to ask the Commission to do so.

The Commission is responsible for drafting EU legislation, but what happens next depends on which legislative procedure is the appropriate one for the proposed legislation. Originally all that the Parliament could expect was that it would be consulted by the Council. The Commission would submit its proposals to the Council and the Council would then consult with the Parliament. If the Council chose to do so, it could amend the proposals to take into account the Parliament's opinion. On the other hand, the Council could disregard the Parliament's opinion and pass the legislation unamended. This procedure is called the consultation procedure.

However, the picture has changed and the Parliament's role in the legislative process has grown considerably. The Maastricht Treaty introduced what was originally called the 'codecision procedure', but following the Treaty of Lisbon it is now known as the ordinary legislative procedure. The procedure is quite complex, and you do not need to know all the details. However, the essential elements of this procedure are as follows:

- The Commission submits its draft legislation to the Council and the Parliament.
- If the Parliament agrees with the draft then the Council can adopt it and it becomes law.

- If the Parliament amends the draft legislation and the Council agrees with the amendments, the Council can adopt it as amended.
- On the other hand, if the Council does not accept all the amendments, it then adopts its own position on the draft legislation which it submits to the Parliament.
- If the Parliament approves the Council's position or does nothing then the legislation is adopted.
- If the Parliament rejects the Council's position then the legislation fails. At this stage the Parliament already has a veto.
- If the Parliament amends the Council's position, a Conciliation Committee is convened, comprising representatives from the Council and the Parliament.
- The Conciliation Committee will try to agree a 'joint text', a compromise between their positions.
- If the Committee cannot agree a joint text then the legislation fails.
- If the Committee agrees a joint text and both the Parliament and Council vote in favour of it, the legislation will become law; if not, the legislation fails.

The ordinary legislative procedure gives the Parliament the power to propose amendments and to veto draft legislation. The power of veto ensures that it has a good track record in persuading the Council to agree to its amendments.

The change of name to the 'ordinary legislative procedure' reflects the fact that is now the procedure most commonly used. The consultation procedure still exists but now falls under the category of special legislative procedures to indicate that it is no longer the norm. Another example of a special legislative procedure is the consent procedure. Where the consent procedure applies, measures can be passed only if both the Parliament and the Council vote in favour of them. It is much less flexible than the ordinary legislative procedure, as Parliament may accept or reject a proposal but cannot amend it. If Parliament does not give its consent, the measure fails.

Conclusion on legislative procedures

The ordinary legislative procedure applies to a wide range of areas, including legislation concerning the internal market, consumer protection, transport, and health and safety. The list was extended substantially by the Lisbon Treaty.

The consultation procedure still applies to some significant areas such as legislation concerning state aids (government subsidies to businesses) and harmonisation of indirect taxation. The consent procedure applies, for example, to the accession of new Member States and action to combat various forms of discrimination.

Unlike the position in the UK, the Parliament cannot be portrayed as the EU's legislature. As the Council is involved in the passage of all major legislation, it is arguably the EU's main legislative body, as no significant legislation can be passed without its approval. Moreover the Commission's right of initiative gives it a key role in setting the legislative agenda. On the other hand, the ordinary legislative procedure is now used for the majority of EU legislation, and the Parliament's right to propose amendments and to veto legislation does give it real power.

Now that we have looked at how the EU makes laws, in the next chapter we consider the types of laws that it makes and how those laws apply in Member States, including the UK. There is also one vital institution that we have not considered yet – the Court of Justice of the European Union – we shall examine it in the next chapter too.

CHAPTER 2

EU LAW IN PRACTICE

INTRODUCTION

The reason why EU law is so important is that it gives people and businesses rights that they may enforce in the courts of their own countries. It operates alongside national law in the legal systems of all the EU's Member States. Accordingly, in this chapter we shall be looking at how EU law confers rights and imposes obligations that are enforceable in national courts, including English ones. But first we shall look at where we find EU law – its sources.

SOURCES OF EU LAW

Primary sources

The primary source of EU law is the foundational Treaties, the Treaty on European Union (TEU) and the Treaty on the Functioning of the European Union (TFEU). As explained in **Chapter 1**, the TEU contains general principles and sets out the broad institutional structure, while the TFEU covers most of the matters of substance, although still very much in outline. For that reason we shall concentrate on the TFEU, though it would be a mistake to ignore the TEU as it does include some crucial principles.

The TFEU may be defined as a 'framework' Treaty. Even though it goes beyond the TEU in terms of substance, its main purpose is to set out broad principles and objectives in relation to the key policy areas, such as the 'four freedoms' (see **Chapter 1**) and competition law (see **Chapters 5** and **6**). It then provides for the institutions to further the achievement of these objectives by passing so-called 'secondary legislation' (see further below). The EU also had to set up a court structure to interpret EU law, the Court of Justice of the European Union (CJEU), and case law is also an important source of EU law (see further below).

STRUCTURE OF THE TFEU

The *Preamble* sets out in very broad terms the objectives of the Treaty, eg 'an ever closer union among the peoples of Europe' and 'the constant improvements of the living and working conditions of their people'.

Then follow the *Treaty Articles* which are divided into seven parts. These include:

- Part One, which sets out general principles and aims, eg establishing a single market, abolition of obstacles to free movement, and common agricultural, fisheries and transport policies;

- Part Two, which creates citizenship of the Union;

- Part Three, which sets out the Union's policies and contains the core provisions concerning free movement, competition policy and common agricultural policy;

- Part Six, which sets out the Union's institutional and financial framework.

Each Part is sub-divided into titles, eg one title for 'Free movement of persons, services and capital'.

The titles are then further sub-divided into chapters, eg separate chapters for free movement of workers, freedom of establishment, services and capital.

There then follow *Protocols* – annexes at the end of the Treaty, eg the UK's opt-out from the single currency.

European Charter of Fundamental Rights

It has recently become apparent that lawyers need to take account of the European Charter of Fundamental Rights. The EU first proclaimed the Charter of Fundamental Rights at the Nice Summit in December 2000. It sets out very much the same rights as are enshrined in the European Convention on Human Rights (see **Public Law, Chapter 6**), but it also adds other rights which are based on the case law of the CJEU, the common constitutional traditions of the EU's Member States and international treaties for protecting human rights to which they have signed up. These rights include:

- the freedom of the arts and sciences
- the entitlement to fair and just working conditions
- the right to strike
- the right to benefit from medical treatment
- the right to good administration.

Originally the Charter did not have binding legal force, but it is likely that it will now become an important source, as the Treaty of Lisbon has given it legal effect and declares that it has the same legal value as the Treaties.

The Charter applies to the institutions of the European Union and to Member States when they are implementing EU law. The UK and Poland have secured a Protocol providing that the Charter:

(a)   will not extend the ability of the CJEU or British and Polish courts to rule that any of their national laws are inconsistent with the Charter;

(b)   will not create any new rights enforceable before British or Polish courts.

It is hard to evaluate the likely impact of the Charter, but there is likely to be case law concerning the attempt by the UK and Poland to secure partial opt-outs. What is clear, though, is that the CJEU is referring to it in an increasing number of its judgments.

Secondary legislation

This is an 'umbrella' term covering the types of legislation the Council, the Parliament and, to a lesser extent, the Commission may adopt. They are secondary in the sense that it is the primary sources of EU law – the TEU and in particular the TFEU – that give the institutions the power to make them. Secondary legislation is subordinate to the primary sources. We shall look at some hypothetical examples to explain what this means.

EXAMPLES

- The Commission wants to propose secondary legislation that makes it easier for businesses to trade in other Member States. Can it do so?

  Yes. One of the basic aims of the TFEU is to promote free movement on the part of businesses, and so it contains provisions allowing the institutions to pass secondary legislation to promote this aim.

- A majority of Member States represented in the Council and a majority of MEPs in the European Parliament want to pass secondary legislation amending the definition of 'theft' in all the Member States. Can they do this?

  No. Remember that they would have to ask the Commission to propose the legislation. In any event, the institutions cannot legislate in areas outside the scope of the Treaties. The EU may pass laws relating to particularly serious types of crime with a cross-border element – eg terrorism, serious organised crime, human and drug trafficking – but it has no power under the Treaties to define the meaning of 'theft'.

- The majority in the Council and European Parliament decide they want to amend the Treaties to allow them to pass legislation defining 'theft'. Can they do this?

  No. Amendments to the Treaties require the unanimous consent of all the Member States. The Union institutions cannot by secondary legislation amend, repeal or extend the scope of a primary Treaty provision. If the institutions try to pass legislation that contradicts the Treaties, or which is outside their scope, the CJEU has the power to declare it invalid.

As the EU is not a state in the sense that, say, the UK and Germany are states, it has been necessary to devise new types of legislation. Sometimes it is possible for the EU institutions to pass laws that apply uniformly across the whole of the EU, but this is not always the case. The EU comprises 27 Member States, each with its own legal system; indeed the UK has three legal systems! Even if the EU institutions have agreed on the aims that proposed new legislation should achieve, it may not be possible to pass legislation that applies uniformly across all 27 countries. An area of law where this is very much the case is employment law. Each Member State has its own system of employment law, with different rules applying to various employment issues. It would be very difficult for the EU to pass a law that applied in all the Member States in the same way. The TFEU therefore enables the EU to pass different types of legislation depending on the circumstances. We shall examine in this chapter the two most important types of secondary legislation – regulations and directives.

Regulations

The EU will adopt a type of secondary legislation called a *regulation* when it is crucial that there should be *uniformity*, ie that a particular law should apply in identical form throughout all the Member States. For example, in the common agricultural market, goods are traded between buyers and sellers in different countries, and the market can operate smoothly only if common rules are in force throughout the whole of the EU.

Cross-border trade in apples would be hampered if there were variations in national rules about the size and quality of apples.

As soon as a regulation comes into force, it becomes immediately binding in all Member States. According to the TFEU, it is 'binding in its entirety'; Member States cannot pick and choose which parts will apply. It is also *directly applicable*, ie it becomes part of the national law of each Member State. So a regulation becomes part of UK law just as an Act of Parliament becomes part of UK law. It does not require the Government to pass legislation to implement it.

PRACTICAL EXAMPLES OF REGULATIONS

Flight cancellations and delays

You may already know that EU airlines may be required to pay passengers compensation if flights starting or ending at EU airports are cancelled or delayed. Non-EU airlines need pay compensation only for flights starting in the EU. Brief details relating to delays are:

- Flights of 1,500 kilometres or shorter:
  Delay: Two or more hours
  Compensation = €250

- Flights within the EU over 1,500 kilometres and for all other flights between 1,500 and 3,500 kilometres:
  Delay: Three or more hours
  Compensation = €400

- For all other flights:
  Delay: Four or more hours
  Compensation = €600

Similar rules apply to cancellations which cause delays, unless the airline has given at least 14 days' notice of the cancellation. The airline must also provide passenger care by paying for reasonable refreshments and meals, accommodation and two telephone calls/e-mails/faxes/telexes. If the delay or cancellation is caused by extraordinary circumstances outside the airline's control, the airline does not have to pay compensation but must still take care of the passengers. Following the closure of much of European airspace following the Icelandic volcano eruption in 2010, airlines had to pay out large sums to stranded passengers.

The reason that the airlines have to pay compensation is that there is an EU regulation, the Denied Boarding Regulation 261/2004, requiring them to do so. In the absence of this regulation, there would be no obligation on the airlines to pay compensation. Similar legislation does not exist outside the EU and passengers are dependent on the airlines' conditions of carriage for any compensation. Indeed, in many countries, airlines accept responsibility for passenger care only once the flight has departed.

Mobile roaming charges

Over the past few years you may have received texts from your mobile phone provider telling you the good news that the cost of mobile calls and text messages within the EU has gone down. This was in response to the EU's Roaming Regulation 717/2007, which introduced an initial cap effective from 1 July 2009 of €0.43 for calls made to other EU countries and €0.19 for calls received (all prices per minute, excluding VAT). Following a series of further reductions, the Roaming Regulation has now reduced the cap to €0.29 for calls made and €0.08 for calls received with effect from 1 July 2012.

The Roaming Regulation has also capped the price that consumers may be charged for sending a text message while abroad at €0.09 (excluding VAT), compared to an average of €0.28 before it came into force. There are also limits on the charges for data-roaming.

Directives

It is frequently not possible for the EU to pass legislation that applies uniformly across all Member States. Account has to be taken of variations at national level. Accordingly, the aim of legislation will be to 'harmonise' the laws of Member States and to bring them into line with EU aims, but not to impose a uniform system across the whole of the EU. Where the EU institutions want to achieve *harmonisation* or *approximation* of national laws, rather than uniformity, they will use a *directive*. Unlike the position where an EU regulation is in force, each Member State will have its own national law on the subject in question, but the national law will have to achieve the aims of the directive.

According to the TFEU, a directive is binding as to the result to be achieved upon each Member State to which it is addressed, but it leaves to the national authorities the choice of form and methods for achieving the result. Accordingly, a *directive requires implementation*, whereas a regulation, which is immediately binding, does not. Each Member State must pass the necessary implementing legislation required to achieve the result envisaged by a directive. The directive will also give Member States a time by which they must pass the implementing legislation, often two years from the date of the directive.

PRACTICAL EXAMPLE OF A DIRECTIVE

You may have heard of the Working Time Directive (WTD). It required Member States to ensure that the maximum average working week should not exceed 48 hours and that workers should receive adequate rest breaks during the working day. Member States had to implement the Directive by 23 November 1996. However, it was left to the individual Member States to implement the necessary measures, to pass the necessary legislation, to achieve the maximum working week. An EU regulation would have been inappropriate as the WTD granted Member States some flexibility, eg in relation to the reference period by which the average number of working hours per week is calculated and the length of rest breaks during the working day.

Further, the WTD also permitted Member States to allow workers to opt out of the right not to work more than 48 hours each week. This has been referred to as the 'British opt-out', but this is incorrect for two main reasons:

(a)   the WTD allows any Member State to permit workers to opt out of the maximum 48-hour working week; and

(b)   it is the worker who decides whether he or she wants to opt out or not.

The UK's Working Time Regulations implementing the WTD allow workers to opt out, and initially the UK was the only Member State that allowed its workers to do so (hence the label originally attached to the opt-out). However, 16 Member States now allow their workers to opt out, either generally or in certain sectors only.

This example shows why it would not be possible to have a single piece of EU legislation applying uniformly throughout the EU. The WTD gave Member States considerable leeway. The WTD prevents workers from being forced to work more than 48 hours per week on average. However, Member States have some discretion over how the average number of hours per week is calculated and whether or not to allow workers to opt out. Conversely, Member States are free to introduce a shorter working week. The WTD lays down minimum standards with which Member States must comply, rather than a rigid EU-wide standard.

The EU passes a lot of legislation. For example, in 2009 it adopted 233 directives and 425 regulations. The foundational Treaties, in particular the TFEU, are documents of considerable substance. The sources of EU law, like all sources of law, sometimes raise complex issues of interpretation which require resolving. The Treaties have therefore created a court system responsible for dealing with issues of EU law.

The Court of Justice of the European Union

Most legal systems have a hierarchy of courts, with the lower courts dealing with the more straightforward cases and the higher courts dealing with the more complex cases and appeals. The EU has a similar structure. At first there was only one court, but its workload meant that other courts had to be set up to help. **Figure 1** below sets out the court structure following the Treaty of Lisbon:

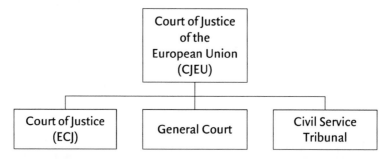

Figure 1: Structure of the EU courts

The Court of Justice of the European Union (the CJEU) is an umbrella term which refers collectively to the Court of Justice, the General Court and the Civil Service Tribunal.

The highest court in the EU's judicial hierarchy is the Court of Justice. As all courts are supposed to be courts of justice, it is often referred to as the European Court of Justice (ECJ) to distinguish it from other courts. This is a convenient abbreviation and we use it to refer to the EU's highest court. Most of the case law referred to in this book comes from the ECJ, and it is on the ECJ that we shall concentrate.

There are 27 judges on the ECJ, one from each Member State, appointed for renewable terms of six years. It is very unusual for all the judges to sit together, and they usually sit in chambers of three, five or 13 judges. The judges elect a President from their number.

Jurisprudence of the ECJ

The approach of the ECJ is rather different from that of English courts. To understand this, it is necessary to examine the two great systems of law in the Western world – common law and civil law:

- Developed primarily in England, the *common law* has been exported to many other countries which were once British colonies. Many former British colonies have common law systems, including, most notably, the USA.
- The *civil law* system is based originally on Roman law. It was chiefly developed in France when Napoleon Bonaparte ruled the country. He introduced the *Code Napoléon* in 1804, and many countries occupied by France in the Napoleonic Wars adopted it; it also spread into parts of what is now Germany. Because the original Member States all had civil law systems, EU law received a lot of inspiration from civil law ideas.

Civil law foundations

Civil law is very different from English law. The ultimate source of law is a Code – such as the French *Code Civil* (based on the *Code Napoléon*) – which aims to be a comprehensive statement of law. A Code is not, however, the equivalent of many English statutes combined into one document, because it approaches its task in a very different way. The Code sets out general principles which the courts interpret and apply to the cases before them. English statutes generally go into much more detail, trying to set out the specific circumstances in which they will apply.

No strict system of precedent

Civil law courts do not have a system of binding precedent. They will consider and respect earlier decisions, but they are free to depart from them. They will respect the need for legal certainty – so once an issue has been decided the same way in several cases, it is rarely decided differently in a later case – but the possibility for departure is there.

It follows that the ECJ does not operate a binding precedent system. The ECJ will attempt to be consistent, but there are some examples where it has changed its mind in later cases. Nevertheless, the judgments of the ECJ are highly persuasive, and it is true to say, despite the absence of a formal doctrine of precedent, that they form an important source of EU law.

Interpreting and applying EU law

As mentioned above, the Treaties are examples of framework drafting, ie they set out general principles rather than detailed provisions trying to cater for all conceivable possibilities. To a lesser extent, the drafting of secondary legislation follows a similar approach.

The judges of the ECJ interpret EU law in accordance with the Treaties, but not just according to the letter of the Treaties, ie their literal meaning, but according to their spirit. The ECJ looks to the purpose behind the law, and interprets it to further the overall objectives of the Treaties. This is known as the *purposive approach*. So, the ECJ will look at the general principles of the Treaties, and interpret Treaty Articles and secondary legislation in a way that will promote the aims of the EU rather than frustrate them. This is different from the traditional English approach, and you will come across cases in this course where the ECJ has been very creative in its jurisprudence. Treaty provisions and secondary legislation are often vague; it is left to the ECJ to fill the gaps. Case law is very significant in the development of EU law.

We have examined the sources of EU law. Now it is time to analyse how they impact on the legal systems of the Member States, in particular the English legal system.

ENFORCEMENT OF EU LAW

You have seen that EU law covers many aspects of business life, ranging from international trade to competition law. It grants businesses the right to trade in other Member States, and it prohibits sex and other forms of discrimination in the workplace. However, these rights would be worthless if there were no mechanism for enforcing them. If the government of another Member State could block imports from the UK with impunity, the free movement of goods (see **Chapter 3**) would be an empty idea. If employees who were victims of discrimination could not take action against their employers, the right not to be discriminated against would be of little value.

The original EEC Treaty envisaged that the European Commission would be the main enforcer of EU law. Certainly, if a Member State breaches EU law by failing to implement a directive or by wrongfully stopping imports, if the Commission cannot achieve a settlement it may refer the matter to the ECJ. Ultimately, if the Member State concerned remains recalcitrant, the Commission is able to ask the ECJ to impose a fine. However, this does little to help the business which has been unlawfully prevented from exporting to another Member State, or the victim of discrimination by an employer. The process takes a long time, and any fine paid by a Member State goes into the EU's coffers rather than being used to compensate those who have suffered harm caused by the breach of EU law. Moreover, the Treaties do not give individuals (including businesses) the right to sue Member States or other individuals in the ECJ. Individuals have very limited rights of access to the Court. The ECJ therefore devised some principles which enable individuals to enforce the rights granted to them by EU law.

Direct effect

One of the core principles of the single market set out in the TFEU is that Member States must not impose customs duties on goods imported from other Member States. In the early 1960s the Dutch customs authorities charged the Van Gend en Loos company, an importer of chemicals, a customs duty contrary to this principle. We shall consider what happened next.

CASE EXAMPLE

Van Gend en Loos

The company sued the Dutch customs authorities in a Dutch court for a refund of the duty paid, relying on its rights under EU law. The Dutch court hearing the case asked the ECJ whether the company could do so. The Dutch Government argued that the EEC Treaty (now the TFEU) was an ordinary international treaty, and while it might be binding on the Dutch Government in international law, its provisions were unenforceable in national courts; the correct means for its enforcement was for the Commission to take the Member State concerned before the ECJ. The ECJ decisively rejected this argument. Why?

The ECJ stated the Community (now EU) constituted a new legal order. In joining it, Member States had limited their 'sovereign rights'. The new system was intended to confer benefits on individuals, and as the Treaty provisions concerning customs duties were clear and unconditional, individuals should be able to enforce them.

This was a landmark judgment. The original Member States had not envisaged that individuals would be able to rely on EU law before national courts in this way. This case established the principle of *direct effect*:

> Where a piece of EU law is sufficiently clear, precise and unconditional, individuals can enforce it before it before their national courts.

It also flagged up the principle of *supremacy* of EU law over conflicting national law. The company could claim back the duty paid even though the Dutch authorities had been acting perfectly legally under Dutch law.

Vertical direct effect

The case of *Van Gend en Loos* involved a claim against an organ of the Dutch Government, ie a private body against the state, sometimes termed a *vertical* claim. **Figure 2** below illustrates this.

Figure 2: Vertical direct effect

Might EU law also be enforced against private bodies as well in a *horizontal* claim?

Horizontal direct effect

The next breakthrough took place in the 1970s in a sex discrimination claim. The original EEC Treaty required Member States to ensure that men and women received equal pay for equal work. On a literal reading, it might seem that it simply imposed a duty on the governments of Member States to make sure that men and women received equal pay. The ECJ had other ideas.

> **CASE EXAMPLE**
>
> *Defrenne v Sabena*
>
> Ms Defrenne was an air hostess employed by the now defunct Belgian airline, SABENA. SABENA paid its female cabin crew less than its male cabin crew, simply because they were female. This was clearly discriminatory on grounds of sex, but Belgian law at the time did not prohibit it. Ms Defrenne sued her employer in a Belgian court. The Belgian courts then asked the ECJ whether an individual could rely on a Treaty Article to enforce rights against another individual in the national courts.
>
> The ECJ followed the purposive approach. The Community (now EU) had not only economic aims but also social ones. It therefore followed that the duty to pay men and women the same for doing equal work applied not just to the Government but also to private employers. **Figure 3** below shows this.

Figure 3: Horizontal direct effect

In subsequent cases the ECJ has decided that many Treaty Articles have not only vertical direct effect but also horizontal direct effect. This means that individuals may rely on them against the state and state bodies (such as local authorities), and also against private bodies. But what about EU secondary legislation?

Direct effect and secondary legislation

Regulations

Consider the example of Denied Boarding Regulation 261/2004. Passengers whose flights had been delayed would not find it to be of much use if they could not enforce the Regulation against airlines that refused to pay the compensation due. Regulations are binding on everyone, not just Member States, so unsurprisingly the ECJ has ruled that EU regulations have vertical and horizontal direct effect. Indeed, at the time of writing a case is being heard in which an airline has refused to pay for passenger care following the Icelandic volcano eruption. The airline has argued that it is unfair to require it to pay passengers considerably more in passenger care than the cost of the ticket. The outcome of the case is currently awaited.

Directives

The position as regards directives is a lot more complicated. After all, a directive is addressed expressly to Member States. It imposes on them the duty to pass national legislation to achieve the aims of the directive in question. Initially the general view was that directives would not have direct effect. A couple of further landmark judgments of the ECJ considered the issue.

> **CASE EXAMPLES**
>
> **Van Duyn v Home Office**
>
> Ms Van Duyn was a Dutch national. Shortly after the UK joined the EEC, she wanted to enter the UK to work for the Church of Scientology. The UK immigration authorities refused her entry, as they regarded the Church of Scientology as socially undesirable. (Note that this is no longer the view of the UK authorities.) Ms Van Duyn challenged her exclusion before the English courts, relying on a directive that limited the grounds on which she might be excluded.
>
> **Marshall v Southampton & South West Hampshire Area Health Authority**
>
> Miss Marshall was a senior dietician employed by the NHS in the 1980s. UK law at that time permitted discriminatory retirement ages for men and women. Women could be forced to retire at 60, while men might carry on working until they were 65. Miss Marshall wanted to carry on working, but was forced by her employer to retire at the age of 62. As her case involved retirement ages and not pay, she could not rely on the Treaty Article granting men and women the right to equal pay, since that applied only to pay and not to other conditions of employment. However, there was a directive, the Equal Treatment Directive (the ETD), that prohibited discriminatory retirement ages. Miss Marshall sued her employer in an English tribunal relying on the ETD, despite the UK law.
>
> In both these cases the English court/tribunal asked the ECJ whether directives could be used in this way.

What arguments can you think of in favour of allowing Ms Van Duyn and Miss Marshall to rely on the directives in question?

(a)   Directives would not be particularly useful if people could not rely on them in their national courts simply because the government concerned had failed to bring its national law into line with them. The 'useful effect' of directives would be weakened.

(b)   Directives had granted Ms Van Duyn and Miss Marshall certain rights. It would be nonsensical if a government could defeat their claims on the grounds that it had failed to implement the directives that gave them those rights. This would allow governments to benefit from their wrongdoing in failing to implement the directives.

The ECJ decided that individuals (including businesses) should be able to rely on directives *vertically* against the state and state bodies. You may have noticed that Ms Van Duyn was relying on a directive directly against the Government, while Miss Marshall was suing her employer, the NHS. Although the NHS is a public body, it was not exercising a governmental function in relation to Miss Marshall; rather, it was acting in the capacity of her employer. The ECJ said that this was irrelevant. Directives could be enforced against state bodies whatever the capacity in which they were acting. (As a footnote, Ms Van Duyn still lost her case. Although she helped to establish a core principle of EU law, on the facts the British Government had not breached the directive.)

Remember that directives give Member States a deadline by which they have to be implemented. The ECJ has accordingly held that directives are unable to have direct effect until this deadline has passed; until then Member States have not actually broken EU law by not implementing them.

So, provided they are sufficiently clear and precise and the deadline for implementation has passed, directives have vertical direct effect. But can they be enforced against private bodies?

Unlike EU regulations which apply to everyone, directives are specifically addressed to Member States. Would it therefore be fair to impose obligations on, say, a private employer where a Member State had failed to implement a directive? After all, it would not be the employer's fault that the directive had not been implemented.

CASE EXAMPLE

Duke v GEC Reliance Ltd

Shortly after Miss Marshall had succeeded in her claim, Mrs Duke tried to follow suit. Her employer had forced her to retire at age 60 as she was a woman, while her male colleagues could carry on working to 65. There was one crucial difference in Mrs Duke's case – her employer was in the private sector. This proved fatal to Mrs Duke's claim. UK law permitted the discriminatory retirement ages, and as her claim was horizontal, rather then vertical, she lost.

This may strike you as unfair. Two women suffered from the identical discrimination: one succeeded in her claim because she was employed in the public sector, but the other lost because she was employed in the private sector. This does seem to introduce a form of discrimination between public-sector and private-sector employees. On other hand, it would have been unfair to have made Mrs Duke's employer liable for discrimination. Whatever the merits of the UK law on retirement ages that existed at the time, the employer reasonably believed it was acting legally, relying on the clear terms of the UK legislation. While UK legislation subsequently removed this anomaly as regards retirement ages, it still remains an issue. However, the ECJ has rejected all suggestions that it should remove the anomaly by extending horizontal direct effect to directives. It has, however, tried to mitigate the unfairness to those involved in the private sector in other ways.

Definition of 'state body'

As noted above, the ECJ held that individuals could rely on directives vertically against states and state bodies. State bodies include not only central government departments, local authorities and the NHS, but also other bodies performing public functions. For example, utility companies such as British Gas and Thames Water are regarded as state bodies, even though they are no longer in the public sector.

Principle of interpretation

An employee suing a private-sector employee cannot rely on the direct effect of a directive; he or she must bring the claim under national law. However, what if national law is not entirely clear on a particular point? Is there some way of introducing EU law by the back door? The ECJ has indicated that there is, as it has told national courts that they should interpret national law in the light of any relevant directive if it is possible to do so. The following provides an interesting example of this approach.

CASE EXAMPLE

Webb v EMO Air Cargo (UK) Ltd

Ms Webb had been sacked by her employer shortly after joining it because she was pregnant. She sued her employer on the basis of sex discrimination. As her claim was a horizontal one, she could not rely on the direct effect of the ETD which prohibited employers from sacking workers because they were pregnant. At the time (late 1980s) UK legislation did not expressly cover the point; moreover, English courts had previously decided that sacking a woman because she was pregnant would not be discriminatory if the employer would also have sacked a man who was going to miss work for a substantial period of time. However, the House of Lords interpreted the UK legislation so as to be consistent with the ETD. Ms Webb therefore won her case.

The principle that the House of Lords applied in this case is termed *indirect effect*. It does to some extent enable the horizontal enforcement of directives. However, it would not have helped the unfortunate Mrs Duke above. Unlike the UK legislation in Ms Webb's case, the UK legislation in Mrs Duke's case expressly allowed discriminatory retirement ages. It would have been impossible for the English court to have interpreted it as forbidding discriminatory retirement ages.

So is someone in Mrs Duke's position left without a remedy?

Liability of the state

In Mrs Duke's case, who was the chief culprit in depriving her of her rights under EU law? Was it her employer? Probably not. After all, it was simply applying the relevant UK legislation. The chief culprit was the British Government. It was the Government's responsibility to implement the ETD properly, and it had not done so. The ECJ has therefore developed the principle of *state liability*. Where a government has broken EU law, for example by failing to implement a directive, anyone who has suffered loss as a result may be able to sue that government for damages. While this came too late to help Mrs Webb, it provides another means of enforcing directives.

The following fictitious example summarises the position.

EXAMPLE

Imagine that the Nurses Directive (fictitious) requires Member States to enact legislation by 1 September 2012 granting nurses the right to take 40 days' holiday per year. Suppose the British Government has taken no action by that date. Assume that an existing Act of Parliament gives nurses in England the right to take 30 days' holiday per year. Lillian is a nurse employed by the NHS: Omar is a nurse employed by a private hospital. They both want to sue their respective employers as they are both given only 30 days' holiday. What are their options?

> (a)   As the directive is sufficiently clear and precise, Lillian may sue the NHS, relying on the *vertical direct effect* of the Nurses Directive. Omar cannot, as his claim is a *horizontal* one.
>
> (b)   Omar could try to rely on *indirect effect* against his employer. This would involve trying to persuade the English court to interpret 30 days' holiday in the existing UK Act as meaning 40 days' holiday. This would be impossible.
>
> (Suppose instead that the UK Act gave nurses the right to take a 'reasonable amount of holiday'. Then it might have been possible for Omar to persuade the English court to interpret 'reasonable amount of holiday' as meaning '40 days' holiday'.)
>
> (c)   Failing indirect effect, Omar could sue the British Government under the principle of *state liability* for failing to implement the Nurses Directive by the due date. His claim appears to be a very strong one.

Note that for direct and indirect effect, Lillian and Omar will sue their respective employers. For state liability Omar will sue the government department that should have ensured the implementation of the Nurses Directive by the due date.

NATIONAL COURTS AND THE ECJ

You will have noticed several mentions in this chapter of national courts asking the ECJ for an interpretation of EU law. On what basis may they do this?

National courts are responsible for enforcing rights granted by EU law. Interpretation of EU law is therefore often relevant to the outcome of cases before national courts, including English ones. It could be left to national courts to interpret EU law in the cases they hear, but this might easily lead to chaos. Suppose the Czech, French, English, Maltese and Bulgarian courts all interpreted an unclear provision in the Denied Boarding Regulation in a slightly different way. Passengers and airlines would not know where they stood. If the single market is to operate smoothly, there needs to be uniform interpretation of EU law. The TFEU accordingly gives national courts hearing a case involving issues of EU law the power, and sometimes the duty, to refer questions of EU law to the ECJ. The national court will suspend proceedings in the case while the ECJ answers the question. The national court will then apply the ECJ's answer to the case in hand.

The ECJ has developed many core principles of EU law in this way, for example the supremacy of EU law, direct effect, indirect effect and state liability. You will have noticed that many of the cases we have looked at in this chapter relate to sex discrimination, so we shall end it by briefly looking at the topic.

Sex discrimination

The cases involving Ms Defrenne and Miss Marshall above were examples of *direct discrimination*: Ms Defrenne was paid less than her male colleagues doing the same work simply because she was a woman; Miss Marshall was forced to retire earlier than her male colleagues simply because she was a woman. Sex discrimination works both ways, and it is equally wrong to discriminate against a man on grounds of his sex. Nonetheless a significant majority of sex discrimination claims involve discrimination against women.

Direct discrimination is hardly subtle, but it is not the only possible form of discrimination. Consider the following example.

EXAMPLE

A company employs part-time workers and full-time workers. They all do the same work, but the company pays the full-time workers £10 per hour and the part-time workers £8 per hour. At first sight this does not appear to be discriminatory, but a closer examination of the workforce reveals that 75% of the full-timers are male, while 80% of the part-timers are female. Although the criterion for assessing pay, the number of hours worked, appears to be neutral, it has an adverse impact on the section of the workforce that is predominantly female. In principle this is an example of indirect discrimination.

Where discrimination is direct, it is very difficult for an employer to defend it, as there are only very limited exceptions that employers may invoke. For example, if the nature of a job demands a person of a particular sex, the employer can employ a person of that sex. Thus a theatre company casting a male role is able to exclude female applicants for the role and *vice versa*.

Indirect discrimination is not necessarily as pernicious as direct discrimination. Accordingly, where discrimination is indirect, it is open to the employer to justify it on objective factors unrelated to sex. So, in the example given above, the company could justify the discrimination, but would have to prove that its different rates of pay were in pursuit of a legitimate business need and were proportionate. Employers have generally found it very difficult to justify apparent indirect discrimination, as the courts require strong evidence from them.

EU law has combated sex discrimination right from the start of the original EEC, and now it also combats discrimination on grounds of age, race, disability and sexual orientation. It also covers many other social and employment issues. English lawyers who ignore the reach of EU law are extremely foolhardy, and are likely to find themselves at the wrong end of a professional negligence claim.

CHAPTER 3

FREE MOVEMENT OF GOODS

INTRODUCTION

Suppose an English company, Widgco PLC, is a manufacturer of widgets. It has factories in Birmingham and Plymouth. If it wants to sell some widgets to customers in London and Manchester, the process is relatively straightforward. Widgco will know that the same rules will govern the sales contracts, whether the customer is located in London, Manchester or indeed in any part of England. There will be no language barriers and transporting the widgets should not pose any serious difficulties. The customers will also probably want to pay for the widgets in pounds sterling.

As explained in **Chapter 1**, the creation of the single market is one of the key aims of the EU. In a fully-fledged single market, it would be as easy for Widgco to sell its widgets to customers in Barcelona and Rome as to customers in Birmingham and Plymouth. However, despite far-reaching developments in EU law, we have not yet reached that position. This chapter will explore how EU law has attempted to break down those barriers and what still needs to be done.

Historically, trading goods across international borders has been complex. There have been numerous barriers to free trade. These may broadly be categorised as tariff and non-tariff barriers. Tariff barriers are taxes on imports, while non-tariff barriers are generally laws and other practices which restrict imports without expressly imposing a financial charge on them. Examples include import permits and other bureaucratic hurdles, quotas and national technical standards with which imported goods have to comply. We shall first look at tariff barriers.

TARIFF BARRIERS

Tariff barriers fall into two main categories (see **Figure 1** below). Each of these barriers is examined further below.

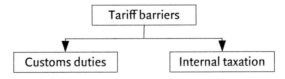

Figure 1: Types of tariff barriers

Customs duties

Customs are a type of tax imposed on imports simply by reason of the goods crossing a border. They are a good way of protecting domestic industries. If widgets imported into the UK face a customs duty of 20% then Widgco will to some extent be protected from competition from cheap imports. Conversely, if Widgco wants to export to other countries, it may struggle to compete with domestic manufacturers if its widgets are subject to customs duties. Clearly, customs duties are incompatible with the single market, where goods should be able to move freely from one Member State to another. One vital element of the single market is therefore a customs union between the Member States.

You may have come across customs duties when coming back from an overseas trip outside the EU. If on your travels you bought goods above the tax-free threshold, eg cameras, computers and clothes, you should have gone through the red channel on your return home, declared the goods and paid customs duty on them. However, in terms of revenue raised, tourists returning from overseas trips represent a minor aspect of customs duties; most of the revenue is raised from imports by businesses. Whenever a container ship arrives at a British port, much of the cargo unloaded will be subject to customs duty. According to HM Revenue and Customs (HMRC), there are around 14,000 categories of goods; on average duties range from 5%–9% of the value of the goods, though the rate may go as high as 85%.

It was relatively easy for the EU to get rid of customs duties on trade between Member States. Although the calculation of duties may have been complex, the duties themselves were simple to identify and Member States abolished them without much delay. However, the EU also had to make sure that Member States eradicated more subtle charges on imports too. For example, some Member States imposed charges for inspecting certain types of imports to make sure they did not pose a public health risk. Sometimes these charges bore little relation to the cost of carrying out these inspections. The EU had to make sure both that the inspections were really necessary and that the charges were reasonable. The EU could not allow Member States to get away with disguised protectionism.

Widgco will therefore be able to export its widgets throughout the EU without having to worry about customs duties. It will be able to compete with other EU manufacturers on even terms, at least so far as customs duties are concerned.

Suppose, though, that Widgco manufactures only its top-quality widgets in England, outsourcing the manufacturing of its basic widgets to China. Assuming that the customs duty on imported widgets is within the average rate of 5%–9%, outsourcing basic widgets to China is likely to be cost-effective due to the lower wages there. Widgco will pay customs duty when it imports the widgets, but once the duty has been paid Widgco will then be able export the widgets to any other Member State without any further customs duties being levied. Could Widgco shop around the EU and import its Chinese-made widgets into the Member State charging the lowest rate of customs duty on widgets? The answer is no, as the rate of customs duties for all imports into the EU is set centrally by the EU itself. Moreover, the Member States do not keep the duties paid – they have to hand them over to the EU.

> **EXAMPLE**
>
> If an electrical retailer imports televisions for resale in the UK, it will pay a customs duty of 14% of the value of the goods to HMRC. Ultimately the British Government will have to account to the EU for the duty collected. If the retailer was based in France, or indeed in any other Member State, the position would be identical.

Accordingly there are two aspects to the customs union:

(a) The *external aspect*. Whenever goods are imported into the EU, customs duties are imposed on them at the same rate in accordance with the *common customs tariff*, irrespective of the point of entry.

(b) The *internal aspect*. Where goods are manufactured in the EU or they have been imported into the EU and any customs duties on them have been paid, they may then circulate freely throughout the EU without any further duties being levied.

Internal taxation

Throughout the EU, when goods are sold to consumers they are subject to value added tax (VAT). The rates vary from Member State to Member State, but all Member States impose VAT on the sale of goods.

A simple way for Member States to protect domestic products would be to charge a higher rate of VAT on imported products than on domestic prducts. This overt form of discrimination is prohibited outright by EU law. Some Member States, realising that they will not be able to get away with blatant discrimination, have used covert forms of discrimination to protect their own producers. For example, suppose Member State A imposes a very high car tax on cars with certain features, but a much lower tax on cars without those features. It turns out that cars with the highly-taxed features are made in Member State B but not in Member State A, whose manufacturers concentrate on different features. Ostensibly the criteria on which the car tax is based are neutral and not dependent on the country where the cars are made. However, on further analysis it is clear that Member State A is using the tax to protect its own manufacturers. Accordingly, EU law also prohibits covert discrimination. Unless Member State A can prove it has a good reason for its tax policy, such as environmental protection, and that the tax rates are proportionate, EU law will prohibit that policy.

Outright bans on imports

Occasionally Member States ban the importation of particular products. The motivation for a ban may be protectionist; on the other hand, the Member State concerned may think it has a good reason for its action. For example, the UK prohibits the importation of certain types of pornography which may nevertheless be permitted in other Member States. It might be argued that the same rules should apply throughout the single market. However, EU law does give Member States some leeway in this field, permitting such bans provided the same rules apply to domestic producers. Even so, Member States may ban imports from other Member States only where there are pressing reasons for doing so, such as public health or public morality. Moreover, the bans must go no further than necessary.

Quotas

Import quotas are another from of protectionism. There are two types of quota, one placing a limit on the quantity of a particular product that may be imported within a given time frame, the other placing a limit by reference to the value of the goods. Clearly quotas are incompatible with the single market, and EU law has banned them on trade between Member States.

NON-TARIFF BARRIERS

The EU has found it relatively straightforward dealing with fiscal barriers, outright bans on imports and quotas. They are easily recognisable and Member States have been willing to eliminate them without much argument. However, there are other forms of protectionism which the EU has had to combat too. These may be labelled *non-tariff barriers*.

Examples include:

- nationalistic public procurement policies (ie state bodies buying only from domestic producers)
- state subsidies to domestic industries
- differences in technical standards/packaging and similar requirements
- nationalistic private purchasing preferences.

Public procurement

Suppose the French Government wants to buy €10 million-worth of widgets for a major construction project. It puts out to tender the contract for the supply of the widgets. Widgco wants to bid for the contract, but discovers that the tender documents specify that the widgets must be made in France. This would disqualify all non-French manufacturers of widgets from the tender process. In a single market, manufacturers from all Member States should be able to bid for the contract. Public procurement rules in the EU require that major government contracts are put out for tender on a non-discriminatory basis. Accordingly, Widgco should be able to bid for the contract on the same terms as its French competitors.

State subsidies

Suppose Widgco also wants to export its widgets to Italy, but discovers that the Italian Government subsidises Italian manufacturers. Widgco would be unable to compete effectively. State subsidies also frustrate the creation of the single market, so EU rules on state aids prohibit state subsidies except in limited circumstances.

Differences in technical and other requirements

Before joining the EU, each Member State would have had its own rules governing a vast range of products relating, for example, to technical standards, packaging, labelling and pricing. These rules would have been very wide-ranging and complex, so we shall illustrate their impact with another fictitious example.

EXAMPLE

Suppose UK legislation specifies a maximum weight for widgets on grounds of health and safety. Most of Widgco's widgets are the maximum weight allowed by the UK legislation. However, the German authorities take a slightly different view from their British counterparts, and the German maximum weight limit is 10% lower than the British weight limit. Widgco will therefore find it difficult to export its widgets to Germany. It will have to develop a separate production run for the German market, losing the benefits of economy of scale. It will therefore be hard for Widgco to compete with German manufacturers who are geared up to comply with the German limit. At first sight the German legislation appears to be neutral, based on the weight of the product and not its origin, but its practical effect is to exclude British widgets from the German market.

One possible way of dealing with this type of barrier is for the EU to develop EU-wide harmonised standards. The EU would decide what the maximum weight for widgets should be, and widgets that complied with the European standard would be able to circulate freely throughout the EU. You may have noticed the C€ mark on some products; it is a declaration by the manufacturer that the product meets the applicable European standard. The letters 'CE' stand for 'Conformité Européenne', meaning 'European Conformity'. However, even when there were only six Member States, it was often difficult, and sometimes impossible, to obtain agreement on a common European standard. In our hypothetical example concerning widgets, the British would argue that the European standard should be based on the British weight limit, while the Germans would argue for their weight limit.

If it proves impossible to agree a European standard for widgets, will Widgco have to adapt to the German standard to export to Germany? A real-life example will cast some light on how to approach this question.

PRACTICAL EXAMPLE

Until the 1980s, German beer purity laws provided that only barley malt, hops, yeast and water could be used in the production of beer. These laws dated back to the ancient reinheitsgebot of 1516. Additionally, there was a blanket ban on additives in beer. While beers from other countries that contained different ingredients could be sold in Germany, they could not be marketed as 'bier' (beer). Ostensibly the beer purity laws were not based on the country of origin of the beer, as they did not stop the sale of beers as bier from other Member States provided those beers complied with them. However, their practical outcome was to exclude many beers from other Member States from the German market as they contained either maize or rice (commonly used in beer), or additives. The effect of the German law was protectionist, as German consumers would be unwilling to buy foreign beer if it was not called 'bier'.

There was no EU-wide standard for beers, so it was left to the European Court of Justice (ECJ) to apply its own case law. The ECJ recognised that where there is no EU-wide standard then Member States are free to set their own standards. Some degree of regulatory diversity is acceptable, even though it may hinder free trade. Nonetheless, there are limits to Member States' freedom of action, as national standards must be compatible with EU law. Germany had to show that its beer purity laws were pursuing legitimate aims and were proportionate. Germany argued that its laws were necessary for consumer protection and public health reasons. While these are legitimate reasons in the public interest, the Germans laws were disproportionate. There were alternative means of protecting the consumer that were less restrictive of trade, for example labelling the ingredients. A blanket ban on additives went further than was necessary to protect public health. Germany allowed additives in other alcoholic drinks, so could not impose a total ban on additives in beer simply on the grounds that beer was consumed in large quantities in Germany.

Could this line of reasoning help Widgco? In the absence of an EU-wide standard, Germany would be able to set its own limit for widgets. However, the weight limit makes it harder for Widgco (and possibly widget manufacturers in other Member States) to sell its widgets in Germany, so Germany would need to justify its rule. Germany would have to produce cogent evidence that its weight limit was necessary for health and safety reasons. If the evidence showed that the higher British limit was equally effective then Germany would no longer be able to maintain its lower limit. If the evidence was inconclusive then Member States would be free to form their own opinion and legislate accordingly.

If Germany is unable to justify its lower weight limit for widgets then Widgco will be able to export its widgets to Germany. It is the users of widgets who will decide whether they prefer to buy the lighter German widgets or the heavier British ones.

Unfortunately, not all of Widgco's problems will be over. It is one thing to have the legal right to sell a product in a new territory; it is another to persuade potential customers to buy it. Widgco will need to develop marketing strategies to persuade German customers to switch to its widgets. Widgco may have to overcome nationalistic private purchasing preferences. Indeed, while Germany had to abolish its beer purity laws, many German breweries still voluntarily abide by them as a marketing technique, and many German consumers still prefer German beer.

Marketing of products

There are various strategies that suppliers of products may use to break into new markets. Advertising is one of the most obvious, but there are others, for example offering price discounts or better-quality goods. National restrictions on marketing techniques may impede Widgco's ability to penetrate into new markets.

As well as exporting to Germany, Widgco would like to export its widgets into other Member States. Unfortunately, it faces a number of problems (all fictitious, but based on actual cases):

- In Poland there is a ban on most forms of advertising of widgets, including on the Internet, direct mailing of potential customers via e-mail and by ordinary post. The reason for the ban is that widgets are a complex product, and so they can be advertised only in trade journals.

- In Slovakia the main outlets for widgets have to close at weekends.

- In Belgium widgets can be sold only in specialised outlets by qualified dealers.

- In Italy there is a minimum price for widgets. Widgco would like to undercut the prices charged by the existing Italian producers, but they are already selling their widgets at the minimum price.

- In Bulgaria there is a maximum price for widgets. Bulgarian widgets are a lot cheaper than Widgco's, but Widgco thinks its widgets are of better quality. However, in order to make a profit it would have to charge more than the maximum price.

None of these national laws affects the product itself. The German law (above) specifying a maximum weight for widgets would force Widgco to modify its widgets for the German market; these laws governing marketing of products would not require Widgco to modify its widgets. Nonetheless, Widgco would argue that these laws are making it harder for it to break into these markets.

Advertising restrictions

How does the Polish law on advertising affect Widgco? After all, Widgco can still advertise in trade journals. While a prominent advertisement in a trade journal may attract some interest in Widgco's products, it may not be enough to enable Widgco to make significant inroads into the Polish market. Unless Widgco is able to advertise more actively, it is unlikely to be able to break into the Polish market in a big way.

Trading hours

The Slovakian law on trading hours raises some complex issues. The Sunday trading saga in England and Wales in the 1980s and 1990s illustrates them. Under the old Shops Act 1950, it was unlawful for most shops to open on Sundays. However, some shops, mainly large DIY stores, started opening on Sundays and were then prosecuted for breaking the law. In their defence they argued that the ban on Sunday trading breached EU law as it restricted the free movement of goods. If shops could not open on Sundays then they would sell fewer goods. And if they sold fewer goods, they would import fewer goods from other EU Member States. At first the courts gave some weight to this argument, but eventually decided that Sunday trading laws did not in fact restrict free movement. Although they might affect the overall volume of sales, they imposed the same burden on domestic goods as on imported goods. They did not make it harder for imported goods to break into the domestic market. As they did not have a protectionist effect, they did not restrict free movement. Moreover, many critics argued that shop opening hours had little to do with achieving a single market. There was no reason why the EU should be involved in deciding when shops might be open or not.

It seems unlikely, therefore, that Widgco has any grounds for challenging the Slovakian law. While it may reduce the number of widgets sold there, it is unlikely to impede Widgco's access to the Slovakian market.

Limiting outlets

The Belgian law limiting the outlets for widgets raises similar issues. Widgco may argue that to break into a new market it needs access to as wide a range of outlets as possible. On the other hand, Belgian buyers of widgets know where they have to go to buy widgets. All widget manufacturers, including Belgian ones, are subject to the same restrictions, and it is hard to see how the Belgian law puts Widgco at a disadvantage compared to its Belgian competitors. Widgco can still advertise its widgets and use other forms of marketing, so it has the means to persuade Belgian users of widgets to try out its widgets.

Minimum price

The Italian law is clearly impeding Widgco's access to the Italian market. It is protecting the Italian manufacturers from competition. A key aspect of the single market is to stimulate competition between manufacturers from different Member States so that consumers will benefit from increased choice. While Widgco may try to persuade Italian customers that its widgets are better quality, price is a key aspect when it comes to deciding whether to buy a product. Unless Widgco's widgets are cheaper than those of its competitors, Italian buyers may prefer to stick with the local brand they know. If Widgco is able to undercut its Italian competitors then it has a better chance of tempting Italian customers to switch.

Maximum price

In Bulgaria Widgco is unable to compete on price, but it can compete on quality. However, even if it is able to find buyers who are willing to pay a higher price for its widgets, it cannot charge that price. If it cannot make a profit then Widgco will be reluctant to try to break into the Bulgarian market. The effect of the Bulgarian law is protectionist, insulating Bulgarian manufacturers from competition from more expensive but better-quality products.

In the past, price controls were common in many countries. However, the prevailing economic view is that effective competition serves consumers better than price controls. Regulators should concentrate on ensuring that there is genuine competition in a given market rather than on setting maximum prices for products.

Summary

National laws on the marketing of products may have the effect of protecting domestic products from competition from products from other Member States. On the other hand, while they may limit commercial freedom, they may not necessarily have a protectionist effect. EU law has had to distinguish between those rules that are protectionist, such as strict bans on advertising and restrictions on prices, and those which are not. The former impede the development of the single market, the latter do not. EU law need be involved only where national rules inhibit the single market (see **Figure 2** below).

Figure 2: EU law and national rules on marketing

CONCLUSION

There are many ways in which States may protect their domestic industries. The EU has been able to eliminate the obvious ones quite easily. So customs duties, overtly discriminatory taxation and quotas have been swept away. Eliminating covert protectionism has proved more difficult.

Member States have legitimate concerns relating matters such as public health and morality. They may justifiably want to exclude products from other Member States on these grounds. EU law has therefore had to balance the promotion of the free movement of goods (a key element of the single market) on the one hand with the legitimate interests of Member States on the other. Many of the cases in this area have concerned national technical standards and rules relating to the packaging of items. Where Member States are able to show that they are pursuing a legitimate aim in the public interest and that their rules are proportionate, they have been able to maintain their national rules, even if their practical effect is to exclude imports. Conversely, if they are unable to do so, they have had to amend or abolish their national rules.

As Member States sometimes have successfully defended national rules which impede free movement, the EU has not yet attained a fully integrated single market. It has achieved a lot, but there is more to do. Where differences in national standards impede free movement, the EU is attempting to introduce EU-wide standards to replace the different national standards. Indeed, about half the trade in the EU is now covered by harmonised EU rules.

Marketing arrangements have needed special attention. Some national rules governing the marketing of products merely limit commercial freedom without harming the single market. Equally, others do make it harder for imported products to compete with domestic products, and so hamper the development of the single market. EU law has had to make sure that it targets only those rules that have a protectionist effect.

Promoting the free movement of goods is merely one aspect of the single market, albeit an important one. The EU is more than a free trade area. It also seeks to promote personal and business mobility, the free movement of persons and businesses (see **Chapter 4** below).

CHAPTER 4

FREE MOVEMENT OF PERSONS

INTRODUCTION

The EU has done much to promote the free movement of goods. Complete free movement has not yet been achieved, but the EU has made substantial progress. Yet even if all barriers to free trade had been swept away, we would still be a long way short of having a complete single market. As well as promoting cross-border trade in goods, ensuring that individuals and businesses can move freely between Member States is also a key goal of the single market. This chapter will examine how EU law has made it easier for individuals and businesses to move between Member States.

When the original Treaty of Rome came into force, the aims of the EEC (which developed into the EU) were primarily economic. So in granting rights of free movement, EU law initially focused on economically active people, workers and the self-employed. We shall start by looking at the position of workers.

FREE MOVEMENT OF WORKERS

Currently in the UK there is a lot of debate about the level of immigration, and indeed the Government is committed to reducing the number of immigrants. Public anxiety in EU Member States about the level of immigration is not something new, so right from the start the EU had to take measures to prevent governments from introducing covert measures that would discourage workers from exercising their rights of free movement.

Obstacles to free movement

There are two main ways in which governments may inhibit free movement or workers: entry and residence requirements; and conditions of residence/employment.

Entry and residence requirements

Suppose that François is a French national who wants to leave France (his home state) and work in another Member State (the host state). He knows that EU law gives him the right of free movement, so he goes to the embassy of his prospective host state to find out if there are formalities with which he has to comply before he can work there. To his dismay he discovers that he will have to cut through a vast amount of red tape before he is able to take up a job in the host state. For example, he has to obtain a visa costing €250 to gain entry to the host state. To obtain a visa he has to fill several application forms in triplicate, and he also has to submit with his application an offer of employment from his prospective employer. Although François is assured that his application is a mere formality, it will take at least three months to obtain a visa as there is a long waiting list. His visa will be valid only for one year, so he will have to renew it annually at a cost of

€200. He will also have to register at the local police station every month. Failure to do so may result in immediate deportation. Moreover, he will be able to bring his wife and children with him only if he can prove to the satisfaction of his prospective host state's embassy that he has sufficient financial resources to support them.

When confronted by this mountain of red tape, it would be no surprise if François decides that it is not worth his while to move to the host state. The host state has successfully frustrated his right to free movement by tying it up with red tape!

EU law makes sure that host states cannot use red tape to frustrate a worker's right of free movement. A worker can obtain entry to host states with the minimum of formality, simply on production of his or her passport or identity card. A worker may be required to register with the host state's authorities, but a worker cannot be deported for failing to do so. Registration is merely an administrative formality; failing to register is therefore not a serious offence and so the host state cannot impose excessive penalties for not registering.

Another way in which a host state might try to discourage workers from exercising their free movement rights would be for the host state to allow workers into its territory, but not their family members. If François could not bring his wife and children with him, he would be unlikely to move to a new country. Members of a worker's family therefore have the right to accompany the worker. Accordingly, François would be able to bring his wife and children with him. To obtain entry to the host state they too would only have to produce their passports or identity cards. François will not have to prove that he can support them.

Conditions of residence/employment

Suppose that François decides to move to the host state and he takes up a job there. He then discovers that life is not particularly easy for foreign nationals, as he faces an array of difficulties. For example, his employer pays its employees who are host state nationals a higher salary than François for doing the same work. When François and his wife try to enrol their children at their local state school, the head teacher tells them that there is a surcharge of €250 per term for foreign children. The national railway company provides railcards to families, enabling them to take advantage of discounted rail fares; François applies for one, but the ticket office staff tell him that only host state nationals are eligible for railcards.

It would be no surprise if François, when faced with this discrimination, decided to pack his bags and return home. Life would be much more pleasant in France. Accordingly, EU law prohibits discrimination against workers from other Member States and their family members. François can claim equal pay from his employer. His children have the right to attend the local state school on the same conditions as apply to the host state's children. He is entitled to a railcard for his family. So EU law provides as a basic principle that workers from other Member States have the right to be treated equally with the host state's nationals.

Permissible restrictions on free movement

Entry and residence requirements

There are various reasons why host states may want to restrict free movement of workers:

- economic reasons
- political reasons
- social reasons
- reasons of public safety.

We shall go on to consider which of these reasons, if any, may be acceptable in EU law.

Economic reasons

During times of economic downturn Member States often want to reduce immigration to protect their workforces from what is sometimes perceived as 'unfair competition' from foreign workers who are prepared to accept lower wages. By restricting immigration, governments hope to alleviate unemployment amongst their own nationals.

Economic reasons such as this are unacceptable as justifications for restricting free movement. Economic theory suggests that labour mobility is a positive factor in promoting economic growth and improving standards of living within the EU's single market. Workers in areas of high unemployment will move to areas of low unemployment to seek work, thereby reducing imbalances within the single market. Even in times of recession, it is counterproductive for governments to take protectionist measures, as protectionism ultimately results in lower growth overall and makes it harder for individual economies to grow.

Restricting free movement for protectionist motives is also completely contrary to the ethos of the single market. In a single state market such as the UK, no government would ever consider measures preventing workers from moving around the country, for example by stopping workers moving from London to Newcastle or Cardiff. Similarly in the single market, the same principles should apply to workers moving between Member States as to workers moving within a single state.

Political reasons

Immigration is a very sensitive political issue in many Member States, and political parties often include in their election manifestos a promise to cut the number of immigrants. Political reasons are just as contrary to the ethos of the single market as the economic reasons discussed above. It is inconceivable that a British government would seek to check the flow of people from the north of the UK to the south or vice versa, even if improbably such a policy were electorally popular.

Social reasons

Sometimes people are worried about the practical impact immigration may have on local communities. One major anxiety is pressure on housing. There have been reports of immigrant families living in overcrowded accommodation. Local families are also anxious that they may lose their place in waiting lists for social housing in favour of immigrants. The stress on public services is another concern, for example sharp rises in the number of primary school children who do not speak the local language well. However, there is considerable debate as to the validity of these concerns.

Again, limiting immigration for these reasons would be contrary to the ethos of the single market. No government in the EU would restrict internal migration for these reasons.

Nonetheless, EU law does make limited concessions to these concerns. When new Member States join the EU, existing Member States are usually permitted to limit immigration from the new Member States for a temporary transitional period. As this is an exception to the usual rules governing free movement, restrictions on immigration from new Member States cannot continue beyond the end of the transitional period.

Public safety

This is a field where EU law does give Member States some leeway. Governments have a responsibility for maintaining law and order within their territory, and may legitimately exclude or deport nationals from other Member States in the interests of public security. Nevertheless EU law does require a balance to be maintained between free movement on the one hand and Member States' legitimate concerns on the other.

Suppose François decides to move to the UK with his family, but the UK Border Agency wants to exclude them for the following reasons:

- François used to belong to an extreme racist political party, but resigned his membership 20 years ago.
- François was convicted 15 years ago of a vicious assault in which he inflicted serious injuries on the victim and served three years in a French prison.
- François' wife Marie was cautioned by French police last month for possessing a small amount of cannabis.
- François regular views pornography on the Internet.

We shall examine these reasons to see if they may justify François' exclusion under EU law.

To exclude an individual, the host state must show that the person concerned constitutes a current threat to public safety. What François may have done in the past cannot be held against him unless it shows that he is a current threat to public safety. The fact that he may have held extremist views 20 years ago cannot justify his exclusion.

Can François' criminal record justify his exclusion? One view is that he committed a very serious offence and so should forfeit his right to be able to move to another Member State. An alternative view is that his past conviction should be taken into account only to the extent that it shows that he is a current threat to society. EU law tends towards the latter view. To be able to exclude François, the UK Border Agency would have to prove that he posed a current and serious threat. If in the 12 years since his release from prison he has not reoffended, it would be very difficult to prove this.

Marie has, however, committed a much more recent offence – possession of a small amount of cannabis. This is a minor offence, and in the UK the police normally give only a warning to someone for a first offence of possession. As Marie's offence is a minor one, she does not constitute a sufficiently serious threat to society to warrant her exclusion from the UK.

While some people may regard Francois' interest in pornography as immoral, it will probably not justify his exclusion from the UK. In the UK it is illegal to watch extreme pornography, such as child pornography. Would it be consistent with the single market to exclude a non-national who is intending to behave in a manner that is perfectly legal in the host state? If British nationals can watch certain types if pornography without facing any sanctions, it would be difficult for the UK Border Agency to argue that François poses a serious threat to society if he watches the same type of pornography. As long as François confines himself to legal pornography, he cannot be excluded from the UK.

In EU law there is a presumption in favour of free movement. If Member States want to limit free movement, the burden is on them to show they have a legitimate reason for doing so and that any restriction imposed goes no further than necessary.

Conditions of residence/employment

Although it is very difficult for host states physically to exclude migrant workers from their territory, to what extent may they impose conditions of residence or employment that might discourage free movement? For example, could a host State seek to justify a surcharge of €250 per term for foreign children attending state schools on economic grounds – the effect on government finances of a large number of immigrants? The answer is no. To impose such a surcharge on the children of migrant workers would be blatant discrimination, direct discrimination based on nationality. Unsurprisingly, EU law takes a strict line against this type of practice. Direct discrimination of this nature is completely contrary to the single market and the principle of equal treatment, and EU law permits it only in exceptional circumstances.

What sort of circumstances might be considered exceptional? Suppose François wanted to join the British army. A nation's armed forces are vital to a state's security, and the British army wants to be sure that its soldiers, who may fight in a war, owe their allegiance to the United Kingdom. EU law recognises that it would not be appropriate to apply the principle of equal treatment to the armed forces, and so does not force the British army to open its ranks to foreign nationals.

A particularly controversial issue is the right for migrant workers and their families to claim social security benefits. The principle of equal treatment allows them to claim the same benefits as the nationals of the host state. If François could not claim unemployment benefits if he lost his job, he might decide it was not worth moving to another Member State to work. 'Benefit tourism' has therefore become a particular concern. It has been claimed that a large number of people have moved from Member States (mainly the newer ones) where social security benefits are relatively low to those where benefits are high. There is considerable debate concerning the prevalence of benefit tourism, with many commentators arguing that its scope has been greatly exaggerated. Nevertheless EU law has recognised that Member States have a legitimate interest in curbing benefit tourism, and allows them to impose eligibility requirements even if they indirectly discourage free movement. For example, residence requirements are permissible as a condition for eligibility for benefits as long as they are reasonable. This prevents immigrants from claiming benefits as soon as they arrive in a host state. On the other hand, EU law does scrutinise eligibility requirements carefully to ensure that they do not go further than is necessary to protect the legitimate concerns of Member States.

The self-employed

Self-employed individuals are also economically active. In the UK a plumber running a business in Plymouth is able to move freely to any other part of the country to pursue his or her trade. Similarly in the EU's single market, a plumber, or any other self-employed person, operating in his or her home state should be able to move freely to other Member States.

EU law therefore grants the same rights of free movement to self-employed persons as it grants to workers. Consequently, Andrea, a self-employed electrician trading in Austria, would be able to bring her long-term partner and their children with her if she decided to set up her business in any other Member State.

Suppose Andrea does move to another Member State with her family. She finds a family house and is ready to set up her electrician's business from premises near home. Unfortunately she discovers that things are not that simple. She runs into the following problems:

- She wants to rent some railway arches from the national railway company. The company refuses to give her a lease because she is a foreign national. As a state-owned company, it has a policy of granting leases only to nationals of the host state.
- She wants to borrow some money from a local government agency that provides low interest loans to new businesses, but her application is rejected as loans are only granted to individuals who have been resident in the local area for three years.
- Local trading standards officials threaten to prosecute her as they claim she does not have a proper qualification. The host state does not recognise her Austrian qualification.
- She wants to bid for a contract to install some new wiring in a new state hospital, but the tender documents specify that sole traders are not eligible to bid. Only firms that comprise three or more electricians are eligible. When she queries this requirement, she is told that it is a government requirement as sole traders are more likely to go out of business than larger firms.

Although all these situations are fictitious, they are based on examples that have occurred in real life and which have been considered by the ECJ. EU law may therefore help Andrea to challenge the laws and practices, as they inhibit her rights to free movement.

Railway arches

The policy of the national railway company is an example of *direct* discrimination based on nationality. Only nationals of the host state are eligible to rent railway arches. No exceptional circumstances exist which would permit this blatant discrimination.

Loans for new businesses

The residence requirement of three years in the local area is preventing Andrea from obtaining a low interest loan. This is making it more difficult for to set up her business as an electrician in the host state. However, it is not as onerous as the nationality requirement for renting railway arches. It does not completely exclude non-nationals from obtaining loans. After three years Andrea would become eligible. Also, the same rule applies to the host state's nationals – a host state national who had not lived in the local area for three years would also be ineligible for a loan. On the other hand, host state nationals are more likely than non-nationals to have lived in the local area for three years. The residence requirement therefore puts non-nationals at a disadvantage compared to host state nationals.

You will see from this example that it is not only direct discrimination that may hinder free movement. While by no means all of the host state's nationals will meet the residence requirement, a far higher proportion of them will be able to fulfil it than non-nationals. EU law on free movement therefore covers laws and practices that are *indirectly discriminatory* on the grounds of nationality. However, indirect discrimination is not usually as severe as direct discrimination, so Member States are able to justify it more easily. If the host state can prove that the residence requirement is pursuing a legitimate aim and is proportionate, EU law will permit it. It is possible that requiring applicants for the loans to have a link with the local authority granting them may be permissible.

Qualifications

The host state does have a legitimate interest in ensuring that only properly qualified electricians trade within its borders. Unqualified electricians would pose a serious risk to the lives and limbs of its residents. A requirement to have the local qualification is another example of indirect discrimination. It is not impossible for a foreign national to obtain the local qualification, but host state nationals are much more likely to have obtained it. However, Andrea does have a qualification obtained in Austria. Can the host state simply ignore it and require Andrea to requalify? The answer depends on the nature of Andrea's qualification. The host state should recognise it if it is similar to its own qualification. If there are differences, the host state may require Andrea to prove that she can make up the gap between the two countries' qualifications.

François, as a worker, is in the same position as Andrea so far as his qualifications are concerned. EU law treats the qualifications of workers in the same way as the qualifications of the self-employed.

Wiring contract – ban on sole traders

As Andrea is a sole trader, she cannot bid for the contract. Here, the requirement that only firms comprising three or more electricians are eligible applies equally to the host state's nationals. An electrician from the host state who was a sole trader would face the same barrier as Andrea. Might Andrea argue that she is being discriminated against indirectly? This seems unlikely, as there is no reason to suppose that foreign electricians are more likely to be sole traders than the host state's electricians. Yet EU law still applies to this scenario.

The ban on sole traders is preventing Andrea, an electrician from Austria, from bidding for the contract. It is therefore making it harder for her to exercise her right of free movement. The host state may argue that it is making life equally hard for its own electricians. However, EU law does not accept this argument. Its approach is to say that the host state's law is making it harder for an electrician from another Member State to exercise her right of free movement. It does not matter that the law imposes the same burden on the host state's own electricians. So EU law covers all laws and practices that discourage free movement, even if they are entirely non-discriminatory.

As with indirect discrimination, the host state may be able to justify this law. First, it would have to show that it was pursuing a legitimate aim. The reason given to Andrea for this law is that sole traders are more likely to go out of business than larger firms. It does seem legitimate for the Government to be concerned about the solvency of businesses who tender for important contracts. It is not enough, though, for the Government to show it was pursuing a legitimate aim. It would also have to show that the law was a proportionate way of achieving that aim. It would need to produce evidence that sole traders are indeed at a greater risk of insolvency than larger businesses, and that there are no less onerous ways of achieving the aim.

You have seen that EU law covers the following situations so far as restrictions on businesses are concerned:

(a)   direct discrimination;

(b)   indirect discrimination; and

(c)   non-discriminatory restrictions.

As direct discrimination is overt blatant discrimination, it is very hard for Member States to justify laws that directly discriminate against foreign businesses. It is only in exceptional circumstances that EU law permits them. It is, on the other hand, easier for Member States to justify indirectly discriminatory and non-discriminatory restrictions on free movement. Such restrictions apply also to a host state's own nationals, albeit, in the case of indirect discrimination, that they have a stronger impact on foreign businesses. Member States may therefore justify them if they have a legitimate aim and are proportionate. The burden, though, is very much on the Member State concerned to produce sufficient evidence.

This section has examined the rights of Andrea, a self-employed electrician. You should also be aware that EU law grants the same rights to companies. A large retailer wanting to open stores in other Member States would also benefit hugely from EU law on the free movement of persons, as would providers of financial and other services.

EXAMPLE

AdStar plc is a leading advertising agency with its headquarters in London and branches in many EU cities. It wants to set up a branch in Bucharest, the capital of Romania, as significant business opportunities have arisen there since Romania joined the EU in 2007. However, it discovers that a (fictitious) Romanian law imposes a limit on the number of advertising agencies in each region of Romania based on the region's population; the limit has already been reached for the Bucharest region. AdStar would therefore have to locate its branch in a different region of Romania, some distance from the capital where many of its potential clients are based. Can AdStar challenge the Romanian law?

We can analyse AdStar's problem in the same way as we analysed Andrea's. The Romanian legislation seems to be indirectly discriminatory. It applies to all businesses, but existing Romanian advertising agencies are likely to have got in first; they would probably have been able to set themselves up in the Bucharest region before foreign ones. The Romanian Government could try to justify its legislation on the grounds that it was pursuing a legitimate aim. For example, it could argue the law ensured that businesses did not become excessively concentrated in Bucharest but were spread evenly around the country. This argument is unlikely to succeed. Even if the aim is a legitimate one, the law is probably disproportionate. The location of businesses should depend on supply and demand, rather than on arbitrary numerical limits.

FREE MOVEMENT AND BEYOND

As explained at the start of the chapter, EU law initially focused on economically active people. We have accordingly looked at workers and self-employed people in some detail. However, the EU is much more than an economic organisation. As the EU's social and political goals have grown, EU law has extended the right to free movement to non-economically active persons. The first to benefit from the extended rights of free movement were students and persons with sufficient means to support themselves, as long as they had adequate health insurance. Students also had to show they were able to support themselves, so they could not claim maintenance and other grants in the host state. Many retired people have taken advantage of their right of free movement, and official statistics for 2011 show that 100,000 British citizens are receiving their retirement pensions in Spain, though the actual number of older British people living there is thought to be much higher. Indeed, the Foreign Office estimates that over 800,000 British citizens live in Spain.

However, the extension of rights of free movement did not stop there, as in 1993 the EU introduced the concept of Union citizenship.

Union citizenship

Everyone who is a national of a Member State of the EU is also a citizen of the EU. Citizens of a state can normally move freely within their own country. British citizens can move freely from Birmingham to Manchester, from Manchester to Cardiff and from Cardiff to Edinburgh. Does Union citizenship therefore mean that British citizens can now freely move to any other Member State, and vice versa? The answer is no: Union citizenship is not identical to being a citizen of a single state. EU law spells out that that rights of free movement are still subject to conditions. However, those conditions have become increasingly relaxed.

Union citizens now have the following rights:

- The right of entry to any other Member State and residence there for up to three months, subject only to producing a valid passport or identity card.
- The right of residence for more than three months if they –
    - are employed or self-employed;
    - are students; or
    - have sufficient resources to support themselves.
    (Students and persons with sufficient resources must also have health insurance.)
- The right of permanent residence after five years' lawful residence in the host state.

Family members of Union citizens are able to accompany them, even if they are not Union citizens themselves.

The ECJ has also interpreted Union citizenship flexibly. You might suppose that if someone stopped working in his host state and did not have health insurance, he would lose his right of residence under EU law. After all, a person with sufficient resources has the right of residence for more than three months only if he has health insurance. However, the ECJ has ruled that this is not the case. As long as the person does not impose an undue burden on the host state's resources, Union citizenship allows him to retain his right of residence. The ECJ has gone beyond the strict letter of the law.

Students have also been able to benefit from the ECJ's generous approach. While they may not be able to claim maintenance grants in their capacity as students, they may be able to claim maintenance grants as Union citizens. Host states who give maintenance grants to their own citizens have to provide good reasons for not giving similar grants to students from other Member States. However, host states may impose reasonable residence requirements as a condition of eligibility.

The Schengen Area

The EU aims to be an area without internal frontiers, yet if you travel from the UK to France you will still go through border controls. However, the UK is one of a small minority of EU Member States that still imposes border controls on travel to and from other Member States. The reason for this is that the UK is not part of the Schengen Area, named after a small town in Luxembourg where the original agreement was signed. Most EU Member States, except for Bulgaria, Cyprus, Ireland, Romania and the UK, are part of the Schengen Area, and indeed Bulgaria and Romania are in the process of joining it. Some non-EU Member States have also joined the Schengen Area, namely Iceland, Liechtenstein, Norway and Switzerland. The Schengen states have agreed to abolish border controls on travel between them, so, for example, when you enter Germany from France you do not need to produce your passport. When you enter the Schengen Area for the first time from a non-Schengen state, you do have to go through border controls, but then you should be able to travel freely between Schengen states.

You may have noticed that when you pass through immigration controls at airports in many other EU Member States there are two queues – the one for arrivals from Schengen states and the other for arrivals from non-Schengen states. If you are arriving from the UK then you have to go through passport control; if you are arriving from a Schengen state, you do not.

Whether the Schengen Area continues in its current form is a matter of debate. France has recently threatened to suspend its participation, and the EU is considering proposals to allow the temporary suspension of Schengen states that are failing to control illegal immigration from outside the EU. Schengen states are also allowed to reintroduce border controls temporarily to deal with serious threats to internal security.

Free movement of persons is likely to remain a highly topical issue. On the one hand, EU law provides a strong framework for extending rights of free movement. On the other hand, concerns in many Member States about the levels of immigration both from within and outside the EU mean that extending rights of free movement may be politically unpopular.

CHAPTER 5

COMPETITION LAW I – COLLUSION BETWEEN BUSINESSES

INTRODUCTION

Competition is at the heart of modern economic life. The chief aim of competition law is to promote effective competition, but before we look at how competition law seeks to achieve this aim, let us first examine why competition is thought to be beneficial. Economics plays a major role in competition law. Economic analysis often proves decisive in competition cases, so we shall examine the benefits of competition briefly from an economic perspective.

The chief benefits claimed for competition are that it promotes efficiency and choice. Businesses, whether they produce goods or provide services, have to compete for customers. **Figure 1** below shows some of the methods businesses use to compete with each other for customers.

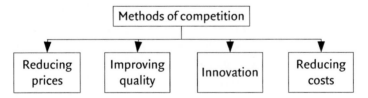

Figure 1: Methods of competition used by businesses

Reducing prices to below those charged by competitors is an obvious means of winning customers. If a business wins extra customers by cutting prices, it may still be able to trade at a reasonable profit despite the price reduction. The chances are, though, that competitors will retaliate by cutting their prices. In the long term a business will be able to maintain a price advantage only if it can reduce its costs by becoming more productive. Accordingly, businesses have to become more efficient to compete effectively.

As well as or instead of competing on price, businesses may also compete on quality. Customers may decide to buy the more expensive but higher-quality product, or the cheaper but poorer-quality version. Consequently, consumer choice increases.

Another way in which businesses can keep one step ahead of the competition is through innovation. The development of new technologies has led to a huge increase in this area. Products that were unheard of even a decade ago regularly appear on the market. Tablet computers such as the iPad and e-book readers such as the Kindle are just two examples of how businesses gain customers through bringing innovative products onto the market.

Competition law aims to achieve 'workable competition'. 'Perfect competition' occurs where there is a complete balance between customer demand and supply. In practice this will never occur, as it is an impossible goal to attain. Instead 'workable competition' is the goal; this occurs where there are enough competing businesses in a given market to ensure that they cannot exploit their customers through anti-competitive practices.

Sometimes there are not enough businesses operating in a particular market to ensure workable competition. Competition law will then step in to ensure that businesses with monopoly or near monopoly power do not use their position of strength to exploit their customers or exclude potential new entrants to the market. We shall examine how competition law curbs the activities of individual businesses with strong market power in **Chapter 6**, but first we look how it deals with businesses that collude with each other instead of competing. We concentrate on how competition law operates in the EU.

COLLUSION BETWEEN BUSINESSES

Suppose Megaco plc ('Megaco'), Fort Entreprise SA ('FE') and Große Hersteller GmbH ('GH') are three major manufacturers of thermoplastics in the EU. Historically they have adopted the following trading patterns:

- Megaco, an English company, markets its products mainly in the UK, the Republic of Ireland and Scandinavia.
- FE, a French company, markets its products mainly in France, the Benelux countries, Spain and Portugal.
- GH, a German company, markets its products in Germany and Eastern Europe.

Megaco, FE and GH may all be in strong positions in their traditional markets. As major manufacturers, they may have faced little competition. However, in a fully-fledged single market, a buyer of thermoplastics would be able to shop around the EU and place its orders with whichever of these three companies offered it the best deal. As the single market develops and barriers to trade weaken, this is more and more likely to occur. However, where businesses have their own established markets, they are sometimes tempted to collude rather than compete.

The directors of Megaco, FE and GH may decide that it is in their respective companies' best interests to come to some form of arrangement. They may agree to concentrate on serving customers in their own established markets; accordingly, Megaco would agree not to market its thermoplastics in the countries served by FE and GH provided they agreed to stay out of Megaco's countries. Megaco would therefore have the comfort of knowing that FE and GH would not actively target its customers. This type of conduct is known as market sharing and would result in a lessening of competition. Also, agreeing to divide markets on the basis of national boundaries is totally contrary to the concept of the single market which aims to break down barriers based on nationality.

This market-sharing arrangement would not necessarily stop the enterprising buyer shopping around the EU for a better price, so the three companies might go a step further to discourage this; they might agree to refer any buyers from outside their established markets to the traditional supplier for that territory. So if a potential French customer were to approach Megaco, Megaco would refer it to FE.

The three companies might go even further and agree to fix their prices. Having split the EU market between them, they might agree to charge the same prices for their products. This would further discourage buyers from shopping around; if all the major producers charge the same prices, shopping around would be a waste of time.

This type of collusion is clearly very harmful to competition. In a competitive single market, the following should happen:

(a) The three companies would try to break into new markets. For example, GH would try to break into France and the UK, as those markets are amongst the largest in the EU. Customer choice would thereby increase.

(b) Megaco and FE could respond to GH's challenge by cutting their prices or by improving the quality of their products. Either way, their customers would benefit from lower prices or better-quality products.

(c) Traditional barriers to trade would break down. Buyers of thermoplastics would no longer be content to buy from their traditional sources but would look for the best deal available anywhere in the EU. This would strengthen the single market.

The collusion between the three companies hampers these desirable outcomes. As a result of the collusion, customers would have less choice and pay higher prices. Secure in their traditional markets, the manufacturers of thermoplastics would not need to improve efficiency or innovate to maintain their market share. Competition law therefore prohibits this type of collusion.

ANTI-COMPETITIVE AGREEMENTS

The directors of Megaco, FE and GH would be fully aware that colluding to fix prices and share markets along national lines is unlawful. For that reason they will not sign a formal contract declaring their intentions to the world and the watching regulators. Instead, they will meet in secret, behind closed doors and avoid putting anything in writing. Competition law therefore catches not only formal, legally-binding arrangements, but also informal collusion. To prove that Megaco, FE and GH have infringed competition law, the regulator would only have to prove that they had contacted each other and following that contact had adopted similar pricing and marketing strategies. Competitors who meet each other and then behave in the market in the same way are likely to land in trouble.

IMPACT ON COMPETITION

It is not the case that every agreement between competitors will breach competition law. Some types of arrangement may be permissible. Unfortunately for Megaco, FE and GH, their price-fixing and market-sharing arrangements are amongst the worst possible infringements of competition law.

Automatically anti-competitive behaviour

Conduct such as price-fixing and market-sharing is by its very nature so harmful to competition that it is regarded as being anti-competitive without more ado. There will be no need to show that it has had any anti-competitive effect. This is sensible as the intention of this type of behaviour is clearly to restrict competition, and businesses should not be able to escape liability for their actions simply because their price-fixing was unsuccessful. Competition regulators should not be forced to devote scarce resources to proving that intentional anti-competitive behaviour of the most harmful type actually had an impact on competition.

Potentially anti-competitive behaviour

Where collusion is not blatantly anti-competitive, it is necessary to show that it does have an effect on competition. Beer ties provide a good example of this type of situation. Breweries have often entered into exclusive purchasing agreements with the operators of pubs. A typical arrangement is that the brewery will lend a pub a large sum of money at a relatively low rate of interest, and in return the pub will agree to buy all its beer from that brewery for the next three to five years. This has the potential of restricting competition as the pub cannot buy its beer from anyone else. Even if a competing brewery were to offer it a significant discount, the pub would be unable to switch suppliers.

A single agreement between a brewery (Brewery A) and a pub (Pub 1) is unlikely to have much of an impact on competition. There are likely to be other pubs in the area, and competing breweries could seek the custom of these pubs. If there is competition from other pubs, Brewery A is unlikely to charge Pub 1 excessively high prices, even though it is a tied pub. If Pub 1 cannot compete with other pubs, it will go out of business and will be unable to repay the brewery. On the other hand, it is still possible that beer ties could operate anti-competitively.

Suppose that Brewery A is just one of three large breweries operating in the area and that the breweries have entered into beer ties on similar terms with all 10 local pubs, as illustrated by **Figure 2** below.

Figure 2: Network of agreements

There will be some competition between the breweries and pubs, but it will probably be limited. As all the pubs are tied to a particular brewery, the breweries will have little incentive to offer their tied pubs significant discounts. They are each likely to offer their tied pubs similar prices, pitched at a level to ensure that the pubs do not become uncompetitive but guaranteeing the breweries an adequate profit. More significantly, it will be impossible for any new breweries to break into the area. If Brewery D tried to enter the market, it would discover that all its potential customers were already tied to a rival brewery. Even if it were willing to offer the pubs substantial discounts, the pubs would be unable to switch to Brewery D.

While the agreement between Brewery A and Pub 1 seems harmless when looked at in isolation, the position changes when you consider the wider picture. As a result of the network of agreements, the three breweries have secured the entire market between them and other breweries will find it very difficult to enter the market. There is clearly an adverse impact on competition.

Distribution agreements

Collusion between competitors is obviously very likely to harm competition. Agreements between non-competitors, such as the agreement between Brewery A and Pub 1 referred to in the previous section, are much less likely to be harmful. It is only when the wider impact of that agreement is considered that its potential to harm competition becomes noticeable. Competition law has therefore drawn a distinction between agreements between competitors and agreements between non-competitors.

Most agreements between competitors are horizontal agreements, because they are entered into by businesses at the same level of the supply or distribution chain. **Figure 3** below shows a straightforward example.

Manufacturer of thermoplastics ⟷ Manufacturer of thermoplastics

Figure 3: Horizontal agreement

In contrast, *vertical agreements* are agreements between businesses at different levels of the supply or distribution chain. **Figure 4** below shows a typical example.

Manufacturer

⬇

Distributor

⬇

Retailer

⬇

Consumer

Figure 4: Vertical agreement

A common type of vertical agreement is a distribution agreement. Suppose that WaterWorld Industries plc (WaterWorld), an English company, is well established in the UK as a manufacturer of electric water heaters. It has invented a new, highly energy-efficient water heater. Up till now, it has concentrated on the British market, but it believes its new water heater provides it with an excellent opportunity to break into new markets, particularly in the EU. It has its own sales force in the UK, and is confident that it will be able to find customers in the UK. However, it does not feel as confident about finding customers in other EU Member States. It believes that there is likely to be strong demand for its products in France and Germany, but it lacks confidence in its ability to penetrate the French and German markets. Its sales force is familiar with conditions in the UK but knows very little about France and Germany. How can WaterWorld break into those markets?

One of the most common types of marketing agreement is the distribution agreement. A manufacturer who wants to break into a new territory will appoint a distributor with expertise in marketing products in that territory. WaterWorld will therefore look for distributors in France and Germany. In France it appoints Distributeurs Nationaux SA (DN) and in Germany it appoints Nord-Elektrohandelsgesellschaft mbH (Nord). **Figure 5** below illustrates the arrangement.

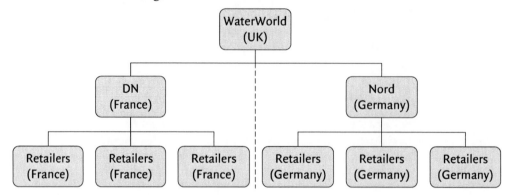

Figure 5: Example of a distribution agreement

WaterWorld will sell its electric water heaters to its distributors, DN and Nord, and DN and Nord will make their profit by re-selling the heaters to retailers in their respective territories. The retailers will then in turn make their profit by selling them on to the end-users, the consumers. In order for the distribution agreement to work in practice, the distributors will have to invest considerable sums in persuading retailers to stock WaterWorld's water heaters. They will have to spend money on marketing and will also probably have to create a local infrastructure, for example renting warehouses to store the products. The distributors will only be ready to make this investment if they are confident that they will be able to recoup it and make a profit by finding enough retailers to stock WaterWorld's products. The distributors will therefore want to take steps to protect their investment.

Suppose that the distributors are successful in finding retailers to stock WaterWorld's products. They would understandably be very upset if WaterWorld undercut their prices and started selling direct to the retailers; WaterWorld would be 'freeloading' on their efforts in finding those retailers. The distributors would be equally upset if WaterWorld appointed second distributors in their respective territories. The second distributors, who would not have incurred the initial costs in finding retailers to stock WaterWorld's products, would also be able to freeload on the hard work of the first distributors and undercut their prices. DN and Nord will therefore require WaterWorld to agree to the following restrictions:

(a)   not to sell direct to retailers in their territories; and

(b)   not to appoint any other distributors in their territories.

The distributors will then feel confident that no one else will be able to cash in on their hard work. On the other hand, WaterWorld may be concerned that it is giving the distributors too much protection. It is putting all its eggs into one basket. It is entirely dependent on DN if it is to break into the French market, and on Nord if it is to break into the German market. WaterWorld may therefore want to impose some restrictions on the distributors. As well as agreeing to do their best to market WaterWorld's products, the distributors will probably have to agree not to market any competing products. WaterWorld will then be confident that its distributors will concentrate all their efforts on marketing its products rather than devoting their energies to a competitor's products. This arrangement is known as an *exclusive distribution agreement*.

At first sight these restrictions might seem anti-competitive: DN will be getting considerable protection in France; it will not face any competition from WaterWorld or from any other distributors in France; Nord will be in the same position in Germany. Additionally, WaterWorld's competitors will not be able to use the services of those distributors to introduce their products into new markets. However, competition law regards exclusive distribution agreements as acceptable. Distribution agreements have considerable beneficial effects. In our example, WaterWorld would probably have been unable to break into the German and French markets if it had been unable to appoint DN and Nord as its exclusive distributors. If competition law banned exclusive distribution, manufacturers would find it very difficult to break into new markets. By enabling them to do so, exclusive distribution agreements increase consumer choice and competition. French and German manufacturers of electric water heaters will now face competition from an English company, WaterWorld. Although DN and Nord will receive some protection from WaterWorld, they will still face competition from manufacturers of other electric water heaters. Although distribution agreements do contain some contractual restrictions, they are not as a general rule anti-competitive.

Unacceptable restrictions in distribution agreements

While most distribution agreements are acceptable, sometimes businesses have gone too far in giving protection to distributors. Although arguably price-fixing in vertical agreements is not as pernicious it is in horizontal agreements, competition law still regards vertical price-fixing as completely unacceptable. Manufacturers are accordingly not allowed to dictate to their distributors the price at which the distributors can re-sell their products to retailers. Similarly, distributors may not dictate prices to their retailers. There are a number of reasons why vertical price-fixing is unacceptable:

(a)   it facilitates collusion between manufacturers. Suppose that manufacturers of a particular product have formed a cartel and fixed the prices for their product. If their distributors charged different prices when re-selling the product, the manufacturer whose distributor charged the lowest prices might gain market share at the expense of the other cartel members; this would nullify the benefits of entering into a cartel. If the members of the cartel are able to impose fixed prices on their distributors, they can stop competition between their distributors undermining the cartel;

(b)   it discourages innovation and efficiencies at the distribution level;

(c)   it results in higher prices. If distributors are able to offer retailers lower prices, the retailers are likely to pass the savings on to their customers; if distributors cannot offer lower prices, this will not happen.

Apart from price-fixing, competition law also prohibits manufacturers from giving their distributors excessive protection. The idea behind distribution agreements is that distributors should concentrate on marketing the manufacturer's products in their own territories. Accordingly, it is DN's task to look for retailers in France to stock

WaterWorld's products, and Nord's task to look for retailers in Germany. WaterWorld would not be pleased if DN started to market its products in Germany, as WaterWorld wants DN to concentrate on France, leaving Germany to Nord. Nord would also be upset if DN moved into the German market, as DN would then be freeloading on Nord's efforts in finding customers for WaterWorld's products in Germany. To prevent this happening, WaterWorld could ban its distributors from selling its products to customers outside their territories. This would mean that DN could sell only to retailers in France, and Nord only to retailers in Germany. This type of arrangement is known as an *export ban*. Why does competition law disapprove of export bans?

Suppose there is especially high demand for WaterWorld's electric water heaters in France, so DN increases its prices significantly, charging higher prices than Nord. Commerces Electriques SA (Commerces), a large French electrical retailer, realises this and so approaches Nord with a view to placing an order. As the distribution agreement between WaterWorld and Nord imposes an export ban on Nord, Nord would have to refuse the order. The export ban therefore has an adverse impact on competition:

- The combined effect of the distribution agreements between WaterWorld and DN and WaterWorld and Nord is to give DN *absolute territorial protection* in France. Commerces is able to buy WaterWorld's products only from DN. It cannot buy direct from WaterWorld, as WaterWorld has agreed not to sell direct to retailers in France. As DN is the exclusive distributor in France, there is no one else in France from whom Commerces can buy WaterWorld's products. The export ban on Nord prevents Commerces from buying from Nord.
- A similar situation would arise in Germany if French prices were lower than German prices.
- There is accordingly an absence of competition in WaterWorld's products – DN can increase its prices, knowing that any French retailer who wants to stock WaterWorld's popular water heaters has no alternative but to buy them from DN.
- This also results in the dividing of markets along national lines. The French market in WaterWorld's products is completely isolated from the German market. This is contrary to the concept of single market, where the aim is to integrate the French and German markets.

The export ban on Nord goes further than competition law permits. Manufacturers and distributors cannot use their agreements to prevent what economists term *parallel imports*. A parallel import occurs where a business, such as Commerces, imports a genuine, non-counterfeit product by buying it from a source in another country rather than from the official source within its own country. Parallel imports are perfectly legal, and indeed competition law encourages them by making it difficult for manufacturers and distributors to stop them.

Competition law in the EU therefore aims not only to achieve workable competition, but also to promote market integration. It shares this second aim with the law on the free movement of goods. EU law wants to stop both governments and businesses from dividing markets along national lines. In a single market, governments and businesses must not be allowed to protect their own domestic markets.

Trade between Member States

If two businesses in a fairly small town such as Accrington in the north of England entered into an anti-competitive agreement, would EU competition law be interested in it? After all, its impact on competition in the EU as a whole is going to be minimal. Also, it would not be reasonable to expect the EU's competition regulators to concern themselves with behaviour that merely has a small, local impact. On the other hand, businesses who behave anti-competitively should not be able to get away with it.

EU competition law applies only to agreements which have the potential to affect trade between Member States to an appreciable extent. A price-fixing arrangement between businesses in Accrington will therefore be outside the scope of EU law. This does not mean that the businesses in Accrington will avoid any consequences for their conduct. While EU competition law will not cover it, UK competition law will. The requirement that conduct must affect trade to be within the scope of EU competition law simply demarcates which legal system has jurisdiction over that conduct – EU or national.

It is in fact relatively easy to show that anti-competitive conduct affects trade between Member States. It is not necessary to show an actual effect on trade but merely a potential effect on the patterns of trade between Member States. In the distribution agreements between WaterWorld, DN and Nord, the export bans would not only restrict competition but also affect trade between Member States. For example, if Commerces in France cannot order WaterWorld's products from Nord in Germany, there will be fewer imports into France from Germany, so the pattern of trade will be affected.

We have now looked at how EU competition law aims to ensure workable competition in the EU by preventing collusion between businesses. Sometimes businesses have sufficient market power to exploit consumers or damage competitors without the need for collusion. Competition law therefore also regulates businesses with strong market power. In the next chapter we examine the dangers of monopolies or near monopolies in a given market.

CHAPTER 6

COMPETITION LAW II – BUSINESSES WITH STRONG MARKET POWER

REGULATION OF DOMINANT BUSINESSES

Suppose that in a particular country there was only one manufacturer of bricks, the Top Brick Company Ltd (TBC), and that for historical and logistical reasons builders in that country did not import bricks from anywhere else. How might this situation harm competition? All builders in the country would have to buy their bricks from TBC. If they refused to buy from TBC, they would not be able to build anything. This might harm competition in several ways, for example:

- TBC would be able to charge high prices for its bricks, knowing that its customers would have no choice but to pay. Builders will simply pass the high prices on to their own customers.
- TBC would have little incentive to become more efficient as it would not need to compete on price to retain its customers or attract new ones.
- Similarly, TBC would not need to innovate to improve its market share.

Whilst it is possible for businesses to acquire monopoly or near monopoly power through their own efforts by developing innovative and popular products, competition law aims to ensure that they do not take advantage of their market power. It does not prohibit monopoly power as such but regulates how dominant businesses use their power. It therefore prohibits businesses from abusing their dominant position.

DOMINANCE

Sometimes it is quite easy to conclude that a business is dominant in a given market. For example, there is little doubt that Google is the dominant player in the online search engine market. However, it is not usually so clear-cut. Accordingly, we must ask the question: 'When is a business dominant?' Before we can answer that question, though, we need to consider what dominance means.

If a business wants to succeed, it needs to take into account its customers and its competitors. If it treats its customers badly then they will go elsewhere. If its competitors reduce their prices or improve the quality of their products, it must respond by taking similar action, otherwise it will lose market share. We may therefore conclude that a business will be dominant if it is able to ignore normal competitive constraints and act independently of its customers and competitors. This is likely to be the case if the business in question has a high market share.

Assessing dominance

Market share is obviously a crucial factor in analysing whether a business is dominant. However, it is not sufficient to conclude that a business is dominant simply because at first sight it appears to have a high market share in a given product. Suppose that market research reveals that ProBike plc's ('ProBike') market position is as follows:

- 60% of the UK market for racing bicycles
- 45% of the UK market for mountain bikes
- 30% of the UK market for bicycles
- 12% of the UK market for quad bikes
- 15% of the EU market for racing bicycles
- 12% of the EU market for mountain bikes
- 7.5% of the EU market for bicycles
- 3% of the EU market for quad bikes.

Is ProBike dominant? It depends on how you define the market. If you define the market as racing bicycles in the UK, then with a market share of 60% ProBike will probably be dominant. If you define the market as bicycles in the EU, then with a market share of 7.5% ProBike will clearly not be dominant. So the first step in analysing whether a business is dominant is to define the relevant market.

Market definition

Economic analysis plays a key role in defining the relevant market. However, the basic principles are reasonably straightforward. The first step is to define the *relevant product market* (RPM). This involves working out which products in practice compete against each other.

Relevant product market

Suppose you go to a shop with the intention of buying a racing bicycle. On arrival you discover that the cost of racing bicycles has gone up by 10%. Would you buy a different type of bicycle, for example a mountain bike? If most customers were willing to switch to a mountain bikes then racing bicycles and mountain bikes would be in the same product market. It would be possible to define the market on the lines of 'bicycles used for sporting purposes'. However, it is unlikely that most customers would switch. Racing bicycles are designed for high speed and competitive cycling along roads; they have light frames, narrow tyres and dropped handlebars. In contrast, mountain bikes are designed for off-road cycling; they are sturdy, have wide tyres and horizontal handlebars. Cyclists use them under entirely different conditions. Indeed, most buyers of racing bicycles would probably not consider any other type of bicycle to be an acceptable alternative, even one less different than a mountain bike. This leads us to the conclusion that the RPM is racing bicycles.

The test we have used to define the RPM is known as demand substitution. We have examined the position from the point of view of buyers of the product. It is also necessary to examine the position from the point of view of suppliers of the product. Consider the following example. Producers of pet food need different types of tin can depending on the content of the can; a tin can for a meat-based pet food is different from a tin can for a fish-based pet food. If you simply applied demand substitution, you would conclude that each type of tin can formed a separate RPM in its own right. A pet food producer who wanted a tin can for meat would not find a tin can for fish to be an acceptable alternative. However, from the perspective of manufacturers of tin cans, one type of tin can is not much different from another. If a manufacturer of tin cans for fish were to put up the prices of its cans, manufacturers of other types of tin can would probably switch production to cans for fish. They would need to make only small adjustments to their production lines and they could start making a different type of tin quickly, at little cost and without taking much risk. Concluding that each type of tin can formed a separate RPM would therefore be defining the market too narrowly, as it ignores the likelihood of supply substitution which acts as a check on the ability of the manufacturer of tin cans for fish to increase its prices.

Nonetheless, in most cases demand substitution will provide the correct definition of the RPM. You need only consider supply substitution where one product, such as tin cans or paper, comes in a variety of different grades or qualities. Even if from the consumer's point of view it is not possible to substitute one grade or quality for another, the different grades or qualities form a single RPM if manufacturers of one type of quality or grade can easily switch to another. However, for many products this is not likely to be the case. In the case of bicycles, you would have to find out what would happen if ProBike put up its prices for racing bicycles by about 10%. If other manufacturers of bicycles could easily switch to racing bicycles, the RPM would probably be bicycles in general. If not, then it would be racing bicycles.

We shall now look at a real case which illustrates the issues very well.

CASE EXAMPLE

United Brands was a large supplier of bananas to the EU. It had a fairly high market share in the banana market, but a considerably lower share in the general fresh fruit market. The European Commission, the EU's competition regulator, argued that the RPM was bananas and that United Brands was dominant in the banana market. United Brands countered that the RPM was fresh fruit in general. The ECJ agreed with the Commission, stating that 'the banana [had] certain characteristics, appearance, taste, softness, seedlessness, easy handling, a constant level of production which enable it to satisfy the constant needs of an important section of the population consisting of the very young, the old and the sick'.

As 'a very large number of consumers having a constant need for bananas [were] not noticeably or even appreciably enticed away from the consumption of this product by the arrival of other fresh fruit on the market', the RPM was bananas and United Brands was dominant.

Although defining the RPM is crucial, it is only the first part of the process of defining the relevant market. Suppose that in ProBike's case we define the RPM as racing bicycles. Would ProBike be dominant? This depends on how you define the relevant geographical market (RGM). If you define it as the UK, ProBike would almost certainly be dominant with a market share of 60%; if you define it as the EU as whole, ProBike would not be dominant with a market share of only 15%.

Relevant geographical market

In a single market, British manufacturers would expect to face competition from manufacturers in other Member States. So in deciding whether or not to put up prices, ProBike would have to consider not only the reaction of manufacturers in the UK but also that of manufacturers in the rest of the EU. If equivalent Italian racing bicycles are cheaper than ProBike's, shops will import the Italian version to meet consumer demand. For a product like bicycles, the relevant RGM is likely to be the whole (or at least a large part) of the EU rather than merely the UK. Transportation costs for bicycles are not high, there are no significant variations in the types of bicycles used in different parts of the EU and there no cultural or language barriers discouraging the use of imported bicycles. Conditions of competition in bicycles are fairly similar throughout the whole of the EU.

For many products the RGM will be the whole of the EU. But this will not always be the case. High transport costs, national variations (resulting, say, from differences in language or technical standards), and local customs and tastes may limit the RGM. Consider a product such as beer.

EXAMPLE

Beer drinking habits vary considerably across the EU. Beer drinkers in the UK are much more likely to drink traditional British ales than are beer drinkers in other parts of the EU. The RGM for traditional British ales is therefore likely to be the UK. Similarly, German beer drinkers have shown a marked preference for German beers, and for beer consumed in Germany the RGM is likely to be Germany.

Market definition is clearly crucial in assessing whether an undertaking is dominant in a particular market. The narrower the market definition, the more likely it is that an undertaking is dominant, as shown by the figures for ProBike.

After defining the relevant market, we need to consider the factors that determine whether a particular undertaking is dominant. The first and most obvious factor to consider is market share.

Market share

If a business has a monopoly or near monopoly in a given market then quite clearly it will be dominant. However, a business does not necessarily have to have a very high market share to be dominant. Consider a business (Business A) with a market share of 45%. Will it be dominant? Look at the figures shown in **Figure 1** below.

Market share

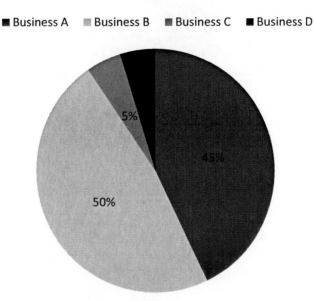

Figure 1: High market share does not mean dominance

Business B in **Figure 1** has a higher market share (50%), so it would be very difficult to argue that Business A was dominant. However, what if the figures were as set out in **Figure 2** below?

Market share

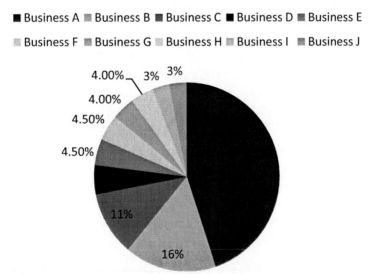

Figure 2: High market share creating dominance

Business A will now probably be dominant. The figures in **Figure 2** are based on those of the United Brands case (see above) where the ECJ decided that United Brands was dominant due to the fragmented nature of the competition. It was a powerful company and it had sufficient financial muscle to withstand attacks from the competition. Accordingly, where a business has a market share of 50% or above, a presumption will arise that it is dominant. Where its market share is less than 50% but 40% or above, whether or not it is dominant depends on the market structure and the ability of competitors to compete effectively. Dominance with a market share below 40% is unlikely (but not completely impossible if only slightly below 40%).

Other factors

Market share is not the only factor to take into account when assessing dominance. As stated above, United Brands was able to fight off its competitors thanks to its large financial resources. Highly profitable businesses with significant spending power are more likely to be dominant than those struggling to make a profit. When faced with the threat of competition, the former are more able than the latter to retaliate by offering discounts and boosting their spending on marketing.

Another important factor is intellectual property rights such as patents. A business that holds a patent on a product has a monopoly right on that product for the duration of the patent, normally 20 years; no one else is able to make it without that business's consent. If there is no viable alternative to the patented product from the consumer's point of view, the ownership of the patent gives its owner the ability to stifle competition.

Conversely, a high market share will not result in dominance where there are low barriers to market entry. In order to obtain a patent, the inventor of the product has to provide details of the invention to the public authorities who then enter the details in a public record. Once the patent has expired, anyone can start making the product based on the details in the public record. Suppose a company (Zetaco) has patented a product which is unique, Blodget Zeta. As it is unique, no other product may be substituted for it and so the RPM for Blodget Zeta will be very narrow – Blodget Zeta itself. Zetaco's market share will accordingly be 100% and it will probably be able to charge very high prices. However, once the patent has expired the position will change. Other businesses will be able to start making Blodget Zeta, and if it is relatively easy and cheap to manufacture, this is very likely to happen. Although Zetaco may initially maintain a high market share, it can no longer charge monopoly prices. If it does, it will face competition from new entrants to the market, as the main barrier to entry, the patent, no longer exists.

Also, where customers have significant buyer power (eg, because a business has a small number of large customers, each of which is critical to its profitability), this is a factor against dominance. A producer of a product may have a market share of 50%, but if it supplies 90% of its products to three large supermarket chains then it may well not be dominant.

Nonetheless, despite these other factors, market share is the decisive factor in the majority of cases. After all, if there are low barriers of entry to a particular industry, a single business is unlikely to obtain a high market share. There are likely to be a substantial number of businesses competing in that industry.

Although assessing dominance is an essential part in deciding whether a business is abusing its dominant position, it is only the first stage in the process. Many businesses become dominant through their own legitimate efforts by providing innovative products or services in a cost-efficient manner; it would be unfair to punish them for their success. Dominance therefore becomes an issue only when a dominant business abuses its dominant position.

TYPES OF ABUSE BY DOMINANT BUSINESSES

There are various ways in which a dominant business might unfairly take advantage of its position; and there are two main classes of potential victims of abusive conduct – the business's customers and its competitors.

Exploitative abuses

A dominant business may well be able to exploit its customers. This type of abuse is known as exploitative abuse. An obvious example of exploitative abuse is charging excessively high prices for products or services. If a dominant business produces an essential or much-desired product, its customers have no choice but to pay up if they want or need the product; it will be difficult for them to obtain it elsewhere. When will a price for a product be excessive? A dominant business may argue that being able to charge a high price is a just reward for its commercial success. Its investors may have taken considerable risks in developing and marketing the product, and should now be able to reap the fruits of their labours.

One way to assess whether a price is excessive is to compare the sale price with the costs of production. If the profit margin is excessive, this may lead to the conclusion that the dominant business is abusing its market power. However, it is very difficult to define when a high price is 'excessively high', and cases where competition authorities have been able to prove excessively high prices are few and far between.

This does not mean, though, that dominant undertakings can charge their customers what they like. Suppose an Italian company, Cuoio Internazionale SpA (Cuoio) produces a specialised type of leather which has become highly popular; as a result, there is now a shortage of supply and Cuoio is in a dominant position. It has built up a cordial relationship with its Italian customers who use the leather to manufacture handbags. Indeed, Cuoio would like to help them survive the current economic crisis so it can secure its customer base when the shortage ends. It has therefore decided not to increase its prices for its Italian customers but only for its non-Italian customers.

Is this pricing policy compatible with the single market? No, it is not. Should businesses be able to charge according to the nationality of the customer? No, they should not. Discrimination without justification on the grounds of nationality breaches basic principles of EU law. Cuoio cannot charge its non-Italian customers more simply because they are not Italian. Competition law prohibits price discrimination, ie charging different customers different prices when the transactions are equivalent. If price discrimination were allowed, it would put non-Italian businesses at a disadvantage compared to Italian businesses. They would find it hard to compete if they had to pay more for their leather. Sometimes there may be a good reason to charge customers in other Member States different prices. If the seller has to pay the transport costs, this may be reflected in the price charged for the product.

Anti-competitive (exclusionary abuses)

As well taking advantage of their customers, dominant businesses may also target competitors.

Once a business has acquired a dominant position, it will want to stay on top. Life is a lot easier if you do not have to worry about awkward customers or competitors stealing trade from you. So the dominant undertaking may develop strategies to stop competitors competing effectively. There are various ways of attacking the competition, some blatant and some subtle.

If a dominant business faces competition from a new entrant to the market, it may respond by cutting prices. That is a perfectly legitimate response. However, what if the business were to cut its prices to below the cost of production? This would mean that it is selling its products at a loss. At first sight this may seem to be acceptable – after all, its customers are benefiting from lower prices. This benefit, though, is likely to be very short-term. The new entrant is unlikely to have the financial resources to sell its products at a loss, so it will probably beat an early retreat from the new market. The dominant business can then put its prices back up to what they were before. This type of abuse is known as predatory pricing and is one of the most serious types of abuse.

Another serious abuse is the refusal to supply an existing customer without a good reason. If the customer does not pay its bills then it is reasonable to stop supplying it. However, there are situations where a refusal to supply is clearly aimed at eliminating competition. Consider the following example based on an actual case.

> **CASE EXAMPLE**
>
> Liptons was a company that serviced and repaired cash registers. One of the brands that it covered was Hugin, a manufacturer of cash registers. In order to service and repair Hugin machines, Liptons had to obtain spare parts from Hugin as no other spare parts were suitable. One day Hugin stopped supplying Liptons with spare parts. Why? Because Hugin wanted to start servicing and repairing its own machines. By refusing to supply Liptons, Hugin was able to eliminate the competition and fill the gap itself. This was clearly an anti-competitive abuse.

The United Brands saga (see above) provides another example of an abusive refusal to supply. United Brands refused to supply one of its distributors because the distributor had taken part in a competitor's advertising campaign. United Brands was trying to discourage its other distributors from cooperating with its competitors, so this too was an anti-competitive abuse.

Other types of anti-competitive abuse are more subtle. Consider the practice that many manufacturers have of offering discounts to their customers. For example, Widgco, the manufacturer of widgets we met in **Chapter 3**, might offer customers who buy more than 500,000 widgets a year a discount of 10% on its standard price, and those who buy more than 1 million widgets a 20% discount. This is entirely reasonable, as it reflects the economies of scale gained by the manufacturer; the average cost of each widget falls, the more widgets it sells. But what if Widgco offered loyalty discounts to customers who bought all, or most, of their widgets from the company?

EXAMPLE

Suppose City Tramways Ltd bought 100,000 widgets a year and obtained a 20% discount because it bought all its widgets from Widgco. On the other hand, Vuvuzela Buses plc bought 1 million widgets but obtained only a 5% discount because it bought a similar number of widgets from one of Widgco's competitors. Why might these discounts be anti-competitive?

The discounts are based not on Widgco's economies of scale, but on its customers' degree of loyalty. Although City Tramways bought only 10% the number of widgets that Vuvuzela bought, it receives a far bigger discount. The aim of the discount is to discourage customers from buying their widgets from a competitor, and not to reward them for bulk purchases. If Widgco is in a dominant position, it will be guilty of abusing it.

Another tactic that businesses use to market their products is to tell their customers that if they want to buy one product that is highly desirable, they have to buy another that they do not necessarily want. This is known as tying.

EXAMPLE

Suppose a company (H) manufactures a popular nail gun used in the construction industry. To use the nail gun, customers must also buy cartridges containing nails to fit the nail gun. The company also makes the cartridges and nails; it is dominant in the market for nail guns and cartridges, but not in the market for nails. Some dealers want to sell the cartridges with another company's nails as they are cheaper than H's. H objects to this and will supply its cartridges only on condition that the dealers also buy H's nails.

This example is based on the case involving the manufacturer Hilti. Hilti had abused its position in the market in which it was dominant, namely cartridges, to force dealers to buy a product in which it was not dominant. This was anti-competitive because it excluded competing nail manufacturers from the nail market. However, it is not always the case that tying is anti-competitive. There may be legitimate reasons for it. It would be unreasonable to require shoe manufacturers to sell shoes and laces separately rather than together. Customers want to buy laced shoes; they have no desire to buy unlaced shoes and then shop around for laces from a different manufacturer.

After it has been established that a business has abused its dominant position, the next point to consider is whether the abuse has had an impact on trade in the EU.

IMPACT ON TRADE AND ENFORCEMENT

The issue here is very much the same as that discussed in **Chapter 5**: EU competition law will apply to an abuse only if it affects trade between Member States. This is usually simple enough to prove. Most distortions in the competitiveness of a particular market will affect trade unless that market is small and localised. Indeed, it is not necessary to show an actual effect on trade; the potential to affect trade is sufficient. Even if an abuse does not affect trade, it is likely that national competition authorities (NCAs) will take action under domestic law.

Figure 3 below summarises abuse of a dominant position.

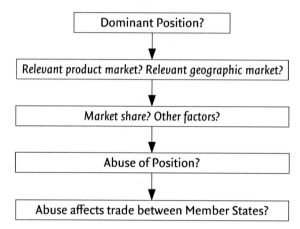

Figure 3: Abuse of a dominant position

We have seen in this chapter and the previous one that competition law prohibits a wide range of anti-competitive practices. However, unless there were effective ways of enforcing it, it would do little to deter businesses from acting unlawfully. The EU currently consists of 27 Member States. It would be very difficult for one regulator to enforce competition law across the whole of the EU. Accordingly, what has developed is a system whereby the European Commission and NCAs cooperate with each other.

Competition regulators

The European Commission has prime responsibility for the enforcement of EU competition law. It makes secondary legislation and issues guidelines in its efforts to combat anti-competitive conduct. However, it does not have the resources to police EU competition law in every Member State. It therefore concentrates on the wider policy issues affecting the EU and on the major competition cases with a significant economic impact. It will therefore investigate large cartels involving companies in several Member States and abuses of dominant positions by large corporations. So it was the Commission which was responsible for the investigations into the conduct of Microsoft and Intel which resulted in the imposition of large fines.

The Commission has delegated to NCAs the responsibility for enforcement of EU competition law for infringements that affect only a few Member States. The leading competition authority in the UK is currently the Office of Fair Trading (OFT), though the Government plans to merge the OFT with the Competition Commission to form the Competition and Markets Authority (CMA). The CMA is due to take over responsibility for enforcement in April 2014. A high-profile example of where the OFT took action is the case against British Airways and Virgin Atlantic for price-fixing of fuel surcharges on transatlantic flights between August 2004 and January 2006. The OFT fined British Airways £58.5 million.

If anti-competitive conduct does not affect trade between Member States then EU competition law does not apply it. However, in the UK and in many other Member States this makes little difference; UK competition law is modelled on EU competition law and the OFT will simply proceed against the businesses concerned under UK law. The sanctions for breaching EU and UK competition law are virtually identical.

Powers of regulators

Competition regulators have significant powers of investigation. Arguably the most feared power is the so-called 'dawn raid', the power to search business premises without prior notice for evidence of anti-competitive behaviour. Major law firms have teams of lawyers on stand-by in case any of their clients are dawn-raided.

At the end of the investigation, the European Commission has the power to fine businesses up to 10% of their annual world-wide turnover for breaching competition law. The largest fine imposed so far is €1.07 billion on Intel for abuse of a dominant position. The Commission has also fined Microsoft €497 million and €899 million (reduced on appeal to €860 million) for abusing its dominant position. It has also imposed large fines on cartel members.

CASE EXAMPLE

In 2008 the Commission fined Saint-Gobain €896 million for taking part in a cartel relating to glass supplied to manufacturers of new cars. In total the four members of the cartel were fined €1.38 billion.

The OFT and other NCAs have powers very similar to those of the Commission. They also cooperate with each other as part of European Competition Network. There is extensive cooperation with regulators outside the EU too, for example with the Department of Justice in the USA.

Despite their extensive powers of investigation, it is very difficult for regulators to prove the existence of cartels. Participants in cartels know that their conduct is unlawful so they meet in secret, use code names in their discussions and avoid putting anything in writing. Accordingly, one of the most powerful weapons in cartel investigations has been the Commission's leniency policy, a policy also adopted by the OFT. A cartel member which is the first to come forward and 'blow the whistle' on the cartel qualifies for 100% immunity from fines. Between 2007 and 2010, 19 out of 26 decisions by the Commission against cartels started with a whistleblower.

CASE EXAMPLE

In 2008 the Commission fined wax producers €676 million for a price-fixing and market-sharing cartel. Sasol was fined €318.2 million. In contrast Shell, as the whistleblower, qualified for a 100% reduction of its fine of €96 million so paid nothing.

Similarly, the OFT granted Virgin Atlantic 100% immunity from any fine relating to its price-fixing arrangement with British Airways.

Dual vigilance – public and private enforcement

You may be wondering who obtains the money from the fines imposed by the Commission and NCAs. The answer is that it goes into the public coffers. Competition fines therefore form part of the revenue received by the EU. This does not help the victims of anti-competitive behaviour. As well as public enforcement of competition law by the regulators, private enforcement is also possible. Many key provisions of EU competition law have direct effect, a concept we discussed in **Chapter 2.**

This means that private enforcement of competition law is possible. Victims may claim damages and other remedies, such as injunctions, before their national courts. While damages claims for competition infringements are relatively undeveloped in EU and English law compared to the position in the USA, competition regulators are actively encouraging them. They take some of the burden off the regulators and enable victims to obtain compensation for the loss suffered.

Whatever happens to the EU over the coming months and years, competition law will undoubtedly remain a major feature of business life. Companies throughout the world have to take it very seriously; otherwise they risk being at the wrong end of large fines and claims for damages.

LAND LAW

CHAPTER 1

INTRODUCTION

There is a common misconception amongst those who have never studied land law that it is 'boring', or 'confusing' or generally 'impenetrable'. Land law is none of these things. It is a cleverly crafted and sophisticated regime, which regulates ownership and usage of land, and satisfies the conflicting needs of owners and users of land.

When you learn land law, you may find it a little tricky to begin with. This is because it encompasses many different elements which must work together in tandem. Any land law course needs to separate these elements artificially for teaching purposes, in order to be able to make sure that students have as full an understanding as possible of each element. Necessarily, a full understanding of how the elements work together cannot realistically develop until further into the course. This is absolutely normal, but may be frustrating for some students.

Land law is probably the area of law which is the most relevant to you right now – and will continue to be relevant to you throughout your life. Property is all around us. We live in houses. We go to school. We go to shops. We go to the gym. If we walk down the street we will see offices, shops and houses. Some property we use even though we do not own it. Some property we cannot use.

Have you ever wondered who owns the pavement on which you walk, or the road on which you drive? Who owns the park in which you relax, or the beach on which you walk your dog? Someone certainly owns these pieces of land. How do you know you have a right to use them? Would you expect to have to let someone else use your house or garden?

Land law sets out a framework to regulate the rights and obligations of different people who own, use and occupy land. Without this framework, there would be chaos. No one would know what their rights were in relation to land.

Property is a valuable commodity. It provides us not only with a place to live or work but – for some people – with a long-term capital investment or a regular source of income. Without the framework provided by land law, purchasing land would become extremely risky. A buyer would not want to spend money on a property if numerous (perhaps unidentified) others had the right to use it. The benefit of being a property owner would be far outweighed by the risks.

The following chapters provide an introduction to land law and demonstrate how it achieves a balance between the rights and interests of owners, occupiers and users of land. Unfortunately we cannot cover the whole subject in **Foundations in Context** – that is not the purpose of this text. The aim is to bring land law into context to help you better to understand its purpose when you begin to study the subject on the LLB course.

Chapter 2 will examine the procedure for buying and selling land. We shall look at the ways in which land law strikes a balance between the interests of sellers, buyers, owners and occupiers of land, and what issues need to be addressed in the process.

Chapter 3 will examine the different ways in which a person may occupy land. An occupier will have different rights depending on the nature of his occupation. This will also have an effect on the rights the occupier will need in order to be able to enjoy and use the property in full.

Chapter 4 provides an introduction to trusts. Trusts arise where the legal owner of a property is different from the beneficial owner of the property. Land law imposes obligations on the legal owner and grants rights to the beneficial owner in these situations.

Are you ready? Then let us begin your introduction to the stimulating world of land law!

CHAPTER 2

Buying a Property

INTRODUCTION

We have already seen from **Chapter 1** that land law provides a framework for the creation and regulation of rights in property. The framework was developed predominantly to give clarity as to how property might be used, both by owners and by third parties.

If a buyer has no idea of who might have an interest in the property he is buying, the risk of buying property would far outweigh the benefits of being a property owner. Someone might already have an agreement to purchase the land at a later stage, or might already have the right to occupy the property to the exclusion of the property owner. Either of these rights could reduce the intrinsic value of the land, making it a less attractive purchase for the buyer.

Land law reduces these risks. It provides a framework which regulates the creation and use of rights in property. It also provides a system whereby rights affecting any property must be registered, to inform potential buyers of their existence.

This chapter will discuss some of the rights which may affect a property, and the relevance of these rights to a buyer before and after he purchases the land. A more detailed discussion of the creation and enforcement of these rights may be found in later chapters.

THE PURCHASE PROCEDURE

Land law has also established a procedure for the purchase and sale of property. In this way, buyers and sellers know what to expect and when, what their rights are and what their obligations are.

Stage One

A buyer will identify a property to purchase. This is usually organised through an estate agent, who acts as agent for the seller. The estate agent will show the buyer the property and, if the buyer decides to buy it, will agree a price between the buyer and the seller. The agent will also inform the seller that he needs to instruct a solicitor to begin the process.

The buyer will then instruct a solicitor and commission a survey. The survey will inform the buyer about the condition of the property. The result of the survey may have an impact on whether the buyer proceeds with the purchase – he might not want to if he knows that significant structural works are needed.

Stage Two

There are many practical issues which the buyer's solicitor will need to uncover – such as whether the property is connected to the mains, or whether the property is connected to gas and electricity. The buyer will also need to establish whether there are any third party rights affecting the property – for example, whether anyone has a right of way over the property. The buyer will also need to know whether, as the property owner, he will have any rights over other land – such as access to the property over a shared driveway for example. These issues are discussed later in this chapter.

Stage Three

If the buyer is happy to proceed with the purchase in light of any issues uncovered in Stage Two above, the buyer and the seller will then negotiate a contract for sale, which will place both parties under an obligation to finalise (or 'complete') the purchase on a certain date. The contract will detail both parties' obligations pre-completion and will outline what will happen if either party fails to adhere to these obligations. The buyer and the seller will then 'exchange contracts', meaning that the contract is dated and the obligations become enforceable. For more details on contracts generally, see **Contract**.

Stage Four

The sale is completed. Stamp Duty Land Tax is paid and the buyer is registered as the new owner of the property at Land Registry. Please see 'Clarity for the buyer', below.

Now that you have an idea of how the purchase procedure works, we need to establish what types of property are available for sale to a buyer.

WHAT TYPES OF PROPERTY?

There are two types of property which a buyer might purchase. The first is called a 'freehold'. If a buyer buys freehold property, he will have it forever. The second is called a 'leasehold'. If a buyer buys leasehold property, this means that he is buying a 'lease'. A lease is a document which permits occupation of a piece of property for a certain period of time (eg 5, 10, 15 or even 999 years). Once the lease comes to an end, the buyer will no longer be permitted to occupy the property. A more detailed discussion of the difference between freehold and leasehold estates appears in **Chapter 3** below.

It will be important for the buyer to know whether the property he is buying is a freehold or a leasehold estate, because this will dictate how long he will be entitled to it. If a buyer is buying a flat, this will usually be a leasehold estate, whereas if the buyer is buying a house, this will usually be a freehold estate.

The nature of the rights needed over other land and the rights which other people may have over the property will vary depending on whether the property is a leasehold or freehold estate. In addition, the nature of rights required may differ if the buyer is a commercial buyer, as businesses have different needs from homeowners. These rights will be discussed in more detail in 'Does a buyer need any rights over other property?' (below) and in **Chapter 3**.

Whether the property is freehold or leasehold, a buyer will need to know what is and is not included in the sale for the purchase price.

WHAT IS INCLUDED IN THE PROPERTY?

A buyer will expect to receive the property and the land upon which it stands for the purchase price. What do we actually mean by 'property'? There are many things in a house – eg, paintings, chairs, beds, showers, fridges; would a buyer expect to receive all or any of these things too?

There has been much debate over the years about what does and does not from part of a property. Land law has evolved on this point through case law, but the answer is not always clear.

EXERCISE

Try to decide whether the following items would be included in or excluded from the purchase:

Item	Included	Excluded
Fridge		
Gas fire		
Curtains		
Lightshade		
Garden statue		
Bookshelves		

You may have found that exercise harder than you thought it would be! You will appreciate that a buyer will need to know what he is getting for the purchase price, and so there has to be a way of working out what is included in the purchase (a 'fixture') and what is not (a 'fitting').

Land law courts have decided that anything which is fixed to the property permanently/semi-permanently will be a fixture, and anything which is not fixed will be a fitting. Therefore a buyer may expect to receive the building, the land upon which it stands and any items in the property or on the land upon which it stands which are fixtures. This gives clarity to a buyer.

The items in the table above could all be fittings, or they could all be fixtures. It will depend on how firmly they are attached to the property and whether the purpose of having these items in the property is to appreciate the items for their own sake, or to enhance the property as a whole. For example, if a worktop in the kitchen had to be broken up to remove the fridge, the fridge would most likely be a fixture; if the fridge were freestanding, it would be a fitting.

Having considered what the buyer is getting for his money, let us now turn to the rights which the buyer might need in respect of the property, as well as how to identify any rights which might affect the property.

DOES A BUYER NEED ANY RIGHTS OVER OTHER PROPERTY?

Earlier in this chapter, we noted that, depending on the type or nature of the property being purchased, certain rights may be needed over other land. In addition, the property might be subject to the rights of others – such as a right of way, for example. As already discussed, these rights will be identified in Stage Two of the purchase procedure. What kind of rights might be identified at this stage?

Rights needed over other property

> **EXERCISE**
>
> Think about the property in which you live. Run through a normal day and write a list of any land which you use in conjunction with that property but which does not form part of the property.

You might have identified many or few examples. This could depend on whether you live in a house (generally freehold) or a flat (generally leasehold).

Wherever you live, you probably need to do all or any of the following things.

Access the property from the main road over any pavement outside the property on foot or by car

If the main road and the pavement are owned by the Highways Authority, they do not form part of the footprint of any property. It is a matter of general law that the public have the right of access by way of licence over these roads and pavements.

If the main road and pavement are not owned by the Highways Authority, for example where they form part of a development where the developer still has not asked the Highways Authority to 'adopt' them, a buyer will need the right to access the property over the road and pavement. The right will need to be given by the owner of the road and pavement to the property owner. This kind of right is called an easement. Once granted, the owner of the property will be able to use the road and pavement for access until they are adopted by the Highways Authority.

Easements attach to a property, and so when the property is sold, any subsequent owner will have the benefit of them (provided that they have been registered at Land Registry where necessary – please see 'Clarity for the buyer', below).

The above would also apply if a buyer needed to park his car outside his house.

Leave your bins/recycling boxes outside the house so that they may be emptied

The same rules apply here as for the use of the main road and the pavement to access the property – see above.

Access the rear of your house via a private lane to reach your garage

In order to be able to use land, you need to have the right to use it. In the case of roads and pavements owned by the Highways Authority, there is an implicit right to use the land, as discussed above. However, with private land, you would need an easement to use the private roadway (and car parking spaces, for example).

Service media (drains, electricity, telephone)

Property owners own the building and the land it is built upon. They will also own limited airspace above and soil underneath the property, but only that which is necessary to enjoy the land as a property owner.

Residential dwellings are generally connected to a water supply, drains, electricity, gas, telephone, etc. The connections to these services will need to cross other land and possibly airspace. Although no one owns airspace, it is regulated and the service providers will need to obtain any relevant consents.

Particular concerns for the commercial buyer

Businesses will need the rights described above, but there may be additional rights which they need by virtue of the nature of their business. For example, shops will need an area where deliveries can be unloaded, if there is no appropriate space to do so within the footprint of the property.

Businesses may also need to cross another piece of land in order to evacuate the building in the case of fire.

Another issue for businesses whose customers visit them at their premises is parking. The availability of parking may be a crucial factor for a commercial buyer deciding whether to buy a particular property. The property may be more attractive to a commercial buyer if there is the right to park on another, adjacent piece of land.

Rights which might affect the property

Restrictions on use

In the same way as a property owner will have rights over land belonging to another person, another person might have rights over his property. These might include easements, as outlined above.

In addition, the property owner's ability to use the land may be controlled by another.

EXAMPLE

David owns property which comprises a house and gardens with an adjoining field. He lives in deepest Dorset, because it is very quiet and peaceful. He decides to sell the field, as he no longer keeps goats and does not need it.

David does not want any buyer of the field to sell it on again to a residential developer, who might build blocks of flats on it. David is worried that if this happens, his peace and quiet will be shattered.

David could prevent this from happening by requiring any buyer of the land to promise not to use the land for anything other than a single house. If the buyer promises this in the sales documentation, it will mean not only that David's buyer will not be able to use the property for anything other than a single house, but also that anyone to whom that buyer sells will not be able to either. In this way, David has control over the use of someone else's land and will have remedies if this promise is broken. This type of promise is called a *restrictive covenant*.

We have seen that the property may benefit from or be subject to other rights. But how would a buyer know about these? This is why the process of land registration was introduced, to give clarity to property buyers.

CLARITY FOR THE BUYER

Unregistered land

Before 1925, all land was unregistered. This meant that there was no system to record who owned which piece of land and, consequently, no sure-fire way of knowing whether anyone else had rights over it. There is still unregistered land in the UK today.

In the unregistered system, in order to be as certain as you can be about rights associated with any particular piece of land, a buyer needs to have a full set of title deeds showing an unbroken chain of ownership of the land for at least 15 years. This is problematic, because in many cases deeds have been lost and there is no way of knowing whether they even exist. As a result, whether a piece of unregistered land is subject to a right will depend on whether a buyer has notice of it. If a buyer does not have notice of and could not reasonably be expected to have knowledge about the right, the right will 'fall away'.

Third parties should register their rights against the property owner at the time that the rights are created in what is called the Land Charges Register. This will constitute notice of any such right and will ensure that the right will stick to the land and last forever. Of course, the success of this system will depend on knowing the identity of the property owners through time.

Registered land

You will appreciate that the unregistered system was a little haphazard, and investigating rights and interests in the land was extremely time-consuming for a buyer. As a result, the registered land system was introduced in 1925. An organisation called Land Registry became responsible for keeping a record of the owners of land. Once registered, each piece of land is given a portfolio of 'registers of title' and a unique identification number. The rights of any third parties are detailed in these registers of title. In this way, a buyer is able to identify the property, the current owner and any rights which affect or benefit the land.

Official copy of register of title

Title number GR946282   Edition date 03.02.2010

- This official copy shows the entries subsisting on the register on 10 September 2011 at 10.10:12
- This date must be quoted as the "search from date" in any official search application based on this copy.
- The date at the beginning of an entry is the date on which the entry was made in the register.
- Issued on 10 September 2011.
- Under s.67 of the Land Registration Act 2002 this copy is admissible in evidence to the same extent as the original.
- For information about the register of title see Land Registry website www.landregistry.gov.uk or Land Registry Public Guide 1- *A guide to the information we keep and how you can obtain it.*
- This title is dealt with by Land Registry Gloucester

A: Property Register

This register describes the land and the estate comprised in the Title

GLOUCESTER   :   COTSWOLD

1. (29 August 1996) The **freehold** land shown and edged with red on the plan **[not reproduced]** of the above title filed at the Registry and being Glebe Farm, Pilgrims Lane, Gloucester GL3 9XX

B: Proprietorship Register

This register specifies the class of title and identifies the owner. It contains any entries that affect the right of disposal.

Title Absolute

1. (29 August 1996) **PROPRIETOR**: SAM RICHARDS of Glebe Farm, Pilgrims Lane, Gloucester.

C: Charges Register

This register contains any charges and other matters that affect the land

1. (29 August 1996) REGISTERED CHARGE dated 15 August 1996 to secure the moneys including the further advances therein mentioned.

2. (29 August 1996) Proprietors(s) DALTON BUILDING SOCIETY of Finance House, London Road, Dalton, Hampshire.

3. (3 February 2010) A deed concerning the land in this title dated 15 January 2010 made between (1) Sam Richards (Covenantor) and (2) Ned James Allen (Covenantee) contains the following covenant:-

"The Covenantor covenants with the Covenantee for the benefit of each and every part of Rose Cottage and to the intent that the burden of the covenant will run with and bind Glebe Farm and every part of it not to build or erect anything on Glebe Farm without the prior written consent of the Covenantee."

_____

End of register

You may wonder whether there are other rights that affect a property which do not appear on the registers of title at Land Registry. It is true that Land Registry can record only the information it is given at the time the property is first registered; if it does not have this information, it cannot appear on the registers of title. However, a buyer may take comfort that the registers of title give all of the information concerning the property (as Land Registry guarantees this). There is also a complex set of rules that apply post-registration of the property, which ensure that if any new rights are created, either they will need to be registered at Land Registry in order to be enforceable, or they will need to be obvious on the ground if the property is inspected.

In this way, the risk in purchasing property is reduced.

HOW WILL THE BUYER PAY FOR THE PROPERTY?

Mortgages

Whether we are talking about leaseholds or freeholds, mortgages play an important part in enabling a purchase. Not all of us are lucky enough to have hundreds of thousands of pounds sitting in a bank account, ready and waiting for when we want to buy somewhere to live (or from which to operate a business). Most of us need financial help to buy a property.

When a lender lends money, there is always a risk that the money will not be paid back – either because the borrower cannot afford it due to a change in circumstances, or because the borrower cannot be found. If nothing were done to balance this risk, lenders would not lend money. This would mean that most of us would be unable to buy a property. What is the solution?

The way in which land law balances the risk is by allowing the lender to use the borrower's property as *security* for his loan. This means that the lender will protect his security by asking Land Registry to note his interest on the register of title in the form of a 'charge'. This means that the lender must be paid back once the property is sold, out of the proceeds of sale. In this way, the lender does not merely have to rely on the borrower's promise to repay the loan. The buyer will ensure that the loan is repaid, otherwise when the buyer becomes the new owner he will become responsible for it (as the charge will remain on the register of title).

Land Registry will enter the details of the loan into the registers of title for the property. If the lender is not paid back on the sale of the property, the new owner takes on the obligation. In this way, any potential buyer will ensure that the lender is paid back – no one will want to take responsibility for repayment of someone else's loan!

In addition, as the repayment of the loan depends on whether the sale price of the property is equal to or exceeds the value of the loan, a lender will be anxious to ensure that the borrower does not do anything to or with the property that might significantly decrease its value. Most institutional lenders – such as banks – will require a borrower to enter into a loan agreement before making the loan. The loan agreement will state that the borrower must not make any substantial alterations to the property (such as the removal of a bedroom, for example) unless the lender has given permission. It will probably also restrict renting, unless the lender has given permission, because tenants tend to take less good care of properties than the property owners.

This may seem harsh, but remember that without this protection, lenders would not lend. If lenders did not lend, a vast number of us would not be able to buy.

Mortgages are normally used to fund the purchase price of the property. The money is not received by a buyer until the day that the purchase is completed. However, a buyer will usually have to pay a deposit when contracts are exchanged. This is normally 10% of the purchase price. How will the buyer fund this deposit?

Other sources of funds

A buyer may borrow the money to pay the deposit for the time between exchange and completion, knowing that when he receives the mortgage funds he will be able to repay the loan. These kinds of loans are called 'bridging loans' because they 'bridge' the gap between exchange and completion. Unfortunately, a very high rate of interest is usually charged as these loans are for such a short period.

The alternative to obtaining a bridging loan would be to rely on the generosity of family or friends in respect of the deposit. This might be in the form of a loan, or it might be a gift; but if it is in the form of a gift, this could create problems for the buyer when he wants to sell the property, because in certain instances a trust may arise. For a discussion of this potential issue, see **Chapter 4** below.

CHAPTER 3

OCCUPATION

INTRODUCTION

In **Chapter 2** we examined the importance of land law to a buyer and the ways in which land law works to reduce the risks involved in a property purchase. This chapter focuses on the different types of property available to a buyer, how occupation may differ depending on the type of property involved and how land law regulates such occupation.

Property is everywhere. Houses, shops, hotels, schools, offices – the list goes on and on. We use these types of property almost every day.

We do not always own property that we use. We might own a house or rent a house, or even be living with our parents in a house which they own. In the last two instances, we do not own the house at all – we simply have permission to stay there.

We do not own shops, but we have permission to go into them and buy goods. We do not own hotels, but we have permission to stay in them. We do not own schools, but we spend a large part of each day in them.

There are different risks associated with any property use. Land law has developed over time in order to reduce these risks for the property owner and the property user. It provides a standard set of rules on which everyone can rely. If a standard set of rules did not exist, no one would know whether he could allow someone else to use his property safely. In addition, occupiers would not know whether their rights would be protected.

We are now going to look at these different types of property in more detail.

FREEHOLD AND LEASEHOLD – RESIDENTIAL OCCUPATION

Most people have a home to live in. They will usually live either in a house or in a flat. Consider **Examples 1** and **2** below.

EXAMPLE 1 – FREEHOLD

Sally owns her own house. She has lived in the house for all of her life. Sally has the 'freehold' of her house, meaning that she can stay there until she decides to leave.

EXAMPLE 2 – LEASEHOLD

Benjamin lives in an annexe of Sally's house. He does not have much money. He does not know whether his new job in the area will work out, so he does not want to commit himself to buying a house. He signed a lease with Sally which allows him to live in her annexe for two years in return for a monthly payment of £100. Benjamin has a 'leasehold' of the annexe, meaning that he has only the right to occupy it for an agreed period of time.

The above examples describe two very different living arrangements. But how are they different in practice? What is the difference between owning a freehold and a leasehold interest in a property?

Sally (the freehold owner)

Sally's position is fairly straightforward. Sally can live in her house forever, and when she dies, she can leave the house to a third party in her will. During her lifetime, she may allow a third party to live in her house, or even sell it and use the money for whatever she likes. Sally is the outright owner of her house and, as such, she can do whatever she likes with it.

Sally is bound to have concerns, though. How can she be sure that other people appreciate that she owns the house? How does she know that some fraudster will not appear, pretend to own the house and then sell it, leaving Sally with no money and nowhere to live?

This is where land law will help Sally. You will remember from **Chapter 2** that Land Registry records details of property and property owners. When land is registered at Land Registry, details of the property address, the owner of the land and any third party with an interest in the land are recorded in the registers of title for the property. Anyone may obtain copies of the registers of title from Land Registry on payment of a small fee.

In this way, property owners like Sally are protected. Unless the seller of the property is the same person as the person registered as the owner at Land Registry, the seller cannot sell the land to another person. This system also protects buyers, who are able to check with Land Registry to make sure that the person purporting to be the owner of the land is in fact the owner.

Benjamin (the leasehold owner)

Benjamin's position is a little different. He does not own the annexe but has a right to occupy it. He therefore has a leasehold interest in it. This means that he is permitted to live in the annexe for (in this example) a period of two years, provided that he adheres to the obligations set out in the lease (most notably, the payment of rent). Sally is the 'landlord' (as she owns the freehold of the annexe) and Benjamin is the 'tenant' (as he has the right to occupy it).

Benjamin could always sell his lease – or his right to live in the property – to a third party, if the lease allows him to do so. However, at the end of the two years when the lease comes to an end, Benjamin will have to leave the annexe. He will not be entitled to stay there any longer.

As a tenant, Benjamin may have concerns. Could Sally ask him to leave the annexe before the end of the lease? Could she increase the rent so that he cannot afford to live there anymore? Could Sally rent the annexe to someone else during the period of the lease? Will Sally be able to enter the annexe whenever she likes?

As a landlord, Sally may also have concerns. Benjamin might not pay his rent. He might damage the property. He might have loud parties at night which will keep her awake. Benjamin might refuse to leave the annexe at the end of the lease.

All of these concerns are valid. If land law did not exist, the transaction might well be too risky for either party to contemplate. The solution is to set out each party's rights and obligations in the lease. In the lease, Sally and Benjamin may agree whatever they like. **Table 1** below gives examples of what they might agree to address their concerns.

	Concern	Lease Clause
Sally	Non-payment of rent	Include a fixed monthly rent figure and state upon which day in each month the rent should be paid.
		State that if the rent payment is late, Sally might terminate the lease and charge interest on any late payments.
	Damage to property	Include an obligation on Benjamin to keep the property clean and tidy and not to damage it.
		State that Sally may enter the property to inspect its repair and condition.
		State that if Benjamin is not keeping the property clean and tidy, Sally may do so herself and charge Benjamin the cost of doing so, or may terminate the lease.
	Loud noise	Include an obligation on Benjamin not to play loud music or make any noise which can be heard outside the annexe.
		State that Sally can serve notice on Benjamin if he acts contrary to this agreement with an ability for Sally to terminate the lease if it happens again.
	Unable to remove tenant at end of term	Sally is entitled to apply to court for an order for possession in this instance.
		The lease could make this clear so that both parties know what their rights are at the outset.
Benjamin	Early termination	The nature of a lease is such that once it takes effect, the landlord cannot force the tenant to leave unless the tenant is in default or if there is a break clause.
		State the length of time that Benjamin is entitled to occupy the property.
		Do not allow Sally to end the lease early (a 'break clause') except where Benjamin is in breach of the lease, as above.
	Rent increase	Unless Sally has the ability to increase the rent under the terms of the lease, she will not be able to increase the rent figure agreed.
		Benjamin should make sure that Sally does not have this ability.
	Sally might rent to another person	Once the lease takes effect, only Benjamin will have the right to live there. This is called 'exclusive possession'. Sally will not be able to rent to another person without breaching the terms of the lease.

	Concern	Lease Clause
	Sally entering the property	Once a lease takes effect, the tenant may control who enters the property.
		The landlord will not be allowed to enter without notice to the tenant.

Table 1: Clauses to address concerns of landlord and tenant

If either Sally or Benjamin does not comply with the terms of the lease, the other will have a course of action. Sally or Benjamin might go to court, or even bring the lease to an end. In this way, both of them have peace of mind. Sally receives money and Benjamin has somewhere to live that he can afford – everyone benefits.

You might be wondering what would happen to Benjamin's lease if Sally were to sell the house. Surely a third party does not have to honour an agreement which was made between Sally and Benjamin? If this were true, the rental market would surely disappear. If a buyer of a house were not required to honour a lease arrangement, the risk of renting a property would be far too high to contemplate.

Land law comes to the rescue once again. We have already seen that a freehold is one kind of interest in land – one that continues forever. A lease is also an interest in land – one that continues for the period decided upon in the lease. Both interests are required to be registered at Land Registry, and once a lease is registered, a buyer must honour it.

In addition, if the lease is for seven years or less, a buyer must always honour it even if it is not registered at Land Registry. Most residential occupiers are protected as a result.

Benjamin can therefore feel secure that whatever happens, as long as he carries out his obligations in the lease, he will be able to live in the annexe for two years and his right to do so will be protected.

FREEHOLD AND LEASEHOLD – COMMERCIAL OCCUPATION

We have examined in some detail the ways in which property law protects residential land owners and occupiers. Property law works to protect commercial land owners and occupiers in much the same way.

Most businesses will lease premises rather than buy them outright. There are two main reasons for this.

The first is that many businesses simply do not have the capital to invest in bricks and mortar – or perhaps do not want to invest such a large amount of capital in bricks and mortar. They would rather plough all profits back into the business for growth, or perhaps into a pension fund for their employees.

The second is economic uncertainty. Many businesses do not want to commit themselves to a particular location for too long a period of time, or to repayments of a mortgage, when the future of their business or the economy in general is uncertain. It is safer for them to commit to a short period of occupation – for example, 10 years – so that if the business does not work out, all they have lost is the rent for the period of the lease. In many instances, a landlord would accept a lump sum to terminate a lease in this situation, or perhaps the tenant might sell the lease to a third party.

If a business does own the freehold of a commercial property, the land must be registered at Land Registry (just like the freehold of residential land). In this way, the world at large is able to find out who owns the land and the property owner is protected.

If a business owns a leasehold interest in a commercial property, the same protection applies as for residential properties. If the lease is for seven years or less, a buyer will almost always have to honour it. If the lease is for more than seven years, a buyer will have to honour it only if it is registered at Land Registry and has its own unique title number.

Of course, the contents of a lease in a commercial context might be very different from the contents of a lease in a residential context. **Table 2** below illustrates some potential concerns of the commercial landlord and tenant, together with lease clauses which might address these.

	Concern	Lease clause
Commercial landlord	Non-payment of rent	Require the tenant to pay 6 months' rent as a deposit.
		Require a guarantor for the tenant's obligations.
		Include the ability to terminate the lease in the event of non-payment of rent.
	Damage to the property	Place an obligation on the tenant to keep the property clean and tidy and not to damage it.
		Place an obligation on the tenant to use the property only for an agreed use (eg offices).
		State that the landlord may enter the property to inspect its repair and condition.
		State that if the tenant is not keeping the property clean and tidy, the landlord may do it itself and charge the tenant the cost of doing so.
		Include the ability to terminate the lease in the event of non-performance of these obligations.
	Selling/leasing	Require the tenant to obtain the landlord's permission before selling or leasing.
		State that the landlord may require a rent deposit or guarantee from the new tenant on sale/leasing.
		Require the outgoing tenant to guarantee the performance of the lease by the new tenant.

	Concern	Lease clause
	Alterations to the property	Require the tenant to obtain the landlord's permission before carrying out any alterations.
		Retain the ability to inspect the progress of the alterations and their finished state.
		Require the tenant to put the property back into its previous state once the tenant leaves.
	Shopping centres	Require the tenant to keep the shop open during normal shopping hours.
		Require the tenant to keep the windows of the shop looking neat, tidy and inviting.
		Prohibit loud music from being played so as to be heard outside the shop.
Commercial tenant	Break clause	Include the ability to terminate the lease at regular intervals in case the business does not do as well as expected.
	Rent increases	Ensure that the rent may be increased only on set dates (if at all).
		State that any rent increase will reflect market rates.
	Repairing obligations	Ensure that the repairing obligation is limited to the condition of the property at the start of the lease. The landlord cannot then force the tenant to improve the property rather than just repair it.
	Ability to sell	Ensure the lease is attractive to a further buyer by ensuring that it: • allows the lease to be sold • allows the tenant to grant a lease to someone else • allows the property to be used for another use (one required by the buyer).

Table 2: Clauses to address concerns of commercial landlord and tenant

We have seen so far that a buyer might buy a freehold or a leasehold property, and therefore may occupy the property as the outright owner or as a tenant. However, there are other types of property that we do not have to buy in order to be able to use them. Again, without land law, the risk to the owner of allowing others to use his property would be too high. This is worth examining in more detail – how does this work?

HOTELS, SCHOOLS AND SHOPS – LICENCES

Imagine if we could claim some kind of ownership right when staying in a hotel, going to a shop, or going to school. The results would be chaotic. There would be so many people with an interest in the property that Land Registry would never be able to keep accurate records. No one would know who was entitled to be at the property at any given point, and the property would become almost worthless to the freehold owner.

As a result, land law dictates that we do not need to claim any ownership in these types of property in order to use or occupy them. We simply need permission from the owners. This kind of permission is known as a 'licence'. When we stay in an hotel, or go to a shop or go to school, permission to use the properties is implied, provided that we use them for the authorised purpose.

The owners of the property may impose conditions on the permission granted in order to keep control of the property. In this way, the owner of a shop or an hotel is entitled to ask a person to leave if that person is behaving in a way the owner does not like. This protects the owners but allows us to use these kinds of properties for a specific purpose.

Licences are useful in a commercial context too. Licences may be used to allow a person to occupy a property for a very short time, or even to enter onto the property to carry out repairs. The owner can take comfort from the fact that the person who is using the property in this way is not acquiring rights in it, and that the owner is able to ask that person to leave whenever he likes.

We are now ready to move on to a slightly more complex issue. Sometimes, the legal owner of the property and the equitable owner of the property may be two different people. What does this mean, and what effect does this have? We are about to find out in **Chapter 4.**

CHAPTER 4

TRUSTS

INTRODUCTION

We have already discussed in some depth the impact of various rights on a buyer, and how land law offers protection for property owners. We have also looked at how land law operates to protect the interests of landlords and tenants. In this chapter, we are going to consider further how land law works to protect other kinds of occupiers.

Land law recognises two sets of interests in any freehold or leasehold estate – the *legal interest* and the *equitable interest*.

> **EXAMPLE**
>
> Imagine a banana. The banana skin represents the legal title and the banana itself represents the beneficial title. The banana (the equitable title) is protected and contained by the skin (the legal title), but the value or interest is not contained in the banana skin – it is in the banana.

Where the legal title and the equitable title of a piece of land are held by different people, a trust arises. The person who is registered as the owner of the property at Land Registry holds the legal title and is a 'trustee'. It is the trustee's responsibility to manage the property. The person who holds the equitable interest in the property is a 'beneficiary'. Only the beneficiary is entitled to occupy the property.

Quite often, the legal owners of a piece of land will also be the equitable owners. They will hold the legal title on trust for themselves as equitable owners. But in what circumstances might there be different legal and equitable owners?

> **EXAMPLE**
>
> When contracts are exchanged for the sale of land, the buyer holds the equitable title to the land from the point of exchange. The seller still owns the legal title, and this will pass to the buyer only at the point of completion. In this way, from exchange until completion, there are two owners of that piece of land – the legal owner (the seller) and the equitable owner (the buyer).

It is important to distinguish between the legal and equitable owners because only the legal owner can sell the land. This means that the name of the legal owner appears on the contract for sale and the transfer deed – not the name of the equitable owner.

LAND LAW IN OPERATION

Imagine that your friend buys a house and registers herself as the new owner at Land Registry. Your friend invites you to move in, and tells you that if you pay to have the kitchen replaced, she will let you have part of the house. If your friend does not honour this promise, you would be out-of-pocket with nothing to show for it.

Land law considers it fair that the person spending the money should have an interest in the property. The person is not a legal owner as he is not registered as such at Land Registry. In this situation the person would be entitled to part of the equitable title of the property. See the examples below.

EXAMPLE 1

Gilbert and Anne want to buy a house called 'Green Gables'. They decide that they will register the property in both of their names at Land Registry.

Gilbert and Anne are the legal owners of Green Gables. They hold the legal title on trust for themselves as equitable owners.

Gilbert and Anne will have their names on the contract for sale and on the transfer deed. Gilbert and Anne will be entitled to the sales proceeds.

You might think that this is a little pointless. Gilbert and Anne own the house. Why distinguish between ownership of the legal and equitable title in this way?

Now consider the next example.

EXAMPLE 2

Gilbert and Anne want to buy a house called 'Green Gables'. They decide that they will own the house jointly. They live in the house together with Miranda, Anne's aunt. Miranda paid the deposit for the purchase.

In this example, Gilbert and Anne are still the legal owners, but this time they hold the legal title on trust for Gilbert, Anne and Miranda as equitable owners.

Gilbert and Anne will have their names on the contract for sale and on the transfer deed. However, in this example, Gilbert, Anne and Miranda will be entitled to a share of the sale proceeds.

Even though Miranda is not a legal owner of Green Gables, she still has an equitable interest in the property. Gilbert and Anne must abide by statutory rules as trustees of 'Green Gables' and must consider Miranda's interests as a beneficiary.

The trustee–beneficiary relationship

We have seen that the legal owners of property hold it on trust for the equitable owners. We have also seen that it is the equitable owners who are entitled to the benefit of the property.

Beneficiaries may be concerned that the trustees are not protecting their interests. As a result, land law places various obligations on trustees to safeguard the beneficiaries' interests. **Table 1** below illustrates some possible concerns of beneficiaries and the corresponding duties of trustees imposed by land law. You may already be aware of some of these from your reading of **Trusts**.

Beneficiaries' concern	Trustees' duty
Trustees will sell the property without their knowledge.	Consult the beneficiaries. Act in the best interests of the trust and the beneficiaries.
Trustees will steal the beneficiaries' share.	Account to beneficiaries for any profit made. Requirement not to make unauthorised profit from position as trustees. Act in the best interests of the trust and the beneficiaries.
Trustees will make unwanted decisions.	Consult the beneficiaries. Act in the best interests of the trust and the beneficiaries.
Trustees will remove the beneficiaries from the house.	Beneficiaries have the right to live in the house unless a court order is obtained.

Table 1: Concerns of beneficiaries and duties of trustees

You can see from the above that once a beneficiary has an equitable interest in a property, land law works to protect that interest. You will learn more about rights of beneficiaries and duties of trustees through your studies in Equity and Trusts.

Once the beneficiary has obtained the right, what happens? Land law not only protects the beneficiary by giving him an equitable interest in the first place, it also helps the beneficiary by offering means of protection of that interest should the property be sold.

Impact on a buyer and protection

In the context of trusts, land law operates to protect the beneficiary. If land law ensures that interests in land arise where fair and proper, what happens to these interests when the property is sold? Do they just disappear?

One argument is that a property cannot be subject to a trust forever, as land is a valuable commodity and should not be tied up. Another argument is that the beneficiary should have a continuing interest because he shares part of the equitable title.

Land law has developed to balance the competing interests of buyers and beneficiaries. A buyer will want to buy an empty house and will want all of the legal and equitable interest from the seller. A beneficiary will want to retain an equitable interest in the house because it will entitle him to occupy it or to receive a share of the sale proceeds.

The position at law is as follows:

(a)   If a beneficiary is in occupation of the property most of the time, the buyer will have to let the beneficiary stay in the property after his purchase. This is not a practical solution, as it would mean that any property which is subject to a trust is very unlikely to be attractive to a buyer. This is not desirable, as property sale and purchase provides valuable support and stimulation to the economy – we all saw what happened when the property market became uncertain during the last recession.

(b)   In a trust situation, a buyer is able to remove the interest out of the property, provided that he follows certain rules. As long as the buyer pays the purchase money to two or more legal owners, the beneficiary's interest is swept off the property and attaches to the proceeds of sale instead. This is because when a buyer pays the purchase money to two or more trustees, the trustees are able to provide good receipt for the purchase money and so the buyer 'overreaches' the beneficiary's interest. If overreaching occurs, the beneficiary loses the right to live in the property, but will be able to claim a proportionate part of the sale proceeds. The buyer then is able to purchase the property knowing that this trust interest no longer affects him.

You may be thinking that this cannot be fair, as the beneficiary will lose his home. However, land law operates to protect property rights and interests at large and to provide a fair solution for the majority. Tying up property in a trust for permanent occupation by a beneficiary is not in general a fair solution. What is fair is that the beneficiary receives a proportionate reward from the money paid for the property.

Of course, when there is only one legal owner, the buyer will need to ensure that another 'trustee' is appointed to ensure that overreaching occurs. This is just a formality; the second 'trustee' might easily be the solicitor acting for the seller in the sale (see (b) above).

If a beneficiary is not in occupation of the property most of the time then the beneficiary might lose his interest in the property. He will still have the equitable interest in the trust, but this has nothing to do with the occupation of the property and so the buyer is unaffected.

If the beneficiary tells Land Registry that he has an equitable interest in the property under a trust, Land Registry will ensure that no buyer can be registered as the new legal owner of the property unless it has evidence that the beneficiary's interest has been overreached. Land Registry does this by placing a 'restriction' on the seller's right to sell the land, making it possible to sell only where the beneficiary's interest is overreached.

Even though the buyer does not take the property subject to the trust, he has to comply with the Land Registry's requirements when he purchases the property, or he will not be registered as the legal owner of the property at Land Registry. We have seen that this is important, as it is only the legal owners of property who can sell.

If the beneficiary does not ask Land Registry to place a restriction on the title and the property is sold by only one legal owner, the only remedy available to the beneficiary is to sue the trustee for breach of trust. This is because the trustee has acted in breach of duty. You will learn more about the remedies available to beneficiaries where there has been a breach of trust in **Trusts**.

PUBLIC LAW

CHAPTER 1

INTRODUCTION TO PUBLIC LAW

This part of the book introduces public law. It explains, in brief, some of the fundamental principles that a student of this area of law must understand. It avoids complex issues, exceptions and detailed consideration of case law so that the reader may understand the historical and practical relevance of these principles.

In the following chapters we deal with law in the UK, focusing on England and Wales. At times there may be consideration of related issues in Scotland and Northern Ireland. The main historical events which have shaped the way that public bodies in the UK are regulated are also explained.

THE RELEVANCE OF PUBLIC LAW

Public law deals with the relationships between individuals and public authorities, and the way in which those who carry out a public function exercise their power or fulfil their public duties.

Authorities financed by public funds may impact on everyone's lives and business. Government ministers, departments and agencies have the power to set and implement wide-ranging political policies for the many public services that we enjoy or processes that we suffer.

Local authorities such as county councils provide social services, social housing and education. They also control land use and development. There are health bodies which decide whether a treatment will be available for use in the publicly-funded National Health Service (NHS). Medical practitioners who work in the NHS also decide how individual patients are treated.

The judges in courts and tribunals determine how disputes should be resolved and whether crimes have been committed. They also decide whether government departments are acting in a lawful way. The police and prisons, on the other hand, are able to imprison suspects and convicted criminals.

There are two important points to remember at this early stage:

- A great number of authorities and organisations carry out a public function.
- Those who are affected by decisions of a public authority cover a wide range: humans beings, clubs, charities and companies.

PUBLIC AND PRIVATE LAW

The public law that regulates the relationship between public authorities and individuals may be divided into three broad areas, shown in **Figure 1** below. Other areas of law are categorised as private law because the rules in those areas also regulate the relationships between individuals. Some examples of private law areas are also shown in **Figure 1** below.

However, the distinction between private and public law is not always easy to draw. Indeed, public bodies may easily be affected by private laws, so the distinction is not solely related to the parties involved. For example, a City Council might enter into a contract to purchase paper for its administrative offices from a supplier. That business relationship would be set out in a contract. As a result, the supplier would be able to use contract law to sue the Council if its invoice for the paper was not paid. Similarly, a claim in tort may be made by a child who is injured after tripping on a badly-maintained footpath owned by the Council, to claim damages for his injury. This part of the book considers only public law.

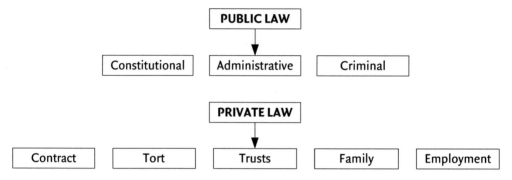

Figure 1: Examples of public and private law

PUBLIC LAW IN OUTLINE

We shall consider what is covered by constitutional, administrative and criminal law in general terms before looking at these areas in detail.

Constitutional law

Constitutional law deals with the internal rules of government. It covers:

- how the state is organised (or in other words how it is 'constituted')
- how government policy decisions are taken
- how laws are made
- how laws are enforced by judges and other public bodies.

When studying constitutional law you will learn how relationships between the major public institutions are regulated, including the relationships between the monarch and the Government, the Government and the courts, the Houses of Parliament and the courts, the UK Government and the European institutions, and the nations which make up the whole United Kingdom.

Constitutional law is relevant to those who work within government and the judges. Knowledge of the rules may also help those who have to deal with government.

Administrative law

Administrative law covers:

- the powers that public authorities may exercise over individuals
- the duties with which public authorities must comply
- how public authorities should make decisions when exercising powers and fulfilling duties
- how those decisions may be challenged by individuals (eg people and companies).

The scope of this part of the book does not allow it to examine in detail the many rules with which public officials must comply when exercising their powers; instead, it focuses on the procedures available to individuals to challenge public officials, especially judicial review. That is a process whereby a court is asked to order a public body to reconsider, or review, a decision. **Chapter 4** also introduces ways of challenging such decisions through an Ombudsman scheme and through judges in the Administrative Court or tribunals.

Criminal law and administrative law

Criminal law practitioners defend clients or pursue prosecutions in the criminal courts. Those who act for the accused may also need to challenge the decisions of a prosecution authority which has imposed restrictions on that person's liberty before conviction. Lawyers may also work to justify the deprivation of someone's liberty to protect the public. This part of the book considers, very briefly, the terminology that you need to understand before studying those restrictions that may be imposed on a person's liberty by the police or courts (bail and control orders), and the process whereby individuals may be sent to another country for prosecution (extradition). Some of these areas may be considered in a criminal law or criminal evidence course rather than under the heading 'public law' itself.

Human rights

Since 1953 the UK has been subject to an international treaty known as the European Convention on Human Rights and Fundamental Freedoms 1950 (the 'European Convention on Human Rights' or 'ECHR'), under which many countries have agreed that their citizens should be able to enjoy certain rights and freedoms. These are commonly referred to as human rights and include the right to a fair trial, the right to freedom of expression, and rights to respect for private and family life.

The UK Government has declared that it will uphold the Convention, so these rights significantly affect the way in which constitutional, administrative and public criminal law is implemented. The ECHR is written in very broad terms and requires careful consideration. This book gives examples of how the rights apply in the context of public law in general and the processes by which the rights may be enforced.

CHAPTER SUMMARY

- Public law deals with the relationships between individuals and public authorities.
- There are three areas of public law: constitutional, administrative and criminal law.

- This book deals with constitutional and administrative law, and introduces the administrative aspects of criminal law in the context of personal freedom and liberty.
- Human rights principles influence many areas of public law.

CHAPTER 2

How the UK's Constitution was Formed

Modern lawyers often know only the current law. They do not need to remember the historical background to their subject because they do not use old principles. However, the way in which the Government, courts and public services operate has been influenced by events over many centuries. Therefore, this chapter describes the events that have shaped the UK constitution. It will help you to understand why we have the system described in later chapters and why particular issues are so important. You could learn more about these events by searching in general online sources.

THE DARK AGES

Weregild in Danelaw, Sarhad and Dirwy in Welsh Law

In Anglo-Saxon times, parts of Northumbria, East Anglia and the East Midlands were subject to Danelaw. If property was stolen, or someone was injured, the guilty person had to pay a fixed penalty, called 'weregild', to the owner of the property or the injured party. A similar system operated among the people who lived in the area which now forms parts of Wales: a fixed 'sarhad' had to be paid by a killer; lesser crimes were penalised by a fixed financial penalty called 'dirwy'.

A stable society may be more likely if everyone knows the consequences of breaking the law, so there is a benefit to having fixed laws. Sometimes, however, the way in which a country is governed needs to adapt to a changing society, so we also have more flexible rules called conventions.

Anglo-Saxon society

Feudalism

In Anglo-Saxon society, the ruling monarch had ultimate power of justice over people who lived in the kingdom according to his own whim. In modern times this has been referred to as a 'feudal society'. Under this regime, the monarch often gave land to a local supporter who became the lord of the manor and is referred to as a feudal lord. This gift also conferred the power to impose rule over the tenants who lived on the land. In extreme circumstances this might include the power to decide whether they should live or die.

Anglo-Saxon law allowed the feudal lords to exercise a range of powers, including:

- *Infangthief* – the feudal lord might choose whether to execute a thief or fine him. Fines were related to a criminal's means, so there was little incentive to spare the life of a poor thief.

- *Frankpledge* – groups of local people agreed to take collective responsibility for the actions of all the people in their group. The feudal lord was able to fine all the men in the group if one of them was suspected of a criminal act but was not presented for justice.

It should not surprise you that it is now rare for such powers to be conferred through mere ownership of land and the favour of the monarch. Even judges and politicians do not have complete discretion over serious criminal penalties, and only the criminal himself is penalised.

Influence of the ordinary person

The feudal lord allowed families to live on his land, in return for service such as taking up arms under his banner, tending his cattle, or granting him hospitality when he was travelling. In return, the feudal lord would consult the heads of these families when taking decisions about how the manor should be run.

Over time a more formal structure of local government developed. Nowadays many government decisions are put out to local and national consultation before making a decision about implementation, and some public functions are run by local councils.

THE MIDDLE AGES

Involvement of religious leaders

Criminal trials were sometimes conducted by putting the accused through a dangerous ordeal, supervised by religious leaders. For one such ordeal the accused had to retrieve a stone from a stream of boiling water. If the accused's wound was healing within three days, he was deemed innocent, because God had allowed the wound to heal; if not, the accused was deemed guilty.

Religious leaders still influence our government but are no longer directly involved in the courts that impose penalties for criminal behaviour.

King Henry II

The deprivation of liberty

King Henry II was King of England from 1133 to 1189 and, like all medieval monarchs, personally controlled how the country was run. He placed his own wife, Eleanor of Aquitaine, under house arrest for 15 years after she encouraged her children to rebel against their father.

Today, our legal system ensures that members of the Government cannot deprive a person of his liberty for protesting about the way the country is run. If such a protestor did commit a crime, only in extreme circumstances would the police be able to keep that person in custody before conviction, and even then, the permitted time-scale is much shorter than the 15 years suffered by Queen Eleanor. An independent court assesses whether suspects have committed a crime and decides any long-term restrictions such as imprisonment. A judge may be asked to decide whether imprisonment is lawful by a process called *habeas corpus*. The representatives of the person who has been imprisoned obtain a written court order (or 'writ') which requires the authorities to bring the prisoner to court. A judge can then examine whether the continued imprisonment is justified in law. This remedy is still available today to challenge the legality of imprisonment.

The murder of Thomas Becket

Medieval monarchs controlled who could own land. They also had the power to levy taxes and to choose who would hold the highest offices in the kingdom. During the reign of Henry II, Thomas Becket was in charge of the collection of taxes as the Lord Chancellor. In 1162, Henry created Becket Archbishop of Canterbury, head of the Church in England (note 'Church *in* England', not 'Church *of* England – this was long before the Reformation, see below). Becket resigned the chancellorship and became a zealous servant of the Church.

At that time there were two types of courts: the religious courts run by the Church, and the royal courts run by the monarch. King Henry proposed laws which would have taken away powers from the Church and removed the privileged treatment given to clergy when prosecuted by the religious courts. Thomas Becket refused to accept this. He was then accused of disobeying the King's commands and of misconduct in his role as a tax collector. Henry put him on trial at Northampton Castle in front of a group of barons appointed as judges by the King. However, Thomas Becket, as a member of the clergy, claimed that he was not answerable to the King's courts. Instead, Becket argued that only a judge appointed by the Pope had the proper authority to decide the matter, and that the trial should take place in a religious court. Becket was eventually convicted by the King's court.

Some years later, Thomas Becket continued to try to extend the influence of the Christian church over the courts in face of growing opposition from the King. Henry's resulting cries of exasperation were (perhaps wrongly) interpreted as commanding the murder of his religious advisor, tax collector and former family friend. As a result, four of Henry's knights murdered Becket in Canterbury Cathedral in 1170 when he refused to submit to the King's greater authority.

The lessons learned by King Henry II after Thomas Becket's murder

Later in his reign, Henry II introduced rudimentary juries whereby a group of local men would bring criminal conduct to the attention of court officials as an alternative to trial by ordeal. These court officials were not involved in the dispute personally and their courts were called an assize. These were similar to our current magistrates' courts, but also determined private disputes such as competing rights of inheritance and reinstated those who had been wrongly evicted from land. This established some of the founding principles of the current legal system in England and Wales of common law.

King John

Was 'Bad' King John really that bad?

Henry II's youngest son, John, had a difficult job during his reign (1199–1216). He continued the aim of fair administration of justice begun by his father. He also tried to remove the power to administer local justice from local lords of the manor by appointing judges who were independent from the Church and were expected to be professional when imposing fines. Some commentators suggest that John tried his best to be fair and independent; others think he used these fines and taxes to raise as much money as possible to fund on-going military campaigns to help him retain land in France. However, it is said that those who became part of John's circle of advisers and officials received favourable treatment from the King and found it much easier to have their cases heard in court. Some believed that friends of the King were more likely to win their cases. If true, this was hardly fair administration of justice.

The Magna Carta

Eventually the lords and barons in northern and eastern England had had enough of King John's ways. They perceived John's behaviour as arbitrary and wrong. After meeting in Northampton in 1215, some travelled to Runnymede near Windsor Castle and signed the document which is now called *Magna Carta* (the 'Great Charter'), to remind King John of his obligations to the feudal lords. In the document it was declared, among many other things, that punishment must be imposed only in accordance with the law of the land (*lex terrae*) rather than on the whim of the King (*lex regis*). The Charter also established a council of 25 independent barons who were to ensure that the King complied with its provisions.

The King largely ignored this, particularly the formation of the independent council, and a civil war ensued. Nonetheless, some principles from the Charter were incorporated into later statutes, and the rule that everyone should be subject to the due process of the law rather than the King's orders has been used worldwide as a founding principle when establishing systems of government. This part of the revised Magna Carta 1297, enacted by Edward I, is still law in the UK and may be viewed at <www.legislation.gov.uk>.

The Magna Carta is now considered to have either embodied or to have reinforced the principles of a fair trial and fair government rather than rule by the will of the king in that:

- government must be conducted according to the law and with consent of the governed
- no one is above the law
- everyone has the right to be protected from unlawful imprisonment.

Conclusion

These events during the reigns of Henry II and King John have influenced the foundations of law and our courts. It is desirable that everyone is required to comply with the law, including those who run the country. The courts are separate from the monarch and from the Church. Judges can only hear cases in which they are able to be impartial and have nothing to gain or lose. They are, in this way, said to be free of bias and independent.

SIXTEENTH AND SEVENTEENTH CENTURIES

By the 16th century England had fully annexed Wales so that what we now call 'England and Wales' was known only as England. So, many references to 'English law' and England exist, and where relevant to the historical context, this book follows that convention.

The Reformation and Henry VIII

At this time many rulers in Northern Europe, including King Henry VIII, became dissatisfied with the involvement of the Catholic Church in Rome in local matters. By making the rules referred to as the 'First Act of Supremacy 1534', King Henry severed the state's connection with the Pope, head of the Catholic Church in Rome, and declared himself 'the only supreme head on earth of the Church in England' with the support of his advisors in Parliament. He had, therefore, become head of the Church in England, as well as the supreme arbiter of secular (ie non-Church) law. Land and property belonging to the monasteries were seized by the King and dissent was brutally suppressed. The idea that the monarch's right to rule is derived from God's will – referred to as the 'divine rights of kings' – was enforced in earnest.

Charles I and Parliament

By 1641, England, Scotland and Ireland were ruled by the same monarch, Charles I (1625–49), uniting certain royal families as a result of marriages and various monarchs having had no children. However, they remained separate states.

In England, the advisers who previously helped the monarch make decisions had evolved into two separate groups. The locally-elected representatives of select landowners met in the House of Commons, and the lords, barons and clergy now met in the House of Lords. The Members of the House of Commons were dissatisfied with the idea of an absolute monarch and the way in which the King exercised his powers. In 1641 they proposed legislation (the Petition of Right) to curtail these powers. If properly enforced, this would have resulted in the Houses of Parliament, rather than the King, governing the Church, government ministers and armed forces. Later that year, the House of Commons also passed a motion (the 'Grand Remonstrance') which set out for Charles a long list of grievances. It included objections to:

- the King's spending
- his exercise of powers to raise taxes, wage war, agree peace and control the availability of goods such as soap, salt and coal
- how land had been confiscated in Ireland
- how lawyers and judges had been oppressed when exercising independence
- the extent of the bishops' influence in Parliament.

Charles I, fighting for his powers, forced his way into the House of Commons to arrest opponents, but they had already escaped. Following these events, and the ensuing Civil War, there remains a convention that the monarch does not enter the House of Commons and has to send her representative (called 'Black Rod') to invite those who are in the House of Commons to see her in the House of Lords.

The Outcome of the English Civil War

The English Civil War culminated with the execution of Charles I in 1649. The leader of the victorious anti-Royalist forces, Oliver Cromwell, abolished the monarchy and declared the establishment of a Commonwealth. In effect, England, Scotland and Ireland became a republic, and Oliver Cromwell became its Lord Protector.

Proposals for the way in which the constituent nations should be governed were drafted, attempted and abandoned. Eventually, the monarchy was restored in 1660 when Charles I's son, Charles II, accepted much-reduced powers. The divine right of the monarch to rule eventually gave way to Parliament as the supreme decision-maker.

In this way, England (and Wales) was one of the earliest countries to resolve the power struggle between the monarchy and the people. The Civil War saw great upheaval, but there was no great revolution where a completely new legal system had to be adopted, unlike in much of the rest of Europe. As a result, our system of laws and government has evolved gradually, based on historical events and practices rather than on a brand-new pre-defined list of rules.

The start of party politics

In Parliament some supported the monarch, and in particular his desire to reunite the English Church with the Catholic Church in Rome, while others did not. Those loyal to the King were dubbed 'Tories' and those opposed to Charles but loyal to the fiercely protestant William, Duke of Orange (see below), were called 'Whigs'. Whilst this division was not as rigid as the current political party structure, parliamentarians had begun the tradition of grouping together to further their political proposals.

William and Mary and the Bill of Rights 1689

Charles II died without legitimate heirs in 1685, so his brother James, who was a Catholic, succeeded him as King James II. William, Duke of Orange was married to James II's daughter, Mary. Protestant parliamentarians negotiated with William to take the throne from James by force, and in 1688 William's army landed in England. However, James had already fled to France, so his daughter Mary was considered his rightful successor.

William was keen to rule alongside his wife, Queen Mary, as king, not merely as her husband. This gave the English Parliament the chance to force William and Mary to restate the most important principles from the Magna Carta and the Petition of Right, referred to above. In return, it recognised William's right to remain king if his wife died before him. These principles were enacted in the Bill of Rights 1689 and provided that:

- Parliament would meet regularly and there would be free elections to Parliament
- Parliament, not the monarch, was the sovereign law-maker
- Parliament alone controlled the raising of taxes, waging of war and the armed forces
- comments made in Parliament could not be subject to court action
- the monarch could not disband or 'dissolve' Parliament on a whim.

THE ACTS OF UNION

1706 to 1707 – the birth of Great Britain

Queen Mary died in 1694. William did not remarry and had no children. By 1701 the English Parliament was concerned about a successor to the throne, given that Mary's sister Anne had no surviving male children. Supporters of the descendants of Mary's father (called 'Jacobites' from Jacobus, the Latin version of James) were pressing for his Catholic descendants to become rightful heirs. Parliament used the Act of Settlement in 1701 to settle the question of succession to the English and Irish thrones. The line of succession followed a protestant granddaughter of James I and those of her descendants who adhered to the Protestant Christian faith, provided they did not marry Roman Catholics.

The Scottish Parliament, in contrast to the English Parliament, created a method of selecting the monarch to ensure that a successor came from the line of former Scottish kings. This person could well have been different from the monarch of England and Ireland. Nonetheless, in 1702 Anne became Queen of England and Ireland and Queen of Scots, which remained separate states with separate currencies and trading restrictions between Scotland and England.

The English Government was keen to create a unified approach with Scotland in its discussions with other European political powers. The Scottish Government was keen to avoid a repeat of the economic collapse Scotland had recently suffered following periods of famine and a failed attempt at setting up a trading colony in central America. So, in the early years of Anne's reign, both Parliaments began to negotiate a union of the two countries, under considerable economic pressure from the English. When both countries finally passed Acts of Union in 1706 and 1707, England and Scotland were joined together under one monarch, with one parliament, one economic regime, one currency and rules for succession to the throne. The Acts of Union removed powers from the separate parliament in Scotland and included provisions to ensure that judges could not be removed from their posts by the monarch, that power being exercised only with the agreement of both Houses of Parliament. Scotland maintained a separate official church and private law system.

1801 – the United Kingdom of Great Britain and Ireland

Ireland, hitherto treated as a colony of Britain, joined England, Wales and Scotland as a United Kingdom in 1801, after Acts of Union were passed in both the Irish and British Parliaments.

REVOLUTION IN EUROPE, REFORM IN THE UK

In the 18th and early 19th centuries, popular revolutions were underway throughout Europe. Philosophers debated how governments should be set up. In Great Britain and Ireland, though, many of the political structures allowing for the people to be in control of the country were already in place. There was less clamour for widespread change, so any reforms were gradual alterations as practices developed.

At that time King George III refused to allow Catholics in Ireland to vote in elections, marking the start of a fight for the right to vote, or 'enfranchisement'. By 1831 only around 400,000 landowners in the UK out of a population of some 20 million were entitled to vote. Between 1832 and 1928 the right to vote was slowly extended to cover all male and female citizens aged over 21. The most obviously unfair systems in the election process were gradually being removed. But it was only after the abolition of an extra vote for some university graduates in 1969 that elections to parliament in the UK truly were based on 'one person, one vote' (for those over the age of 18). As a result, it is now essential for politicians to gain the support of ordinary citizens in order to obtain the power to govern, and political issues have become highly influential over law reform.

The Parliament Act 1911

It used to be that new laws had to be agreed expressly by both Houses of Parliament. Nonetheless, the House of Lords usually agreed to proposals from the House of Commons about financial matters as a matter of course. Despite this convention, in 1909 the Lords rejected the annual budget that had been approved by the Commons, including some new welfare benefits for the poor.

The Lords gave in only after a general election showed that the electorate also supported the proposals. As a result, Henry Asquith, the Liberal Prime Minister, proposed a new rule that the House of Lords could never oppose budget proposals and could not delay other laws agreed by the House of Commons for more than two years beyond the year in which the Commons agreed them. The (mainly Conservative) House of Lords opposed the change, fearing that it would eventually be used to push through proposals for a separate government for Ireland. Asquith then persuaded the King, George V, to agree (in principle) to appoint many new Liberal members of the House of Lords if necessary to force the measure through. Rather than suffer a large change to their membership, the Lords relented and the rule became the Parliament Act 1911. This also reduced the maximum period between elections to the House of Commons from seven years to five years.

Irish independence and the Parliament Act 1949

By 1949 the southern part of Ireland had gained full independence from the UK and became the Republic of Ireland. Northern Ireland had resolved to remain part of the UK until a majority of its citizens favoured independence.

In the same year the Labour Government used the Parliament Act 1911 itself to force through a reduction in the maximum period for which the House of Lords might delay laws approved by the Commons. The resulting Parliament Act 1949 provides that the House of Lords cannot delay proposals for more than one year. The House of Commons had become the dominant law-making institution in the UK.

Growth and control of the public service

The 'welfare state' system of benefits for the poor and needy was part of an ever-growing public service. In the 1960s, the courts recognised the growing influence of government and started to allow challenges to government decisions. Administrative law began to develop in its modern form.

European Communities Act 1972

The UK wished to join the organisations which now form the European Union in the 1960s, but membership was vetoed by the French. However, the need for free trade with continental Europe was strong, and the UK finally became a member of the European Economic Community (or 'EEC') as it was then called in 1973. In joining, the UK Parliament had to accept that the institutions of the EEC could create laws for the UK, or require that the Europe-wide laws were implemented in a local version. The House of Commons was no longer in complete control of law-making for the UK, and the UK courts became bound by decisions of the European Court of Justice (now the 'Court of Justice of the European Union').

HUMAN RIGHTS

Quite apart from its membership of the European Union (as it is now called), the UK was a founder member of another European body, the Council of Europe. This was set up in 1950 as a reaction to atrocities perpetrated during the Second World War. The Council drafted the ECHR, mentioned in **Chapter 1**.

Anyone who feels that their rights under the ECHR have been violated by a state that has signed the Convention may bring a case before a central court in Strasbourg called the European Court of Human Rights. However, that person must first exhaust any potential remedies in the courts of the country against which he makes the allegations of breach. In the UK, the Convention rights were not originally part of our national law so could not be applied by the domestic courts. Consequently, some claimants had to follow the lengthy process of going through all stages of appeal in the national courts before their case could properly be heard on the basis of their Convention rights.

In the 1980s, some commentators, legal academics, judges and politicians considered that the Conservative Government, led by Margaret Thatcher, had been using its powers to implement laws which breached human rights but which the national courts could not overturn. There followed pressure to incorporate human rights into national law, to provide citizens with practical access to a national court which had the power to enforce Convention rights.

As a result, the Human Rights Act 1998 now requires all public bodies to comply with the Convention. This also means that courts and tribunals must interpret and apply laws in a way which is compatible with the ECHR. When that is impossible, a court may make a 'declaration of incompatibility'. Such a declaration does not actually change the law; it may, however, result in the Government making necessary changes in the future.

DEVOLUTION TO THE REGIONS OF THE UK

Ever since the separate kingdoms of the UK first joined together, there have been those who seek to draw back power from the Parliament in London. In 1999, national governing bodies were established in Scotland and Wales. There is a Scottish Parliament to make legislation and a Scottish Government to govern Scotland. In a similar fashion, Wales now has a National Assembly for Wales and a Welsh Government. Each body has a website which explains more about its powers and functions.

In Northern Ireland devolution has been more problematic. There were several attempts to create a peaceful devolved government, culminating in the Northern Ireland Assembly in 1998. Political opposition and disputes resulted in its operations being suspended several times. There is also a Northern Ireland Executive which carries out governmental functions in the permitted areas. The current system sets out some areas of government that it is intended should never be transferred from Westminster's control, such as tax, defence and immigration.

As there has been no great popular call for it to date, there is no separate parliament or executive for England.

GREATER SEPARATION OF THE COURTS FROM PARLIAMENT

The courts in medieval times were influenced by the king or the Church, and the Lord Chancellor was an adviser to government, collector of taxes, and also involved in the Church and the court system. In more recent times the Lord Chancellor has been a member of the government, in charge of the courts and the appointment of judges. In a similar cross-over of positions, the most senior judges used to hear the final appeal in court cases within Parliament, as a committee of the House of Lords.

Politicians, judges and legal theorists have been concerned that courts should be independent of governmental influence. Between 2005 and 2009 reforms were introduced so that the Government has no direct control over the judges. The Lord Chancellor's duties were separated and redistributed to other office-holders. The most senior judges moved to a new Supreme Court, and an independent Judicial Appointments Commission was established to recommend new judges. The Lord Chancellor became simply a formal name for the Secretary of State for Justice, the minister in government who is in charge of the administrative functions in the courts, among other things.

CHAPTER SUMMARY

The way in which people in the UK have been governed has evolved gradually over the centuries without the need for a major revolution, because each set of rules and practices can be changed as times change.

Centuries ago: The King, the Lord Chancellor and feudal lords enjoyed immense power. King John's excessive taxes led to his barons drawing up a document to remind him of their rights and his obligations. The most important principles in this document are now referred to as the Magna Carta.

Mid- to late 17th century: Following the restoration of the monarchy and after the Civil War, the Bill of Rights 1689 set out principles to safeguard Parliament from the monarch's interference.

Late 17th and early 18th centuries: Parliament was able to demand more power from William III and Mary II. The desire to maintain peace and have a common monarch for the British Isles culminated in the union between Scotland and England and Wales. The same Acts of Parliament secured the independence of the judiciary from royal interference.

Late 19th and early 20th centuries: The number of bodies which carry out a public service increased substantially, having an ever-growing impact on our daily lives. The right to elect representatives to the House of Commons was extended to all adults because it was considered unfair to limit this right to landowners. The House of Lords accepted the superiority of the House of Commons.

Mid- to late 20th century: Administrative law developed in its modern form. The House of Commons accepted restrictions on powers when the UK joined the European Communities (now the European Union). The European Convention on Human Rights made public bodies take human rights into account. The Human Rights Act 1998 provided that national courts can interpret and apply laws in a way that is compatible with the ECHR, but must follow unambiguous national laws.

End of the 20th and early 21st century: Law-making and administration were devolved to national bodies in Scotland, Wales and Northern Ireland. The Lord Chancellor's powers were reduced, giving him less direct influence over the judges. The judges in the House of Lords separated from Parliament to form the independent Supreme Court.

CHAPTER 3

THE CHARACTERISTICS OF THE UNITED KINGDOM CONSTITUTION

In **Chapter 2** we looked at how the current system of government has evolved. This chapter sets out the most fundamental principles and concepts that are relevant today and which you will consider on a public law course. Many courses begin by looking at these principles. They are:

- The constitutional institutions.
- Written and unwritten constitutions.
- Conventions.
- Sources of the UK constitution.
- The rule of law.
- Separation of powers.
- Checks and balances.
- Parliamentary supremacy.

Lawyers who work in the Government Legal Service need to know these principles because they work for politicians and civil servants who are subject to these concepts every day of their working lives. Other lawyers may act for clients who deal with such public bodies.

You may find it helpful to read this chapter quickly at the start of your studies and return to it after reading the rest of this book. Some areas involve philosophical issues and may appear complex if they are new to you. Others require a relatively wide understanding of the law-making and political systems in the UK, as well as of the historical events that shaped these concepts. They are best considered in depth once you know more about the subject. For now, read about the issues and make a reminder to review this chapter again later in your studies.

THE CONSTITUTIONAL INSTITUTIONS

There are several different ways of organising a country's government or state. In the UK, we have a monarch and three branches of government with specific functions.

The executive, legislature and judiciary

There are, essentially, three branches of government within the state:

- The *executive* formulates policy and decides how it is implemented. It is made up of all those people who exercise day-to-day power over how the country is run. This is often referred to as 'the government'. It includes the central government departments, the police, councils, local bodies that carry out a public function and businesses who are contracted to provide public services. The head of the executive is the Prime Minister, who has a group of colleagues selected to run the government departments, called ministers. The most senior ministers attend meetings called the Cabinet. As most power is controlled by the executive, references to the 'Crown' now mean the ministers and their departments, rather than the Queen herself.

- The *legislature* comprises the law makers. In the UK there are two debating chambers in which political events and proposals for law reform are discussed and draft laws are finalised. These are the democratically-elected Members of Parliament who meet in the House of Commons, and appointed members of the House of Lords (see **Chapter 4**).

- The *judiciary* comprises the judges in the courts and tribunals. They decide the outcome of formal disputes between individuals as well as grievances that individuals may have with the way that the executive has acted. **Chapters 5** and **6** summarise relevant constitutional issues.

As a result of the devolution of power to the separate nations comprising the UK, the legislative and executive functions of government are carried out in Belfast, Cardiff and Edinburgh as well as in London.

The monarch

The monarch is the head of state, currently Queen Elizabeth II. She has a place in all three arms of government but today has principally a ceremonial role. The monarch signs Acts of Parliament to make them law (the Royal Assent). Judges sit in what are, at least nominally, the Queen's courts. Civil servants who implement policy for the executive are servants of the Crown and ministers are 'Her Majesty's Principal Secretaries of State'.

THE UK CONSTITUTION

Written and unwritten constitutions

A constitution is the rules that set out how government is established and how it is regulated.

Many countries have a written set of governmental rules, for example the USA has the US Constitution as amended by the Bill of Rights. This form of written constitution is often given a more important status than all other laws, which means that so-called 'ordinary' laws may be challenged in court if they do not comply with the 'constitutional' principles. Often, written constitutions may only be changed if a special procedure has been followed, requiring the agreement of a high proportion of representatives of the people in that country. In this way, such constitutions are referred to as being 'entrenched'.

The rules under which the UK Government operates are different. They are not all written down in one document, or even in a complete collection of documents. While there are some documents to which you can refer, there are also some unwritten rules. Even so, the unwritten practices are still observed and respected by politicians and judges just as much as any other law. None of the written or unwritten constitutional rules has special status such as being 'entrenched' or being superior to other laws.

There may be advantages to having unwritten principles that are not entrenched, such as being able to change quickly with the times. However, there may also be the disadvantage of uncertainty as to how unwritten rules apply.

Sources of constitutional rules

Many constitutional principles are derived from political philosophy which developed after the restoration of the UK monarchy in 1660, during the 17th, 18th and 19th centuries. As a result, much of the UK system had been established before the desirability of a written constitution had been considered elsewhere. There was no need to follow the example of France or the USA and create a completely new political establishment, nor to make a formal declaration to signify independence from colonial rule. So we have a constitution derived from common law customs, historical documents, procedures, traditions, conventions and the structure of governmental institutions.

Common law customs and case law

Some laws in our common law system are derived from principles which are considered always to have been the law of the land. Many of the powers exercised by the monarch and some exercised by government ministers are of this nature and are not written in a formal document.

Judges have referred to these kinds of principles in cases of constitutional significance. One such concept is the principle that an individual is permitted to do anything unless it is forbidden by law, while the state may take only such actions as are authorised by law. The case most often referred to as setting out this concept is *Pepper v Hart*, so this is referred to as 'the rule in *Pepper v Hart*'.

Institutions and their internal rules

The way in which government works is influenced by how the branches of government are set up and the powers that they exercise, including their powers over each other. As such, each institution's internal rules affect how its members carry out their role and interact with the other institutions. The book which sets out Parliamentary practice is called *Erskine May: Parliamentary Practice* (or simply *Erskine May*). In a similar fashion, judges have protocols and guidelines to follow when deciding civil cases and the punishment of criminal offences.

Legislation

In **Chapter 2** you read about a range of written laws created by Parliament (called 'legislation') to set out the rules of government, such as the Acts of Settlement and Parliament Acts. Other pieces of legislation have special constitutional significance, including:

- Habeas Corpus Act 1679 (which enshrined the courts' ability to determine whether a prisoner was being held lawfully).

- Crown Proceedings Act 1947 (which removed some of the monarch's privileges so that it is possible to sue the state for certain actions taken by civil servants).
- Representation of the People Act 1983 (which sets out who can vote and how voting is conducted).

Conventions

Some practices are historical conventions that make political or practical sense, such as the practice that judges do not get involved in political debates. Take as another example the procedure that the Queen follows when appointing the Prime Minister.

She has the legal right to appoint the Prime Minister. However, rather than choosing according to her own whim, by convention she appoints the leader of the party which holds the majority of the seats in the Houses of Commons. It would be impractical to select the leader of the losing party after an election because it could generate enormous public protest.

Doctrines

Political philosophy influences how government is run and law is made. An example of such a philosophical principle is that everyone should be subject to the law, so the monarch is not above the law.

All of the sources mentioned here combine to create a large body of rules which affect how public services operate. The rest of this chapter considers some of these sources in detail. Others are considered in later chapters.

THE ROYAL PREROGATIVE AND STATUTORY POWERS

Certain common law legal powers are invested in the Crown. These are called royal prerogative powers, under which either the Queen or government ministers may:

- enact a bill into law once it has been agreed by Parliament (Royal Assent by the Queen)
- confer honours to recognise special public service, such as a knighthood
- pardon convicted criminals
- declare war and peace
- finalise treaties with foreign states
- appoint ministers to the executive.

The Queen herself exercises some of these powers but no longer takes any decisions about how the country is run. Her remaining powers are associated with a ceremonial role and are exercised only following the recommendations of more democratically accountable people, such as Parliament, ministers or the Prime Minister. These usual practices or 'conventions' are explained further below ('The Nature of Conventions').

The royal prerogative has been diminishing gradually as replacement Acts of Parliament set out new rules for departments to follow. These may even give the minister a statutory power to introduce laws, called statutory instruments (SIs), which set out technical or administrative points (see further **Chapter 4** below). For example, there is an annual statutory instrument to update the amount paid as compensation for redundancy.

Sometimes, to make implementation of new laws easy, Parliament gives a minister the statutory power to change or remove Acts of Parliament. Ministers have such a power if a court has decided that a statute contravenes the Human Rights Act 1998 (see **Chapter 2**). Powers like this are sometimes referred to as a 'Henry VIII power', after the autocratic rule of that monarch.

THE NATURE OF CONVENTIONS

Conventions are practices that have not been written down as rules but are followed as a matter of tradition. As a result of the way in which UK constitutional practices have developed, a convention may well contradict the strict legal position.

When the Queen exercises her legal powers (the royal prerogative), she does not actually make the relevant decision. Following the settlement achieved during the restoration of the monarchy and the later reductions in the monarch's powers, it is a well-observed convention that she exercises these powers only on advice and at the request of the relevant minister or Prime Minister.

Table 1 below summarises some examples of the rules alongside their related convention, so that you can see that the legal rules do not necessarily give the full picture.

The legal position based on case law or statute		The convention in practice
The Queen has the prerogative power to create or veto an Act of Parliament.	but	The Queen always signs bills which have followed the correct parliamentary procedure, on advice from the Prime Minister.
The Queen can appoint the people who become ministers in the executive.	but	The Queen appoints the leader of the party with the most Members of Parliament in the House of Commons to be Prime Minister. The Prime Minister then selects the ministers and the Queen sanctions their appointment.
Parliament must meet at least once every three years.	but	Parliamentary business is actually carried out in Westminster every day of the year, for most of the year.
The Queen can declare war.	but	The Cabinet of the most senior ministers would decide whether to begin a military campaign. A convention is developing that the Cabinet should consult Parliament beforehand.

Figure 1: A comparison of legal rules and related conventions

There is a significant difference between laws and conventions. Laws are enforceable in court, conventions are not. Laws do not change just because they are ignored, but conventions are flexible and may be adapted to new circumstances without being breached. For example, in 2010, the Conservative Party had more Members of Parliament in the House of Commons than any other party but did not hold an overall majority. The Conservatives formed a coalition with the Liberal Democrats, and the Queen appointed the Conservative leader, David Cameron, to be Prime Minister even though his party did not hold a majority of seats.

To a large extent, conventions are only followed now because they have been followed in the past, so those involved feel that they are obliged to continue the tradition. Therefore, conventions can develop over time, like the convention that the Prime Minister should not normally be a member of the House of Lords. This has been observed since the Parliament Act 1911 gave supremacy to Parliament.

Other practices that were originally followed only by convention have been enshrined in formal legislation so are now law. A recent example includes the point that the Queen must not exercise her prerogative power to enter into (or 'ratify') the international agreements between nations called treaties until Parliament has had an opportunity to consider the terms and indicate its approval or disapproval. This was enshrined in the Constitutional Reform and Governance Act 2010.

As the prerogative powers and conventions that adapt them are not written down it can be difficult to identify and understand them all. The Ministry of Justice's 2009 Report on *The Governance of Britain: Review of the Executive Royal Prerogative Powers* provides a helpful analysis.

AN INTRODUCTION TO CONSTITUTIONAL THEORY

Every public law course considers the detail of broad constitutional doctrines, especially by reference to the views of Professor AV Dicey, first published in 1885 in his *Introduction to the Study of Law of the Constitution*. Some courses consider the views of other political philosophers.

The principles underpinning constitutional theory include:

- The Rule of Law
- The Separation of Powers
- Parliamentary Supremacy (or Parliamentary Sovereignty).

This chapter introduces the fundamental points behind these theories or 'doctrines'.

The Rule of Law

The Rule of Law doctrine is the idea that law applies to everyone and that everyone should be treated according to a proper legal process. Note that this does not mean that everyone is treated in exactly the same way. For example, children cannot go to a pub and buy beer, but adults can. Similarly, a shop-keeper cannot imprison an employee he has seen stealing from a till, but the criminal courts can. In the same way, politicians and judges may be treated differently from ordinary people when carrying out their specific roles in government.

Dicey explained the concept of the Rule of Law as follows:

- 'No man is punishable or can be lawfully made to suffer in body or goods except for a distinct breach of the law established in the ordinary legal manner before the ordinary courts of the land ...'
- 'It means ... the absolute supremacy ... of regular law as opposed to the influence of arbitrary power.'
- 'No man is above the law ... every man and woman ... is subject to the ordinary law ... and amenable to the jurisdiction of the ordinary tribunals ...'

As a result of these ideas, we are able to draw other general principles. They are expressed in different terms by different commentators but may be summarised as follows:

- law should be clear and accessible
- government officials must not have any exemption from the ordinary law
- there should be no unjustified discrimination in government action or the exercise of judgment in the courts
- imprisonment should only result from a clear breach of the law
- the judiciary and legal profession should be independent from the executive.

Dicey's book is not the source of these points; some are based on ancient philosophy. Dicey himself noted that many of the principles are part of the common law derived from judicial decisions. Therefore, related case law is just as important as Dicey's distillation of the concepts.

The Rule of Law is discussed by some in more liberal terms than Dicey's views. Some theorists expound wider-ranging ideas about the Rule of Law to include the concept that laws must only be implemented in a fair and impartial way, which could include the right to a fair trial and guaranteed access to legal advice. Others say that the Rule of Law theory means that laws must be interpreted in a way which upholds all fundamental rights and freedoms, such as human rights.

The Separation of Powers

The Separation of Powers is a constitutional doctrine formulated (though not invented) by a French political theorist called Montesquieu in the 18th century. He suggested that government should be constrained by certain restrictions to avoid oppression and tyranny.

The restrictions are:

- the executive, legislative and judicial functions of government should be assigned to different bodies so that:
  - only the executive executes (or authorises execution of) policy;
  - only the legislature makes law;
  - only the judges decide how law should be applied
- the people in these three arms of government must be separate so that no one works in more than one branch at a time.

In the UK Government, powers are not completely separate in this way. There are sometimes benefits to having an incomplete separation. If each arm exercises influence over the others' roles, it may result in a system of 'checks and balances' that limits the risk that power may be abused.

Incomplete separation of powers

The judicial function is well separated from the executive as a result of the Acts of Settlement and the more recent reduction in the Lord Chancellor's powers (see **Chapter 2**), albeit that the Lord Chancellor still controls the administration of the courts. The judiciary and Parliament are also quite independent from each other following the creation of the Supreme Court, so that the final court of appeal no longer hears cases as a committee in the House of Lords. This is further supported by the convention that courts will not interfere with Parliament's own proceedings and the fact that judges may be (and are) disciplined by the independent Office for Judicial Complaints if they make inappropriately political comments in court that are not related to the case they are hearing.

However, the legislative function is not carried out by one body alone. While legislation becomes law after a debate in Parliament, most proposals for new laws are first made by ministers in the executive. Further, by convention, those ministers in the executive must also be Members of Parliament in the Commons, or sit in the Lords. In this way they play a role in both the executive and the legislature. Ministers also have powers to introduce some laws without a debate in Parliament. **Chapter 4** considers the extent to which this gives excessive power to the executive.

So, the executive may be in an inappropriately dominant position in that the same political party controls the House of Commons as runs the government departments (including the police and prison service).

Judges may also be considered to interfere in the legislature. The common law system means that judges carry out a law-making function and do not just decide how law made by others should be applied. Politicians and journalists regularly criticise judges who decide cases in ways that they did not anticipate or desire. In fact, for many years Parliament has disagreed with a decision of the European Court of Human Rights, in which that Court declared that the denial of voting rights to prisoners was incompatible with the ECHR. Thus, you can see that the legislative function is not completely separate.

Checks and balances

The Constitution of the USA was specifically drafted to avoid a perceived scope for tyrannical and arbitrary government by the British executive in the British American colonies. Even then, however, the founding fathers created a system with incomplete separation of powers. The US Supreme Court may stop actions by the President (the executive) by declaring them unconstitutional, and Congress (the legislature) controls funding of the judiciary. Similarly, in some circumstances the President has the power to grant a pardon to criminals after their conviction by the judiciary and to veto some laws made by Congress.

In the UK, the unwritten nature of the constitution makes it more complicated to determine the extent of our separation of powers and related checks and balances. Even so, there are certain features that have the potential to comprise a system of checks and balances or limit excessive power:

- Parliament decides whether to introduce new legislation (proposed by the executive).
- Legally, no more than 95 ministers can come from the Commons.
- Ministers appear in Parliament to answer questions about their decisions and how their departments are run. An example is Prime Minister's Question Time.
- The House of Lords is not always dominated by members who support the same political party as makes up the executive government, so this may keep the executive in check.
- Judges decide how to interpret and apply legislation (created by Parliament).
- Judges also decide whether actions by the government departments (the executive) are valid. Judicial review is one way in which they achieve this. Another is the court's power to determine whether imprisonment by the police or prison service is lawful in *habeas corpus* applications.

Chapter 4 explores these themes in greater detail to help you understand whether there are effective systems in place to limit the exercise of arbitrary power.

Parliamentary Supremacy

Parliamentary Supremacy (sometimes called Parliamentary Sovereignty) is another doctrine described by Dicey. He suggested that:

(a)   Parliament may make any law whatsoever, even if unfair, unjust or impractical.

(b)   The courts or any other body may not question Acts of Parliament.

(c)   An Act of Parliament is not binding on a future Parliament.

In practical terms this means that new Acts of Parliament prevail over old ones. For example, while the original Act of Union with Ireland suggested that that union was to be permanent, the later law which created the Republic of Ireland is entirely valid. Even if a conflict between the new and old Acts is not expressly resolved in the new one, the new Act prevails. This is called the doctrine of implied repeal.

Acts of Parliament also prevail over case law. For example, in 2008 a House of Lords decision interpreted the law on discrimination in a way which made it more difficult for disabled people to make a claim. Parliament reversed this decision in the Equality Act 2010. The doctrine of parliamentary supremacy means that the rules in the Equality Act prevail over the decision of the House of Lords. This raises three related issues:

(a)   Judges are not considered as having broken this doctrine if they interpret ambiguous legislation in a way which complies with conventions and international obligations.

(b)   UK courts cannot change an Act of Parliament or declare it invalid even if it breaches human rights. The Human Rights Act 1998 maintained parliamentary supremacy by allowing UK courts to issue only a *declaration of incompatibility* with human rights principles if Acts of Parliament cannot be interpreted in a way which is compatible with the ECHR.

(c)   Statutory powers given to ministers override any common law prerogative rights.

These points may bring politicians and judges into conflict when the line between ambiguity and judicial innovation is unclear.

Lastly, parliamentary supremacy also means that international agreements made by the executive with other countries are binding only once made part of UK law with the consent of Parliament. This even applies to laws emanating from the European Union. Parliament gave advance consent that some EU laws might become national law automatically. However, the European Union Act 2011 enshrined the parliamentary supremacy principle that whatever Parliament can do, Parliament can always undo, by providing that EU law is recognised in the UK only by virtue of the Acts of Parliament that accept this to be the case. Parliament could, in theory, decide that European law no longer applies.

Limitations on Parliamentary Supremacy

While Parliament may enact or reverse any legislation that it wishes, there are very good reasons why politicians would not necessarily do so:

(a)   *Political pressure and practicality.* It would be politically unpopular if, say, the Westminster Parliament withdrew powers delegated to the Scottish Parliament. In a similar way, it is extremely unlikely that Parliament would withdraw the independence granted to Canada and other countries which have left the British Empire. Political pressure associated with probable reduction in popularity at the next election prevents a political party from implementing laws which were not part of its election proposals or 'manifesto'.

(b)   *International pressure and the European Union.* While it is now clear that Parliament could decide that it is no longer bound at all by European law, or is not bound in relation to a particular matter, withdrawal from the EU would have such a wide-ranging impact on the diplomatic relations, law and economy of the UK that it is extremely unlikely. This also applies to the UK's other international obligations.

(c)   *Human rights.* Parliament has decided to limit Parliamentary Supremacy by deciding that, in normal circumstances, any new legislation should only be implemented if compatible with fundamental human rights. The fact that politicians may want to uphold the Rule of Law doctrine would also prevent completely unfair laws.

CHAPTER SUMMARY

The UK state comprises the monarch, Parliament, the executive and the judiciary.

The constitution

- A constitution is the rules which set out how government is established and how it is regulated.
- Our constitutional rules are unwritten and derived from legislation, common law cases, doctrines, conventions, and the structures and rules of the institutions themselves.
- Conventions are binding only because they are observed and considered to be binding. In contrast, laws are binding whether or not obeyed.

Constitutional theory

Dicey and Montesquieu are influential political theorists:

- They wrote works in which they formulated (but did not invent) the doctrines of the Rule of Law, the Separation of Powers and Parliamentary Supremacy.
- Dicey's formulation of the Rule of Law is only one version. Other theorists set out additional points or alternative versions of the doctrine.
- It is difficult to apply the doctrine of the Separation of Powers to the UK's unwritten constitution.
- Parliamentary Supremacy is limited by political, practical and international pressures.
- Parliamentary Supremacy is also limited by the requirement that new laws must comply with human rights principles.

THE ROLE OF PARLIAMENT

INTRODUCTION

This chapter is concerned with Parliament in its current form. It introduces three of the main areas relevant to the study of constitutional law:

*   the structure of Parliament
*   how Parliament makes law
*   the effectiveness of Parliament at keeping the executive in check.

It is a brief introduction to the structure and issues related to the UK Parliament in Westminster.

Why is it important to learn the role of Parliament? New laws are created in Parliament. All lawyers need to understand how laws are formed because they will have to deal with those changes in practice. In particular they need to know when new rules become law, ie 'come into force'.

You will also need to know how Parliament works if you:

*   become a Member of Parliament, as some lawyers do;
*   work for a business, charity, pressure group or organisation which is trying to influence those within government and Parliament to create or amend laws;
*   work in the Government Legal Service preparing new laws in draft, considering the impact and legality of proposed wording;
*   work as a civil servant in the Houses of Parliament, in a government department or as part of the devolved administration in Wales, Scotland or Northern Ireland;
*   advise a journalist who is reporting on political events, new law or political reform; or
*   advise a politician or an official who has been accused of a misdemeanour.

People in these roles need to know how Parliament creates law in order to do their jobs, or to ensure that they are effective when trying to influence those who make policy and law. If you work as a lawyer in local government, understanding this background will help you advise those who implement policies set by central government.

Knowing how Parliament works will also help you understand other areas of public law. For example, in **Chapter 6**, when considering freedom of speech, you will learn about the related Parliamentary rules which allow politicians to speak without fear of retribution.

In this chapter we examine:

*   the structure of Parliament;

- how Parliament makes law;
- how Parliament scrutinises proposals from the executive; and
- the extent to which Parliament keeps the executive in check.

Reference is also made to issues and sources of law that you might investigate in greater depth to expand your knowledge and views.

THE STRUCTURE OF PARLIAMENT – THE TWO HOUSES

The Parliament of the United Kingdom contains two debating chambers, the House of Commons and the House of Lords. These chambers pass new laws. The House of Commons is directly elected by the people. The House of Lords is not. Most of the Lords are appointed by political parties and keep their position for life. Some critics are concerned that it may be undemocratic to allow people who have not been elected to play a role in forming the laws that affect us all. Others are concerned that even the election process for seats in the House of Commons is unfair.

The House of Commons

The UK public currently elects 650 Members of Parliament (MPs) to sit in the House of Commons (or 'the Commons'), although there are proposals to reduce this number to around 600 'seats'. Under the present system for elections, the candidate with the most votes in each area, or 'constituency', becomes the MP for that area. Members of Parliament represent the concerns of the people in their constituency, as well as those of businesses and other organisations. They split their time between their local constituencies and the House of Commons in London.

In the House of Commons, MPs consider and vote on new laws. When they consider new laws, only a handful of MPs are independent of a political party and are free to vote as they wish on every occasion. Most of the time MPs are expected to vote according to the instructions given by the political party to which they belong. The MPs who enforce this expectation are called the 'whips'. They receive their instructions from the leaders of their political party. If an MP does not obey the whip, he or she may be denied the support, publicity, reputation and financial resources of his or her party. George Galloway defied the Labour whips and voiced strong opposition to the war in Iraq on many occasions from 2001–03. In consequence he was eventually ejected from the party.

Member of Parliament also sit on committees to scrutinise government policies and proposals.

As explained in **Chapter 3**, government ministers are appointed from the political party or coalition of parties which holds the majority of seats in the House of Commons. The political party with the next largest number of MPs appoints a 'Shadow Cabinet' of MPs, each of whom becomes a spokesperson on matters related to a particular government department. Those MPs who are ministers or members of the Shadow Cabinet are called 'frontbenchers' because they sit on the benches at the front of the debating chamber. The other MPs are called 'backbenchers'.

Reform of the election process for MPs is often on the political agenda. Change was rejected in 2011 in a UK-wide referendum. If you consider the merits of different voting methods, the potential effect of changes to constituency boundaries and reductions in the number of MPs, you will be able to discuss whether adopting an alternative system would be better. You might start by finding out about the Boundary Commission for each region of the UK.

The House of Lords

There is debate about the role that a second chamber in Parliament should play and who should have a right to vote in that chamber. Indeed, doubt has been expressed in some quarters whether a second chamber should exist at all. To deal with these discussions, you first need to know about the current role and make-up of the House of Lords (or 'the Lords').

The main role of the House of Lords is to propose amendments to new laws so that they are well-drafted and work effectively. It also has the potential to keep the House of Commons in check. There is a helpful explanation of this process at <www.parliament.uk/about>.

Those who sit in the House of Lords debating chamber have a variety of titles, such as Lord, Baroness, Viscount, Bishop and Earl, but all are referred to as 'peers'. The chamber used to include the leaders of the Church of England (the archbishops and bishops) and hereditary peers. The hereditary peers were originally chosen by the monarch for a variety of reasons, including favours, power, knowledge, military service or reward for good deeds. A deceased hereditary peer's seat passed to his descendants, so the Lords became a chamber dominated by landowners, who obtained that position only as a result of their long-dead ancestor's relationship with the monarch of the time.

Since 1999, only 92 of the hereditary peers are allowed to sit in the chamber at any one time, pending further reform. As a result, as at July 2012, the Lords is made up of the individuals set out in **Table 1** below.

Bishops and Archbishops of the Church of England	Life Peers	Hereditary Peers
Maximum 26	There are 698 life peers. They hold the position for life and do not pass the seat to their descendants.	Maximum 92. Most are now selected by a political party.

Table 1: Composition of the House of Lords

New life peers are appointed in recognition of loyal political service, legal experience or expertise in a particular area. They are appointed by the Queen, on request from the Prime Minister. An independent House of Lords Appointment Commission makes recommendations for non-political appointments and confirms the suitability of those recommended by a political party. For example, Oona King was appointed after recommendation by the Labour party in 2011 following a laudable political career. In 1991, the writer PD James became a life peer so that the chamber could benefit from her expertise in criminal justice, hospital administration and the forensic science service.

The exact number of peers varies from year to year as a result of deaths and new appointments. The political make-up of the chamber may vary but is usually relatively stable. Occasionally there are many changes. You can gain an insight into the current political and religious influence in the Lords by accessing <www.churchofengland.org> for information about the bishops' role, and <www.parliament.uk> for recent appointments and the political alignment of the Lords.

Further reform of the House of Lords

Since the 1999 changes, the pace of reform has slowed. In May 2011, the Coalition Government published proposals to make the Lords into a chamber of around 460 Lords, where 80% of the members would be elected, 20% would be appointed, and each member would serve for no more than 15 years. There would still be 12 Bishops from the Church of England. In a multicultural United Kingdom, this privilege afforded to just one denomination of the Christian Church may be considered unsustainable. Many life peers have a religious perspective (such as Jonathan Sachs, a long-serving Chief Rabbi of the Jewish faith), but no faith other than the Church of England enjoys a guaranteed number of representatives selected by the leaders of the faith itself.

HOW PARLIAMENT MAKES LAW

This part of the chapter explains how laws are created in Parliament. It is essential background to any discussions about who really holds power and whether Parliament should be reformed.

New laws are embodied in:

- Acts of Parliament agreed by the Houses of Parliament ('primary legislation'); and
- instruments, like regulations, issued by government departments ('delegated legislation').

Statutory instruments (abbreviated to 'SI' when being cited, eg 'SI 1994/187', which is statutory instrument number 187 of the year 1994) are the most common form of delegated legislation. They are called statutory rules (SRs) in Northern Ireland, but for the sake of brevity we refer only to statutory instruments here.

Deciding what becomes an Act of Parliament

The party or coalition which controls the Government decides the content of most Acts when they are first produced in a draft form. At this point the Act is called a Bill. The frontbench MP for the relevant department usually presents each Government Bill to Parliament for debate. Bills proposed by backbench MPs are called Private Members' Bills and are presented for debate only through limited methods. Twenty Private Members' Bills are selected by ballot each year; some are squeezed into a 10-minute debate and a few are raised on the rare occasions when another debate concludes earlier than expected. In most years, fewer than 10 Private Members' Bills go on to become an Act. In contrast, the majority of Government Bills become law, and those which do not in their first year are often reconsidered the following year.

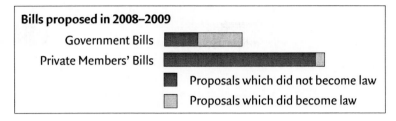

How is a Bill drafted and passed?

Initially, there is public consultation on policy that will become a Government Bill. Then civil servants, advisers and lawyers work together to produce the first draft. The civil servants and lawyers may also assist in the production of a Private Member's Bill. During this drafting stage, Bills are usually discussed with interested groups, experts and relevant committees in Parliament.

The Bill is then formally debated several times in the Houses of Parliament. Most Bills are considered by the Commons first, but some non-controversial Bills are considered in detail by the Lords only. The Commons alone deals with Bills covering tax and government spending. If the Bill passes all stages of debate, the Queen's signature or Royal Assent finalises it and turns it into an Act. Laws usually come into force on a date set out in the Act or a separate statutory instrument. You can currently find out more about the steps through which proposals and policies become law at <www.parliament.uk/about/how/laws>.

Overruling the House of Lords

Sometimes the Lords repeatedly reject legislation supported by the Commons. In that event, the Commons may use the Parliament Acts 1911 and 1949 to ask the Queen to give Royal Assent to the law, disregarding the views of the Lords. This procedure has been used only very occasionally. A relatively recent example occurred between 1998 and 2000. A proposal to make the the age of homosexual consent the same as the age for heterosexual consent was supported by an overwhelming majority of MPs. Most of the Lords were aligned with the Conservative party, though, and repeatedly rejected the legislation. As a result, the Commons invoked the Parliament Acts and the proposal became law.

You should refer to course textbooks and <www.parliament.uk> to discover more about the legislative process and the Parliament Acts, and to consider which chamber is the more powerful. The Parliament Acts are available on <www.legislation.gov.uk>. Course textbooks also give more examples of the occasions on which they have been used. Some of these consider whether it is theoretically possible to use the Parliament Act 1911 to amend itself, just like the provisions of the Parliament Act 1949.

The purpose of delegated legislation

Delegated legislation, such as a statutory instrument, allows ministers to create law without consulting Parliament, so it saves a lot of time. However, it can only be created after an Act has given the relevant power to a minister.

The Government uses delegated legislation for a number of reasons, including:

-     setting the date when each provision of an Act comes into force;

- creating technical regulations and detailed administrative rules which implement the broad policy or legal requirements set out in an Act;
- increasing financial limits in line with inflation; or
- removing an unnecessary provision from an Act of Parliament.

You can find out more about these by researching 'Regulatory Reform Orders' and 'Henry VIII powers'.

How delegated legislation is created

The legal officers of the relevant government department usually draft a statutory instrument in consultation with relevant people and organisations. It is then laid before Parliament and becomes law on a specified date. Those instruments related to financial matters are considered by the House of Commons alone. Most statutory instruments come into force automatically, subject to a 40-day period during which Parliament has an opportunity to annul the legislation by passing a 'negative resolution'. Some statutory instruments are prepared under a power which requires a specific or 'affirmative' resolution from both Houses before they come into force. While committees do look at delegated legislation, in fact very few statutory instruments are actually voted upon in the Houses of Parliament.

HOW EFFECTIVE ARE THE HOUSES OF PARLIAMENT?

As extensive power is vested in the UK executive, Parliament is usually expected to fulfil two specific functions as part of the system of checks and balances. It should scrutinise new law and keep the power of the executive in check. It is common to analyse whether our form of strong executive government is beneficial and whether Parliament fulfils these two specific functions.

First, you need to understand the limits on Parliament's power of legislative scrutiny and on Parliament's power to keep the executive in check. This background and further investigation will help you to develop arguments about:

- whether Parliamentary Supremacy or Parliamentary Sovereignty still exists as a valid concept in the UK
- whether Parliament should be reformed
- how to influence law reform, or how to bring errant ministers to account for their failings.

Legislative scrutiny

How does Parliament represent our views?

Set out below are some of the procedures that individuals, businesses, charities, pressure groups, political parties and other organisations may use to make their views known in Parliament and so have them brought to the attention of ministers, as part of the democratic process:

- We can all write to, or e-mail, our MPs, encouraging them to vote as we might wish in a debate, or to ask them to discuss our concerns with the relevant government official.

- We can ask an MP to discuss our concerns with a particular minister, or to raise formal oral and written questions with the minister in the House of Commons.
- Specialist committees of both Houses of Parliament scrutinise the detail in legislation, which may influence wording or lead to the proposal of amendments. Select committees consider specific areas, and occasional parliamentary debates consider wider issues.
- If more than 100,000 people sign an on-line petition on <www.epetitions.direct. gov.uk> then the House of Commons may hold a public debate about the issue. The website explains how the process works. For example, in 2011 a petition by families and friends of Liverpool football fans who died at the Hillsborough stadium in 1989 resulted in a change in government policy.

Consider how effective these methods might be. Your MP may be too busy to assist, or may not be involved in taking the relevant decision. Highlighting the issue in a public forum may result in positive government action, particularly if it is televised or reported in the press, but only if the minister listens to the views expressed and does not find a way to avoid the issue. There may also be many other MPs who are subject to the influence of organisations with considerably larger resources which campaign, or 'lobby', for legal or political change. Worse still, oral questions asked by MPs in the House of Commons may be more concerned with political point-scoring (by the opposition) and sycophancy (by the governing party's backbenchers) than highlighting injustice or the need for reform.

The limitations of parliamentary scrutiny

Ministers have a lot of power in theory and in practice. Ultimately, what the executive branch of UK government decides to do is what happens. The executive sets the legislative agenda, holds a majority in the House of Commons and controls MPs who are ministers, and the whip system ensures that backbenchers vote according to their party leader's preference. Only on particularly contentious matters is the Government's preferred option likely to be defeated in the chamber.

Parliament has little influence over delegated legislation. Typically there are more than 3,000 statutory instruments every year. Few are considered in the debating chambers themselves. Committees of Parliament check them but have little power to make changes to the draft beyond merely asking for amendments. The scrutiny process has not prevented a statutory instrument from becoming law since 1980.

Ministers decide what is put into proposed legislation and control the government departments. Rather than lobbying an MP, you may exert greater influence by contacting ministers directly when they consult the public on proposals.

Influencing the legislative process and the executive – an alternative strategy

There are less direct ways to influence government decisions and laws made by Parliament:

- Some campaigns are pursued by large media organisations like the tabloid press.
- Others are driven by those with a special interest in an issue. Publicity may gain popular support, leading to media coverage and, eventually, political support. For example, Sara Payne gathered media support to allow parents access to information

about local sex offenders following her daughter's murder. This led to a pilot scheme which might be applied country-wide.

- Large-scale protests might influence debates and government action. However, worldwide anti-war protests by millions in the early 21st century raised the issue in the press but did not result in any changes to policy of the US or the UK Governments regarding military action.

Keeping the executive in check

This section considers the extent to which Parliament balances the power of the executive to prevent the worst excesses and whether Parliament is effective in bringing general government failures to account.

The strength of the government departments

Unfortunately, Parliament probably has neither the time nor the expertise required to scrutinise anything but the most excessive of government actions, and is relatively weak because:

(a)   it is the minister of the relevant department who is accountable to the Houses of Parliament, so the civil servants are sheltered from negative public scrutiny by the minister;

(b)   government departments are now so vast and specialised that decisions taken by anonymous civil servants within a department are far-removed from the minister anyway; and

(c)   much of the work of government is actually carried out by bodies which are not part of the Civil Service. For example, many public services are run by private companies and charities.

Why should the government be accountable to Parliament?

The executive has wide prerogative powers. Some government decisions are taken by individual ministers, but many are made by unelected employees, the civil servants. If MPs are to represent the concerns of their constituents, businesses and organisations who contact them, they need to be able to make ministers accountable in a public forum for their decisions and those of their civil servants. When ministers know that they may have to defend themselves in Parliament, they might also ensure that their actions are justifiable in the first place. Sadly, some ministers may take advantage of their power for their own gain, or act in a way which is inappropriate for someone with such power. If a minister were to be exposed by MPs as unfit to hold such a powerful position and was forced to resign, we might be governed by a better person.

Individual ministerial responsibility and the Ministerial Code

Parliament, in particular the House of Commons, provides a debating chamber in which unpopular decisions, poor administration or inappropriate ministerial behaviour may be raised to exert pressure on the party leaders and bring the issue to the attention of the public.

There is a convention, called 'ministerial responsibility', which provides that government ministers are publicly accountable not only for their own actions but also for the actions of those who work in and for their department. They have a duty to explain to Parliament and to justify policies, decisions and actions. There are conflicting views about the extent of this concept. The 'Whig' view includes the idea that ministers should take account of Parliament's views and act accordingly. Another theory, the 'Peelite' view, is that ministers have autonomous control over decisions and, in Parliament, only have to justify those decisions. Understandably, those who exercise power in the executive often subscribe to the Peelite view.

Allied to this concept of ministerial responsibility for actions of those who work in his department is the *Carltona* principle, that ministers accept responsibility for the actions of the civil servants in their department. This followed a case where government officials closed Carltona Ltd's premises during the Second World War so that the land and employees could be used for other purposes.

There is a Committee on Standards in Public Life, which promotes high standards of behaviour in the public sphere through seven principles by which those in public office should abide. These principles are:

*   Selflessness
*   Integrity
*   Objectivity
*   Accountability
*   Openness
*   Honesty
*   Leadership.

The Committee has no real powers but its views are taken into account. Every executive in the central and devolved governments has adopted a Ministerial Code which supports these principles.

How should ministers be responsible?

In light of the desire to make ministers accountable for their decisions, departments and personal failings, you need to understand how ministers might be brought to account. Consider the following incidents and what you think the relevant ministers should do.

EXERCISE
(a)   A government project costs more than anticipated. There is less money available for other things.
(b)   Hundreds of foreign violent and sex offenders are not deported after release from prison.
(c)   A minister arranges for officials to speed up an immigration application by his foreign lover.
(d)   A minister says that an expenses claim is within the rules but the popular press think it is inappropriate.

Should the relevant minister in each case only have to explain the matter in Parliament, or should the minister reconsider the department's policies and procedures? Should the minister have his or her powers curtailed, or be forced to resign from his or her post so that a more suitable person may take over? By investigating old press coverage of ministerial actions and failures, you can discover what really happened in these and other situations and use your views about the incidents described to develop arguments about whether Parliament has enough power in practice.

Parliament's powers to make the executive accountable

The UK Parliament is described as being weak when considering failures like those described above. It is referred to as merely an 'arena' in which issues may be publicised. It is only able to ask the executive to justify its actions, with little opportunity to limit what the executive actually does. In contrast to this, a chamber which is able to act independently of the executive or exert significant influence over what the executive does is referred to as 'transformative'. You might research an example by finding out about the powers of the US Congress.

So, the UK Parliament has no power to force a minister's resignation. However, a minister is expected to resign if he or she knowingly misleads Parliament, is personally responsible for the failings of his or her department, is involved in personal dishonesty or abuses his or her position for personal gain. It is unlikely that a minister would resign over poor administration by civil servants. In fact, few resign until they have lost public credibility or the support of their party's leaders.

A recent ministerial resignation was that of Liam Fox, the Defence Minister, in 2011. He accepted that he had breached the Ministerial Code in his dealings with a friend and former flat-mate, Adam Werritty. There were no questions over Mr Fox's decision-making as Defence Minister and his work was even complimented by the Prime Minister. He remained in post but, eventually, the continual publicity about Mr Werritty's connections with professional lobbyists in the defence industry, and goading of the Conservative Party about Mr Fox in the House of Commons, eroded his credibility in public and in Parliament so much that he had no option but to resign.

News coverage of similar issues and finding out more about the Committee on Standards in Public Life will help form your views and arguments in this area.

Greater influence of Parliament

In some situations, Parliament may be able to exert greater influence so that the government policy changes. Examples to consider include:

- Many of the Government's own backbench MPs may oppose contentious elements of a policy (perhaps as a result of lobbying), or the Government's majority may be quite small in the House of Commons. In the face of such opposition, the Government may change its policy.

- A policy may be so unpopular that MPs use mechanisms in the Fixed-term Parliaments Act 2011 to force an early general election. One such method is a confidence vote, which triggers a general election if the political parties cannot re-group or become reconciled within 14 days and pass a further resolution to the effect that confidence in the Government has been restored.

In 1979 the Labour Government had a very narrow majority and lost a similar confidence vote by one vote. A general election followed, bringing the Conservative Party led by Margaret Thatcher to power. This resulted in many changes to policy and society in general.

Collective Ministerial Responsibility

The confidence vote is part of a convention called 'collective ministerial responsibility'. That convention means that the whole Government should resign if Parliament passes such a vote. In other words, all the ministers take responsibility as a collective. However, that convention also expects ministers to work as a collective, so they should not disagree with policy laid down in the Cabinet. Neither should any ministers who were involved in the confidential Cabinet meetings disclose details of any internal discussions or disagreement. This was originally a way to prevent the monarch taking action against individual ministers. Today, the convention helps the Government garner strong support for its proposals by ensuring that all ministers will vote in favour of its proposals when considered by Parliament.

Do elections to the House of Commons keep the executive in check?

Elections to the House of Commons happen relatively infrequently, and the numbers of MPs from each party rarely reflect the proportion of support for each party across the entire country. However, do not underestimate the power of elections, because a party needs to hold a majority of seats in the House of Commons in order to form the Government.

The public and press rarely forget a very bad decision, so politicians need to take decisions that maintain their popularity if their party is to keep (or gain) an overall majority of seats in the Commons.

CHAPTER SUMMARY

All lawyers have to deal with the law that Parliament creates in their everyday work.

Some lawyers work in and with Parliament, creating or influencing the content of new law.

Understanding how Parliament works underpins other areas of public law.

The structure of Parliament

- The House of Commons: elected MPs, the front bench, backbenchers, the whips.
- The House of Lords: bishops, archbishops, hereditary peers and life peers.
- Many peers support the views of a particular political party but are not democratically elected.
- Committees scrutinise detail.

How Parliament makes law

- Most new laws are initiated by ministers in the executive.
- The Houses of Parliament follow a set procedure to debate the content of Bills in public before enactment.

- The House of Commons may ignore the views of the House of Lords.
- The system of delegated legislation (eg statutory instruments) gives power and flexibility to the executive to introduce new law with minimal involvement from Parliament.

Parliament's roles

- Scrutinises legislation.
- Makes the executive accountable.
- Does not control the executive.

Issues

The main areas that you may discuss in connection with Parliament are:

- Future reform of the House of Lords.
- Is Parliament effective when scrutinising legislation?
- Is the UK's system of separation of powers and checks and balances effective?
- How might you and your clients influence law reform?
- Does Parliament keep the excesses of executive power in check?
- Reform of the voting method for MPs at general elections.

How might you and your clients influence law reform?

- Lobby an MP so that he or she asks an informal or formal question in Parliament.
- Influence a political party or raise concerns with members of the relevant committee.
- Sign an online petition on <www.epetitions.direct.gov.uk>.
- Lobby the minister, or respond to consultation papers issued by the Government.
- Make contacts in the press and other news media to gather wider support.

Does Parliament keep the executive in check and make politicians accountable?

- Many decisions of Government are made within government departments and private organisations. Parliament does not usually decide how to implement the laws it creates.
- Despite individual ministerial responsibility, ministers rarely resign over poor decision-making.
- Parliament may highlight concerns in the debating chambers, but is a relatively weak arena.
- Parliament's powers are sometimes increased when the ruling party holds a small majority.
- General elections are infrequent, but politicians prefer to remain popular so that they can form the executive.
- Collective responsibility, in theory, means that a Government should resign after a no-confidence vote, but it also means that up to 95 MPs who are ministers are guaranteed to support the Government.

CHAPTER 5

CHALLENGING GOVERNMENT DECISIONS AND ACTIONS

INTRODUCTION

Across the world, political systems interfere with the lives of citizens. Some regimes routinely imprison those who speak out against their rulers. Citizens of the UK are fortunate in that respect, in that the head of state and the Government can no longer take whatever action they desire. Even though violent and bloody actions by rulers are now a thing of the past, many parts of the state and organisations nevertheless may make decisions to which people may object.

Remember that in the UK, the fact that there is only partial separation of powers (see **Chapter 3**) results in laws being made and implemented by:

(a)   the Houses of Parliament (the legislature);

(b)   Ministries of Government, councils and government agencies (the executive); and

(c)   the courts and tribunals (the judiciary).

In addition, our lives may be affected by a very wide range of bodies that carry out a public function. Central and local government sometimes even delegate their powers to private companies and organisations, to fulfil particular public functions.

There are generally six ways in which to raise objections to an official decision, action or failure. This chapter introduces each of these methods of challenge, focusing on the most complex one, judicial review.

(1) Make an internal complaint

Those who are adversely affected by government actions and who object to the way they have been treated, may follow a complaints procedure. There is a complaints procedure in the NHS, for instance, and an independent complaints handling service provides support for complainants throughout this process.

(2) Raise an appeal

As an alternative, public bodies may have an internal review or appeal process. At the end of the appeal the original decision may be overturned or changed, in a similar way to the appeal process in a court. Many of these appeals take place in an administrative tribunal.

For example, anyone who has suffered an injury inflicted by a criminal may apply to the government-funded Criminal Injuries Compensation Authority (CICA) for compensation. If the CICA refuses the application then the victim may ask for it to be reviewed by another member of staff, or may appeal to a formal tribunal. In this particular process a final appeal is available to a court called the Upper Tier Tribunal.

(3) Apply for a judicial review

Appeals are often allowed only on very restricted grounds (eg on the basis that the law was incorrectly applied or new facts have come to light which mean that the decision should be reconsidered). So an appeal may not be available for every complaint. Those who want to challenge a decision, action or failure of a public body on the basis that it was made illegally may, instead, be able to use a legal mechanism called judicial review. A judge in the Administrative Court would then consider whether the public body acted within the law.

EXAMPLE

The Minister of Justice might reduce the maximum amount that the CICA is able to pay as compensation for particular injuries. It would then be illegal for the CICA to award more money than the Government allows. The minister's decision is never going to be one that may be appealed under the CICA's own process. Instead, a victim might want to challenge the minister's decision itself. A judicial review would allow a judge to check whether the Act of Parliament that gave him the power to set the level of compensation also allowed him to reduce it in the way that he did.

Notice that judicial review is different from an appeal because the judge cannot make a different decision, only decide whether or not the original decision was legally valid.

Judicial review is covered in more detail below.

(4) Complain to the Ombudsman

As an alternative to challenging the legality of a decision via judicial review, it may be possible to ask an official called an Ombudsman to consider whether the body acted improperly, unfairly or provided a poor service. More information is available at <www.ombudsman.org.uk>.

Note that some private bodies also use the term 'ombudsman' when referring to their complaints service, eg the Property Ombudsman for complaints about estate agents, but such schemes should not be confused with the government Ombudsman which considers actions by public bodies covered by that scheme.

(5) Pursue a civil claim

If a government body has affected your client's private law rights, it may be possible to pursue a claim in the civil courts. For example, if Network Rail decided to scale back the maintenance regime for the railways and this caused an accident in which your client was injured, you might be able to raise a negligence claim in the county court on your client's behalf. A claim for breach of contract might be available to a client who entered into an agreement with a public body that has subsequently been breached.

If an action by a public official is so outrageous that it amounts to an oppressive or arbitrary decision, it might be possible to raise a claim for the tort of 'misfeasance in public office'. In one example, this claim succeeded when a decision was based on the officials' own self-interest and was intended to cause the claimant damage. Swansea Council refused a commercial tenant's request to change the permitted use of her premises. The tenant's claim succeeded because the council's refusal was based on opposition by some councillors to the political activities of the tenant's husband – a consideration that should have been utterly irrelevant to their decision.

These civil claims may achieve the right outcome for your client without public law having to be taken into account, because the court may award compensation or issue a statement setting out how the body should have acted. Sometimes, however, judges have decided that a civil claim should not be allowed against a public body for sound reasons of policy. For example, the police are not usually liable in the civil courts to individual members of the public. This furthers a policy that police should be able to go about their duties of crime detection and prevention without worrying about potential legal claims being raised by the general public. In another example, a court has decided that a local council would not be liable to homeowners if their homes were worth less than they hoped because a building regulations inspector had failed to spot defective building work. A rationale for this might be that these inspectors are supposed to be protecting the public in general and not specific homeowners, or that the potential cost to local authorities would be prohibitive.

(6) Raise a defence to criminal prosecution or civil proceedings brought by a public body

Your clients may not be particularly bothered about the actions of public bodies until they themselves are brought before a court. In such circumstances they might be able to win their case by raising a complaint about the way in which the public body has acted. For example, in the 1980s, protesters at Greenham Common were prosecuted in a magistrates' court for breach of a local bye-law which prohibited them from entering a protected military area. In 1990 they successfully argued that they did not have to apply for judicial review in the Administrative Court before arguing that the local bye-law was invalid; they were allowed to raise this as a potential defence in the magistrates' court itself.

Also consider an example in the civil courts. If a council sues to repossess a tenant's home because council officials think he has not paid the rent, the tenant might ask the court to determine whether the decision to evict him is in accordance with all of the laws applicable to that process. The judge who hears the eviction case may then consider issues similar to those considered in a judicial review, explained below.

JUDICIAL REVIEW IN CONTEXT

The rest of this chapter focuses on judicial review, to help you become accustomed to the rules for this complicated but important area of public law.

Constitutional context: the Rule of Law and the Separation of Powers

In some countries there is a written constitution against which the validity of all laws and actions of the state may be measured. There is no such written constitution in the UK. Instead, judicial review is part of the judiciary's role in the system of checks and balances which ensures that no branch of government is more powerful than any other. It underpins the theories of the Separation of Powers and the Rule of Law. Asking a judge to review actions and failures made as part of a public function supports fundamental legal and constitutional concepts, including the following:

- Parliament should be the supreme law-maker.

- The state may take only those actions that are authorised by law, and citizens should not be subject to the exercise of power in an arbitrary way.

- Decisions of a judicial nature should be taken by following common-law principles of natural justice, which have been developed by the courts.

- However, the Government needs to be able to act in a way which is administratively effective.

Before the 1960s there were very few applications for judicial review, but central and local government have expanded enormously since then. Now, half of the cases in the Supreme Court concern judicial review. Expansion of this area and the new powers for judges to interpret laws in line with the Human Rights Act 1998 have resulted in some commentators and politicians suggesting that the judges now interfere far too much in law-making.

Practical context: judicial review of incorrect use of government powers

It is worth considering some examples of judicial review to help you understand how useful this process might be for a wide range of people and organisations:

- A junior police officer in North Wales obtained a court order confirming that he should not have been forced out of his job when the Chief Constable threatened to discharge him from the police service on the basis of unfounded rumours about his personal life.

- A taxpayer used judicial review to stop money being wasted by a council when it was running a subsidised public laundry service in Fulham.

- Judicial review may help organisations as well as individuals. A rugby club retained a right to use a Leicester City Council practice ground. It was decided that the Council's decision was unlawful when it withdrew permission to use the ground because three of the club's players intended to play in South Africa at a time when that country was subject to the apartheid regime that oppressed people of non-white racial origin.

- Judicial review may have long-lasting effects. An application for judicial review by a Catholic campaigner led to the rule that local doctors (general practitioners or 'GPs') must consider whether to consult parents before giving advice or treatment to children under the age of 16. This was not quite what the campaigner had hoped, because she wanted to stop GPs giving any contraceptive advice to girls aged under 16 without their parent's knowledge. The court accepted, however, that GPs may conclude that some children would be sufficiently knowledgeable as to give valid consent to treatment without involving their parents.

- Judicial review may help companies and pressure groups too. An installer and an owner of solar panel generation systems, supported by the environmental campaign group, Friends of the Earth, managed to persuade a court to cancel a reduction in the subsidy for solar power generation when the Government introduced the change before the relevant consultation period had ended. The court also ordered that lower rates set in April 2012 could not be applied retrospectively (ie back-dated) to installations made between December 2011 and that date.

- Judicial review is often used in immigration cases. A refugee Iraqi Kurd was convicted of several criminal offences so was liable to be deported back to Iraq. He was kept in a detention centre pending deportation because the Government had decided that it was unsafe for security staff to take such people back to Iraq. In 2012 the refugee used judicial review to secure his release from the detention centre, because it had been unreasonable of the Home Secretary to order his detention when she ought to have realised that his deportation would not be possible within 18 months.

- Sometimes just applying for judicial review is enough to persuade an authority to change its approach. In 2011, the charity National Deaf Children's Society applied for judicial review of the decision by Stoke-on-Trent Council to reduce the services provided in schools by teachers of the deaf. The Council agreed to reverse the plans and (among other things) to consult local parents of deaf children and the charity before finalising alternative arrangements.

Judicial review – the legal process and grounds for review

The law regarding judicial review and the available remedies is to be found in s 31 of the Senior Courts Act 1981. The related procedure is set out in Part 54 of the Civil Procedure Rules. Principles used to decide cases are derived from a great volume of case law. Learning the wide range of complex grounds and detailed reasons for judicial review is probably the most difficult area of public law. This chapter includes a brief overview so that you may become familiar with the general themes.

In determining the case, the judge will not consider whether the act, decision or failure is right, neither will he or she make a replacement decision. Decision-making is reserved to the executive. The judge merely examines the legality of the decision, and will decide in favour of the claimant if the decision is illegal, irrational or procedurally unfair (ie 'improper'). In simple terms, the judge will assess whether the decision has been made by the correct person, using the relevant power correctly and following the correct procedure.

When will a court overturn an administrative decision?

Judicial review is based, to a great extent, on common law principles, so there is no defined list of grounds on which claims may be raised. Cases are generally grouped into the three areas of illegality, irrationality and improper procedure. Some examples are set out below, but much more detailed study is required for a full understanding of the subject. The website for the Public Law Project <www.publiclawproject.org> contains helpful summaries and leaflets.

Illegality

A judge will overturn an action by an administrative official or body if it is illegal. Examples include where:

- the official misunderstood the law, or failed to apply it correctly to the situation;

- the official did not have the power to take the action in question, or went beyond the limit of his or her power (this is referred to as acting *ultra vires*, ie 'outside the power');

- the official refused to act in a mistaken belief that he or she was not able to act;

- the official who had responsibility for taking a decision did not exercise a discretion properly, eg being influenced by the impact of the decision on his or her own interests, or merely following the recommendation of an adviser without considering the matter in person;

- the official took irrelevant issues into account, or did not take into consideration relevant issues that should have been examined, including the Human Rights Act 1998;

- an Act of Parliament is incompatible with the Human Rights Act 1998.

Irrationality

Cases grouped under this heading include decisions which were obviously illogical, irrational or absurd. The judge will overturn a decision which is:

- so unreasonable that no reasonable authority could reach it; or

- so outrageous that it defies logic.

The first of these principles is derived from the case of *Associated Provincial Picture Houses v Wednesbury Corporation* and is referred to as '*Wednesbury* unreasonableness', after this case about restricting a cinema licence so that no child under 15 was allowed into the cinema on Sundays. The second was explained in a case related to the GCHQ government security establishment in Cheltenham (*Council of Civil Service Unions v Minister for the Civil Service*). This case is often referred to as the 'GCHQ case' and related to a decision prohibiting GCHQ employees from joining a trade union.

Procedural impropriety

A judge will overturn an administrative decision if the decision-maker did not follow the correct procedure. This area is closely related to the Rule of Law theory (see **Chapter 3**) and ideas of natural justice, including the right to a fair hearing.

Successful cases have included defects where:

- the official did not follow a procedure set out in an Act of Parliament or regulations;

- people who were affected by a decision were ignored or not allowed to make formal oral representations at a hearing (this might also contravene the right to a fair trial in Article 6 of the ECHR);

- the decision was taken by someone who had a personal interest in the matter or a close connection with the parties (this is called 'bias');

- without good reason the public body tried to renege on previous promises ('legitimate expectations');

- the decision-maker did not give any reasons for a very unusual or unexpected decision.

Time limits and administrative expediency

Judges accept that the Government sometimes needs to operate without interference from the courts. Administrative convenience may even be more important than allowing judicial review. Thus the availability of judicial review is limited as follows:

- The courts have required that applications for judicial review are made without undue delay. In 1972, Parliament imposed a long-stop time-limit of three months. These very short time-limits avoid the problems that might result from overturning a decision long after it has been implemented. If the case involves questions that might be raised under the Human Rights Act 1998, the time-limit is extended to one year.

- Judges will not allow judicial review if another remedy of the types described in the 'Introduction' to this chapter is available, or the complaint is about a matter which does not relate to a public function.

- Judges will sometimes refuse a review if Parliament has passed related legislation to prohibit judicial review completely. This kind of rule is called an 'ouster clause'. As the Rule of Law and Separation of Powers doctrines mean that the court's constitutional role is to ensure that public bodies comply with the law, judges often ignore an ouster clause in legislation, but will accept it if it merely imposes only a different time-limit.

- Judges will not interfere with high-level political policy, such as decisions taken about whether to go to war or how to safeguard national security.

Who can apply?

Normally, an applicant for judicial review has to show that he has sufficient interest in the matter (referred to as 'standing') to make the application. This is relatively easy requirement to fulfil. For example, the Catholic campaigner whose case might have stopped doctors giving contraceptive advice to girls aged under 16 had sufficient interest because she had daughters of that age, whether or not they had actually asked their doctor for contraceptive advice. In recent times, pressure groups and charities have even been allowed to bring claims or make representations to the court in cases in which they are interested. For claims based on the Human Rights Act 1998, the claimant has to show that he or she is a 'victim' of the breach of the Act.

What sorts of decision are susceptible to judicial review?

Only actions, decisions and failures related to a public function may be challenged via judicial review. Public authorities like the Government, local councils, state school governors, health authorities and prisons are obviously covered. So are magistrates' courts, coroners and county courts. Increasingly, however, public functions are carried out by private companies under supervisory arrangements with a public authority. Private bodies which carry out a public function are also susceptible to judicial review.

Not every decision of a public authority relates to a public function. For example, contract law governs local authorities' relationships with their suppliers, so it is not possible to bring judicial review proceedings against a council for deciding to pay an invoice late. A lot of our public life is subject to rules of other organisations, like professional bodies, clubs and religious organisations, which we may choose to join. When these bodies, etc do not provide something that is usually required from government and do not carry on a public function, they are not subject to judicial review.

How might judicial review help our clients?

After considering a claim for judicial review, the judge chooses which remedy is appropriate in the circumstances. Some of these are derived from ancient royal prerogative powers. Others were first awarded in private law disputes but may now be awarded in judicial review. The old names of the prerogative remedies are included in **Table 1** below, so that you will know what they are when they are mentioned in old cases.

Remedy	Characteristics	Prerogative name
Quashing order	A judge may invalidate a decision as if it had never been made in the first place.	Certiorari
Prohibiting order	A judge may force the public body to refrain from taking an action which contravenes its legal powers.	Order of prohibition
Mandatory order	A judge may require that the public body carries out its duties in accordance with its legal powers.	Mandamus
Declaration	A judge may make a statement of the law or of the complainant's rights so that it is clear what the public body can or cannot do. This may be a helpful alternative to a quashing order (above) where the judge does not want to overturn the entire decision. The court may also declare that an Act of Parliament is incompatible with the ECHR (a 'declaration of incompatibility').	
Damages	The judge may set the level of compensation that should be paid by the public body to the complainant. Damages may be awarded only when the claimant has suffered financial loss or injury as a result of a breach of the Human Rights Act 1998, or following a private law claim such as negligence or breach of contract.	
Interim injunction	The judge orders the public body to stop acting until the case has been heard properly. In other words, this preserves the status quo.	

Table 1: Remedies following judicial review

When a challenge is made to a decision to imprison someone before he or she is convicted of a crime, this process is called a writ of *habeas corpus*. In simple terms, the authorities are required to bring the prisoner to the court to determine whether he or she should be released (see further **Chapter 2** above).

Be aware that the judge will not necessarily grant exactly what the applicant requests and has discretion as to which remedy to award, taking account of such matters as the applicant's behaviour and circumstances.

How would I make an application for judicial review?

Court procedural rules require the applicant to write to the public body to seek reasons for its decision, warning that an application may be made for judicial review. Fourteen days should be allowed for a response.

The formal judicial review process then comprises two stages. First, the applicant has to submit papers to a judge, in the part of the High Court called the Administrative Court, setting out a summary of the case. The judge considers whether there is an arguable case by reference to the paperwork only. Then, if the judge grants permission for the case to proceed, the papers are served on the opponent and a date is set for the court to consider all the relevant evidence from both parties.

Applications for an order of release under the *habeas corpus* regime follow a slightly different procedure. The first stage is omitted, so that the prisoner may be brought to court and all the evidence considered as soon as possible.

More details about the process in the Administrative Court may be found at <www.justice.gov.uk>.

A note on judicial review case names

Remember that the *Carltona* principle requires that ministers accept responsibility for the actions of the civil servants in their department. Therefore, the named defendant in many claims for judicial review is a Secretary of State or a Minister for a particular department, even though the disputed action may actually have been taken by a civil servant.

An application for judicial review is made in the name of the Queen (*Regina* or 'R') on behalf of the applicant. So, a case which is reported as *R on the application of Singh v Secretary of State for Home Department* is a case where Mr Singh has asked the Queen's courts to consider an action taken by or for the Home Secretary. Until relatively recently, this case would have been given the less easily understandable title *R v Secretary of State for Home Department, ex parte Singh*, but which means exactly the same. Some old cases are reported in the traditional way, with just the name of the applicant and the name of the relevant body or official, such as *Wheeler v Leicester City Council*.

CHAPTER SUMMARY

Alternative methods of challenging official action

- Complain. Many public bodies and officials have an internal complaints procedure.
- Appeal. Raise an appeal if possible, but be aware that grounds may be very restricted.
- Judicial review. Apply for judicial review if the decision, action or failure is illegal, irrational or procedurally unfair.
- Ombudsman. Complain to the Ombudsman if the public body is subject to the scheme and has not acted properly or fairly, or has provided a poor service.
- Pursue a civil claim. It may be possible to sue for negligence, breach of contract or misfeasance in public office.

- Wait until you are pursued by the authority. If a public body pursues a criminal prosecution or a civil claim against you, you may be able to defend the court case by raising an argument that the action taken was illegal.

Claiming judicial review

- Judicial review cases are complex and varied.
- There are obstacles to overcome when making a claim for judicial review:
    - time-limit
    - standing
    - permission stage before the substantive hearing
    - ouster clauses.

Judicial review remedies

Courts will not dictate how government should implement policy or law. The judges have a choice over granting the following public law remedies based on prerogative powers:

- Prohibiting order – orders a body to refrain from acting in an illegal way.
- Quashing order – quashes a decision so that it has no legal effect.
- Mandatory order – orders the public body to perform its duties in a legal way.

Applicants may also be able to pursue remedies which are derived from private law:

- Declaration – declares the legal position of the parties.
- Damages – compensation for losses suffered by the applicant.
- Injunction – very similar to a prohibiting order. An injunction is sometimes awarded to protect the applicant pending the full consideration of the evidence from both parties.

CHAPTER 6

FUNDAMENTAL FREEDOMS IN CONTEXT

This chapter sets out a brief summary of some of the rights that constitutional theorists expect all citizens to have the freedom to exercise, called fundamental freedoms. Some of these are human rights derived from the European Convention on Human Rights (the 'Convention' or 'ECHR'). The chapter also explains the ways in which these rights may be enforced in the UK.

The need to draft laws which comply with human rights and to make amendments following related court cases has shaped many changes in the law. For example, schools no longer punish pupils using corporal punishment such as the cane; it is now for judges who hear a criminal case, rather than the Home Secretary, to set the minimum sentences offenders are expected to serve; the state no longer retains DNA samples from suspects who are acquitted of criminal offences or against whom charges are dropped; transsexuals may now marry someone who is of the opposite sex to their assumed gender; there is an equal age of consent for homosexual and heterosexual activity; and employers are no longer permitted to insist that employees join a particular trade union in order to keep their jobs.

This law is relevant to many lawyers. Government lawyers need to ensure that their organisation complies with legal rights. Lawyers in private practice need to know about these principles so that they may raise them in argument when relevant.

THE EUROPEAN CONVENTION ON HUMAN RIGHTS

The states which signed the ECHR agreed to abide by Articles which set out (amongst others) the following rights and fundamental freedoms:

- Everyone's right to life shall be protected by law (Article 2).
- No one shall be subjected to torture, or to inhuman or degrading treatment or punishment (Article 3).
- No one shall be held in slavery or servitude. No one shall be required to perform forced or compulsory labour (Article 4).
- Everyone has the right to liberty and security of person. No one shall be deprived of his liberty save in accordance with a procedure prescribed by law (Article 5).
- Everyone is entitled to a fair and public hearing within a reasonable time by an independent and impartial tribunal established by law (Article 6).

- No one shall be held guilty of any criminal offence on account of any act or omission which did not constitute a criminal offence at the time when it was committed (Article 7).
- Everyone has the right to respect for his private and family life, his home and his correspondence (Article 8).
- Everyone has the right to freedom of thought, conscience and religion (Article 9).
- Everyone has the right to freedom of expression, to hold opinions and to receive and impart information and ideas without interference by public authority (Article 10).
- Everyone has the right to freedom of peaceful assembly and to freedom of association with others (Article 13).
- Rights and freedoms in the Convention shall be secured without discrimination on any ground such as sex, race, colour, language, religion, political or other opinion, national or social origin, association with a national minority, property, birth or other status (Article 14).

This is not a comprehensive guide to all of the rights. In addition to the rights agreed in the Convention, many countries have signed additional agreements called Protocols. For example, many countries agreed to abolish the death penalty by signing Protocol 13. There is therefore no substitution for reading the Convention and the Protocols themselves, available at <www.echr.coe.int>.

Many of the rights include specific exceptions. Most may also be overridden on defined grounds, such as a public emergency or in times of war. These general reasons for overriding the rights are called 'derogations'. Article 15 sets out the rules about derogations and includes provisions which state that some Articles, like the commitment to protect the right to life (Article 2), are so fundamental that they cannot be overridden. These are called 'absolute' rights.

The European Court of Human Rights

The European Court of Human Rights (ECtHR) is the Court in which complaints may be raised that there has been a breach of human rights by a country which agreed to abide by the ECHR (the 'High Contracting Parties'). It is possible to apply to the ECtHR only after the applicant has pursued all possible remedies at a national level. Until 1998, applicants had to apply for permission to have their case taken to the Court through a body called the European Commission of Human Rights. The Commission has now been abolished and the role of checking whether cases are eligible to be heard by the Court is carried out by judges in the Court itself.

Remedies from the ECtHR

The ECtHR is able to award 'just satisfaction' to a victim of a breach of human rights. This usually involves a declaration that the state's action breached the rights alleged, may include a statement about how the relevant government should implement the Convention and may include an order for compensation. These remedies are not always awarded, though.

Some examples of how useful the remedies have been are set out below:

- Compensation awarded can make a difference to a victim. In 1999, the UK Government was ordered to pay £10,000 to a boy who was bruised from beatings by his step-father. The UK law at that time allowed the step-father to avoid prosecution for assault occasioning actual bodily by raising the defence of reasonable chastisement. The order was made because the UK courts had failed to protect the boy from treatment prohibited by Article 3, namely the prohibition of torture and/ or inhuman or degrading treatment or punishment. In another example in 2000, Duncan Lustig-Prean recovered compensation of more than £90,000 for lost earnings and pension benefits after the UK used the fact that he had admitted to being gay as justification for his dismissal from his job as a naval commander in 1995. This was a breach of Article 8 relating to respect for private life.

- Many cases are brought in an attempt to force changes in government policy. Mr Lustig-Prean's case, with others of a similar nature, resulted in a change in policy, so that a person's sexual orientation no longer prevents him from serving in the armed forces. The Court does not specifically order this change in the law or policy, but it is often the natural result, so that the High Contracting Party concerned may avoid multiple claims of a similar nature.

- The ECtHR will not always award compensation. The families of suspected Irish Republican Army (IRA) terrorists sought compensation after the UK breached the right to life under Article 2 because the Special Air Service (SAS) shot dead the three IRA suspects in the mistaken belief that they were about to detonate a car bomb in Gibraltar. The Court did not consider it appropriate to award financial compensation to these particular families.

- It might be possible to avoid extradition or deportation. Extradition is the process whereby someone is sent to another country so that he may be tried for a crime under the laws and in the courts of that country. Deportation is the process whereby an illegal immigrant is permanently returned to another country. Article 3 of the Convention is commonly used to avoid extradition from the UK to a country where the punishment given to an offender may be inhuman, or where evidence may be used that was obtained through torture. In 1989, a German national called Jens Soering avoided extradition from the UK to the USA to face murder charges because the relevant US official provided insufficient assurance that he would not receive the death penalty and be made to submit, pending execution, to the degrading prison regime known as 'death row'. As a result of this case, commentators refer to the rule that a suspect cannot be extradited where there is a real risk that he will face treatment or punishment which breaches Article 3 as the '*Soering* principle'.

- The applicant may want to feel that justice has been done. Sometimes cases are brought simply to obtain an order setting out a principle. Siwa-Akofa Siliadin, a woman from Togo who worked as an unpaid domestic servant for four years in France, brought a claim before the ECtHR but did not seek any financial compensation, only her legal costs. In domestic French law, she had been awarded just over €45,000 for damages and unpaid wages, but the people for whom she worked escaped a prison sentence. Ms Siliadin asked the ECtHR to order that France had breached Article 4 of the Convention by failing to provide adequate protection in the criminal law. That is exactly what she achieved.

- The Court decision may result in a criminal trial having to be re-heard. In 2001, Kudlip Sander tried to achieve this but did not succeed. He was convicted of conspiracy to defraud, and the ECtHR decided that the judge had breached Article 6 of the Convention because he should have been more robust in emphasising the need for the jury to be impartial after a juror had brought another juror's racist comments to the judge's attention. Despite the breach, Mr Sander was awarded only his costs; the ECtHR did not recommend a retrial because the European judges did not consider that the original judge's failure caused the conviction. People in other situations may achieve a different result.

Principles considered by the ECtHR

Before you study human rights cases in detail, it is important to understand three principles that are used by the ECtHR (as well as national courts) when considering arguments about human rights.

- *Proportionality.* The ECtHR will permit interference with a Convention right only if the state has imposed the interference for a proper and practical purpose, and even then only if it was done in a way that is rational and necessary to achieve that particular aim. For example, it is legitimate to try to maintain security and safety in a prison, so it might sometimes be necessary to keep particularly violent prisoners locked in their cells all day to achieve that aim. However, it might not be necessary to apply that restriction to every single prisoner who happens to be on that wing.

- *Margin of appreciation and judicial deference.* The ECtHR recognises that some legal principles are best left to national institutions, because they will have a better understanding of relevant cultural values, historical issues and philosophical attitudes. This is called the 'margin of appreciation', or sometimes a 'margin of discretion'. It tends to be applied to issues about religious observance or personal morality. Judicial deference is similar. The ECtHR recognises that in some instances the Court should defer to the opinion of democratically-elected representatives where a balance needs to be struck between the rights of an individual and the needs of society, rather like how the UK courts accept Parliamentary supremacy.

HUMAN RIGHTS ACT 1998

The ECHR is part of international law and is not directly enforceable in UK courts. Instead, the UK law is set out in the Human Rights Act 1998. The Act is designed to ensure that there is a remedy for people who allege that the UK Government or a related body has breached a right in the Convention, without requiring them to complete the entire UK appeals process before applying to the ECtHR. So, it makes it unlawful for a public body to act in a way which is incompatible with a list of rights which are identical to those in the Convention. The Act may be used by anyone who is a victim of a breach, which essentially means that the applicant or a member of the applicant's family must be affected. The time limit for any application is one year.

Remedies in the UK courts under the Human Rights Act 1998

Because of the need to respect Parliamentary supremacy, the UK courts are able to take only limited action. Power over decision-making remains with the executive. Courts can either interpret Acts of Parliament in a way which is compatible with the Convention, or, if that is not possible, make a declaration that the UK law is incompatible with the Convention. It may be possible to interpret existing UK rules in a way which allows the court to award another remedy, such as compensation, based on that law, but there is no specific right to compensation based solely on a breach of human rights.

Once a court has made a declaration of incompatibility, the government can (but is not obliged to) amend the law in an accelerated procedure by passing a statutory instrument called a 'Remedial Order'.

Horizontal as well as vertical effect

The relationship between the state and individuals or non-governmental organisations is said to be a 'vertical' relationship, whereas a horizontal relationship exists between different individuals or organisations. These are represented in **Figure 1** below.

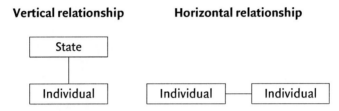

Figure 1: Vertical and horizontal relationships

Clearly, human rights are relevant to vertical relationships as the state should uphold the human rights that it has agreed to observe. However, they may also be relevant to horizontal relationships. This is because the 1998 Act expressly applies to the courts, so judges must always interpret and apply law in a way which is compatible with human rights. Therefore, judges sometimes have to consider human rights issues when deciding how to resolve a dispute between parties even where they have no connection to the state. This is called 'horizontal effect'.

OTHER LAWS WHICH SUPPORT FUNDAMENTAL FREEDOMS – THE WIDER INFLUENCE OF HUMAN RIGHTS

Before a Bill is passed in the Houses of Parliament, the relevant minister must issue a statement of compatibility to confirm that the legislation complies with the Human Rights Act 1998. As a result, the rights may influence developments in law without the need for a court case. Article 5 of the Convention has influenced the way that police exercise their powers to arrest and detain a suspect before trial. The Convention allows arrests made on a reasonable suspicion that the suspect has committed an offence. It requires that anyone arrested must be informed promptly of the reasons for the arrest and brought promptly before a court. The UK law includes provisions to the same effect, but with more detailed rules about how to achieve these things.

It is also important to appreciate that the Human Rights Act 1998 is not the only law which supports fundamental freedoms in the UK. Freedom of speech in the UK's Parliament was enshrined well before the Convention. Parliamentarians have the right to say whatever they like in Parliament, and they can never be sued for defamation for doing so. This right is called 'Parliamentary Privilege' and also means the public and media have a right to report what is said in Parliament.

A NOTE ABOUT READING HUMAN RIGHTS CASES

When you are reading human rights cases, remember the historical context. Until the Human Rights Act 1998 came into force, the UK courts could not always deal with human rights arguments, so many cases failed in the UK but succeeded in the ECtHR. Cases heard after the 1998 Act came into force may consider human rights arguments, but the UK courts cannot always grant a useful remedy. Also remember that an old case heard by the European Commission of Human Rights would only have related to arguments about whether the case should even proceed to the ECtHR in the first place.

CHAPTER SUMMARY

Context

- Human rights arguments are relevant in a wide range of contexts.
- Governments' agreement to uphold human rights has as much influence over changes to the law as over specific court decisions.
- Arguments in court are particularly common in immigration, deportation and extradition cases.

Sources of human rights

- The Convention may be accessed at <www.echr.coe.int>.
- The same rights as are in the Convention appear in the Human Rights Act 1998.

Court powers and remedies

- In the UK, the national courts are allowed now to consider arguments about human rights and may base their decisions about other legal issues, particularly judicial review, on these rights.
- UK courts cannot change an Act of Parliament if its provisions are clear. Courts may only interpret laws in a way which is compatible with the Convention, or issue a declaration of incompatibility.
- A declaration of incompatibility triggers a procedure to allow the Government to change the offending law quickly via a remedial order, if it so wishes.
- It is possible to apply to the ECtHR after exhausting national remedies. That Court may award 'just satisfaction' but has discretion over whether to award any remedy at all.
- The effects of an order of 'just satisfaction' from the ECtHR have been quite varied, depending on the issues in the case.
- Courts may allow interference with human rights where it is proportionate to do so.
- The courts also recognise that it may be best to leave some decisions to local bodies, to democratically-elected officials or to the national parliament.

TORT

CHAPTER 1

RIGHTS AND WRONGS

WHY HAVE A LAW OF TORT?

Take three common events: an all-night party; a car crash; a newspaper article exposing a scandal.

Take three frequently-heard statements: 'No-one is allowed to take risks anymore'; 'We live in a compensation culture'; 'We have an unhealthy obsession with celebrities.'

Tort law is closely connected with all these events and controversies.

The invisible matrix – rules of the game of life

We live our lives surrounded by a web of rules. This matrix of rules is often invisible to us. We only really notice it when something goes wrong – when a rule is broken and someone gets hurt.

All societies are bound together by rules. However, not all rules are rules of law. We live by vague social rules about how we should behave which largely control what we wear, how we eat and what we think of as good manners. You will have come across many more formal types of rules. School rules and the rules of sport are two we all know well.

Most of us also share an understanding of the moral rules about how people ought to act. Many religions and secular thinkers have developed sophisticated ethical rules about how people ought to interact.

Legal rules are limited to those which may be enforced through the courts. Therefore these legal rules are much more limited than moral rules. 'Love your neighbour as yourself' may be a widely admired moral rule, but we generally cannot take our neighbour to court for failing to love us. Similarly, it may be good manners to say 'thank you', but we do not take people to court for failing to do so.

Moreover, legal rules do many different things. Some laws enforce promises, such as the law of contract. Others punish people for anti-social actions, such as criminal law. The rules of tort law aim to protect people from non-criminal harm. They enforce our right not to be harmed or wronged by other people's actions.

Practising lawyers become experts at working with rules. They earn their living explaining these rules to clients, and helping them to win or defend cases using these rules of law.

Legal wrongs

'Tort' means 'wrong'.

Tort law is concerned with what happens when people suffer wrong in the form of harm done to them by other people. In a typical tort case, an individual who has been harmed goes to court to complain that another person has done him harm and asks that the other person should be made to pay compensation for the injury. The judge must decide what to do about the complaint.

Therefore, tort law potentially involves all of us nearly all the time, because we may harm and be harmed in so many different ways. Each one of us suffers harm at some time. Sometimes we cause harm to others.

> **EXAMPLE – BROKEN BACK IN A CAR CRASH**
>
> A typical example of a tort claim arises when there is a serious car crash. Here people are hurt and property is damaged, and this will very often lead to a claim in the tort of negligence.

Thinking about a physical injury such as a broken back in a car crash provokes some questions:

* What has the injured person really suffered?

  Probably severe physical pain and discomfort.

  Probably financial loss in the form of expenses or lost earnings.

* Who might be to blame for the injury?

  The list might include the other driver or the victim himself, or the manufacturer of the car if it was defective; or you might decide that it was a pure accident and that no one should be blamed.

* After someone is harmed what should happen next?

  Who should bear the cost?

  What are the alternatives?

We might have a system whereby the injured person simply put up with the injury. Friends and family or charities could be expected to look after the victim out of pure kindness. The victim alone might be expected to cope with the costs of the injury.

We might encourage everyone to insure against harm happening to them. When the injury happens, the victim simply claims on the insurance policy.

Alternatively, we might decide that the state should always help out by compensating people who suffered harm with benefits. In this case, the taxes paid by the whole community would be used to compensate the victim.

We might also have a system whereby the victim could use the law to obtain compensation by suing the person responsible for the injury. This is where tort law comes in.

At present we have a system where all these options are possible. On many occasions the victim simply puts up with it. Sometimes people are able to make claims on their insurance policies. Some people become eligible for state benefits as a result of being injured. But we also have tort law, which enables some people to seek compensation some of the time from the person responsible for their injury.

THE PRINCIPLES OF TORT LAW

The first principle of tort law is:

> The law should protect people from harm.

How does the law do this?

In a tort case there is always a claimant and a defendant. The claimant comes to court seeking justice against the defendant.

The judge sits in the middle and has to decide who wins. The judge has to apply the rules of law to the facts and try to reach a just decision. If people do not think that the judge decides fairly, there is a danger that people will take the law into their own hands, and this ultimately leads to a world of anarchy and private vengeance.

The second principle of tort law is:

> The law must try to strike a balance between the interests of the claimant and the defendant.

The famous statue on top of the Old Bailey represents Justice. She holds scales and a sword. The sword illustrates that the law must be enforceable. Judges have to make decisions. One party wins, another loses. The judge cannot sit on the fence. The scales represent the attempt to balance the interests of the parties fairly. Lawyers will come up with powerful arguments for both sides. The judge must weigh these arguments and decide who has the stronger case. Justice must be seen to be done. Both sides need to know that they have been heard, then there is a better chance of the loser accepting the outcome.

However, it is often difficult for the judges and Parliament to develop really good legal rules that do justice to both parties.

It is worth thinking about what makes a good rule. In football the 'off-side rule' and in cricket the 'leg before wicket rule' have always been difficult rules for referees, umpires and players. Although these rules are necessary for the two games, they give rise to plenty of controversy and argument, and they have been changed frequently over the years. Similarly, legal rules develop when they attract wide criticism.

In tort law the rules are mainly created by judges trying to decide whether or not to make the defendant pay compensation to the claimant for an injury. The judge has to understand the facts and then make the decision. Each case must be decided by applying rules, otherwise the law would be arbitrary. Any judge will probably have a basic feeling or gut reaction about who should win. The rules may be created so that they offer some flexibility.

However, the rules should also produce sufficient certainty so that people may be advised about the likelihood of winning or losing. The rules of tort try to achieve this.

The third principle of tort law therefore is:

> The law should provide clear rules, but these rules should be sufficiently flexible to take into account a variety of circumstances.

> **EXAMPLE**
>
> How do judges decide when someone has breached their legal obligation? Striking the balance between certainty and flexibility is not easy. Take a fundamental rule of the tort of negligence: the defendant has to pay damages only if he is at fault. The defendant will be at fault if his behaviour fell below the standard of how the reasonable person would have behaved in the same circumstances. Is the rule flexible? Yes, the judge has a very wide discretion in deciding how the reasonable person would have acted. Is the rule sufficiently clear? In extreme cases it is fairly easy to say when someone has broken the rule, but there will be many cases when it is very hard to say whether or not the defendant is in breach of his duty.

So the main purpose of tort law is to build up a just system of rules that enables the law to right wrongs by providing compensation to people hurt by the actions of others.

LAWYERS AND REALITY

Tort lawyers

All tort law is a form of litigation. Tort lawyers advise claimants and defendants. They also advise businesses on how to minimise their exposure to being sued.

All lawyers are bound by a code of conduct, which includes a commitment to uphold the rule of law. For a tort lawyer this means trying to develop and apply the rules that build a world in which harmful behaviour is discouraged and victims receive justice.

The reality

In spite of a widespread perception that we live in a compensation-seeking culture, studies find that many people simply accept their injuries rather than seeking any sort of compensation. A recent study suggests that only in about 12% of cases did accident victims seek legal compensation. However, note the following figures:

- In a typical year, between 600,000 and 900,000 accident claims are made.
- In 2008, there were 625,072 road traffic claims. In the same year there were 86,957 claims against employers, 86,164 claims against public authorities and 9,880 claims for clinical negligence.
- In 2009, road accidents made up about 76% of these legal claims and claims against employers amounted to approximately 11%. One-third of road traffic accident victims and one-fifth of those injured at work finally succeeded in obtaining compensation in that year.
- In 2010, there were approximately 850,000 legal claims arising from accidents as well as over 15,000 disease claims. Claims about diseases may vary widely, from 15,000 up to 200,000 per year.
- These tort claims cost employers just under £8 billion in 2010. In many years the NHS pays out over £6 billion in damages because of successful medical negligence claims.
- Over 90% of the damages were paid by insurance companies.

CHAPTER 2

What Types of Harm are Protected?

INTRODUCTION

In the previous chapter we established some of the key underlying principles of tort law.

The first three were:

- The law should generally offer people protection from harm.
- The law must try to strike a balance between the interests of the claimant and the defendant.
- The law should provide clear rules, but these rules should be sufficiently flexible to take into account a variety of circumstances.

We can now consider a fourth principle:

> The law must be realistic and set limits to the types of harm against which protection is given.

Looking more closely at the idea of injury and harm provokes the enormous legal question of what types of harm should be compensated.

If you think for a moment about the many different ways in which people are injured, you can start to build up a picture of which types of injury are the most significant in any legal system. For instance, try to rank the following harms in order of importance:

- Physical injury.
- Psychiatric injury.
- Property damage.
- Financial loss.
- Damage to reputation.
- Invasion of privacy.

Even attempting to rank these types of harms raises difficult questions, as it is not easy to compare something like a broken leg with an allegation of dishonesty which damages someone's reputation. Within each area of harm there will be different levels of seriousness. Physical injury can range from a scratch to brain damage, and property damage can range from a torn shirt to a burnt-out house. Faced with this challenge, the law of tort has come up with a pattern of rules which are used to decide which harms may be compensated in different situations.

As we start to examine this subject, we focus first on one of the most significant areas of harm – physical injury.

PHYSICAL INJURY

There are numerous different contexts in which people suffer physical injury throughout their lives. Every day people die and are physically hurt. Many of these deaths and injuries are either purely accidental, or the result of natural causes beyond anyone's control. Tort law is involved only when people think that someone else should be asked to compensate for what has happened to the victim. Frequently, people who are injured or who have lost someone they love look to law to obtain some sort of justice as a result of the physical injury. This happens especially when people are injured or killed on the road or at work.

To understand how the rules of law develop in relation to physical harm, we need to look at the various contexts in more detail.

Physical injury in childhood – around the home

Children are often injured in the home. These injuries can range from minor scrapes and bumps to broken bones, or devastating injuries such as burns after fires or scalding. Some children also suffer abuse and neglect. The law could treat these injuries to children in a number of different ways. We could decide at one extreme that children should not receive compensation from anyone at all. Alternatively, we could decide that children should be treated in exactly the same way as any other person. We could decide that some childhood injuries are so trivial as to be outside the law entirely. Which injuries should receive protection and compensation?

EXAMPLES

Examples of serious injuries giving rise to claims by children include the following:

- A mother leaves a 1-year-old baby in a high chair and goes into another room. The baby manages to climb out of the high chair and then falls head first onto a hard kitchen floor and suffers a fractured skull.

- A council fails to remove an old boat that has been dumped on its land. Two children decide to play with the boat and try to renovate it. One of them takes a jack from his family's garage and jacks up the boat. The other goes underneath the boat to fix it. The jack slips and the boat falls on the child, fracturing his spine.

Physical injury in childhood and the concept of a pure accident

Some incidents of physical harm to children might be described as pure 'accidents'. The very word suggests that no person is responsible and that the event arises from bad luck or fate. However, in each of the examples given above there may well be someone who is legally responsible for the incident.

You will find that in our legal system we have decided that a minor, ie someone aged under 18, does have the right to claim for injury and that a minor can be held legally responsible for harming others. So a child may sue or be sued in tort.

Naturally this raises a host of other legal issues:

- Who actually makes the claim on behalf of the injured child?
- When a child receives compensation, which person should control the money? (Here the law of trusts is immediately relevant.)
- Should an adult be held legally responsible, even when the adult has not taken any specific action but simply failed to stop the child being harmed?
- Which adults should be held legally responsible? Would this cover only parents, teachers and babysitters, or does it apply to anyone in the vicinity?
- At what age is a child responsible for his or her own actions?
- When children are playing together and one gets hurt, should the law be involved at all?

Children, when challenged by an adult after causing damage, will often provide explanations and/or excuses for their actions, such as: 'I didn't mean to!' or 'Sorry, it was an accident!' Should children be held responsible for clumsiness? What standards of behaviour should we expect of children?

Physical injury in childhood – sport and school

Many injuries to children occur in the context of sport or on adventurous school trips. Sports which involve lots of physical contact, such as rugby, football and boxing, present obvious dangers. Skiing and swimming also have the potential to cause serious injuries. So what should the law say when injuries arise in these contexts? To what extent does a person's willing participation in sport take away his legal right to complain and seek compensation when something goes wrong?

In this area most people would argue that some risks are justified to ensure that children have an interesting and challenging experience of life. However, there are clearly some risks which would be unjustified. Many people have now become familiar with 'risk assessment' forms that try to anticipate the sort of injuries that might occur. Some fear that the threat of liability, and the administrative demands of such form-filling deter teachers and others from organising the sort of trips that generally benefit pupils.

EXAMPLES

The following examples concern children making claims after injury at school:

- A rugby match is taking place at school between two teams of under-16s. The match is bad-tempered and chaotic. The referee is inexperienced, but offered to referee as no one else was available. The referee is not bringing the scrums together correctly. There are many scrum collapses. In the second half there is another collapsed scrum and one of the prop-forwards breaks his neck. The boy will be paralysed for life.
- After a maths lesson two teenage girls start having a play fight using their plastic rulers as swords. A bit of plastic breaks off and flies into the eye of one of the girls, blinding her in that eye. Amongst others, she sued the girl with whom she was fighting.

PSYCHIATRIC INJURY

Should the law treat physical and mental injuries differently? It may sometimes be hard to separate physical and mental harm. A broken leg can cause a great deal of pain and frustration. A bad facial scar can cause severe embarrassment. There are also times when the victim is not physically touched at all but nevertheless suffers a severe reaction. Shell-shock and post-traumatic stress disorder are familiar examples of this type of harm. Sometimes a shock to the mind may have an effect on the body, such as possibly inducing a miscarriage. We are familiar with the idea that many illnesses are psychosomatic, and this reflects the difficulty of drawing a clear distinction between bodily and mental injury. In the area of pure psychiatric harm the law does allow people to sue, but the rules are more restrictive than for physical injury. This is a good example of the interweaving of the first and second principles of tort law discussed above.

Two aspects of this type of harm give rise to particular difficulties with putting limits on the possible claims:

(a)   Occasionally there are big public disasters which have a traumatic effect on numerous people, both those involved in the disaster and those who witness it, eg the hijacked planes flying into the twin towers on 9/11, and the disaster at Hillsborough when 95 football supporters were crushed to death at a Cup semi-final that was being televised as it happened.

(b)   Frequently people find that they suffer from psychiatric injuries which they claim are caused by stress at work. This raises a host of intriguing questions. Should someone who suffers from an illness caused by stress at work be able to sue the employer? This question alone raises many of the key issues in tort law.

Is a 'stress-induced injury' too vague a concept? On the other hand, there clearly do seem to be cases where people are so badly affected that they have a mental breakdown from which it can take years to recover.

To what extent do employees genuinely consent to undergo the stresses they experience at work? If we compensate people who are physically injured by negligent employers, why should we not compensate people who suffer psychiatric injury as a result of their employer's negligence?

You will see that once again tort law does allow such claims, but there are specific rules which limit the circumstances in which the claims can succeed.

PROPERTY DAMAGE

The most frequent tort claims, such as car accidents, often cause not only physical injury but also property damage. The car may be a write-off; clothes may be covered in blood and oil. Sometimes there is no physical injury but only property damage. A broken pipe can lead to flooding which destroys all the property in a flat. One casually dropped cigarette may start a fire which destroys thousands of pounds' worth of property. Someone wandering around an antique shop might easily bump into valuable artefacts and break them. With damage to vehicles and property in the home, the owner will often have taken out insurance. So should the owner (or his insurance company) obtain compensation from the careless person who caused the loss? In this area, as with physical personal injury, the law sets very few restrictions. As a result, each year there are claims for millions of pounds' worth of property damage.

FINANCIAL LOSS

Sometimes there is a combination of physical injury, property damage and economic loss. For instance a self-employed builder who breaks his neck when he crashes his van will experience physical injury, property damage and loss of income. Sometimes, however, there is no harm done to a person's body or possessions; instead, the person loses only money.

Each day trillions of pounds change hands in the global markets. Businesses make investment decisions. Banks decide whether or not to lend money. Investors decide which shares to buy in different companies. Boards of directors decide whether or not to acquire another company. Many businesses and individuals seek advice from experts about how to develop the business or make the best use of their wealth. Sometimes the advice given is bad. Not surprisingly, the person who has lost money as a result of someone else's bad advice will consider seeking compensation.

Sometimes there is a contract between them and the advice is so bad as to amount to a breach of one of the agreed terms of the contract. Frequently there is no such contract. So the law must come up with the solution to a number of questions when people seek compensation for pure economic loss.

The biggest question is: Should the law allow people who have lost money through what they consider to be the carelessness of an adviser, to sue that adviser and seek compensation even when there is no contract between the parties?

The answer to the question has absolutely enormous financial implications. Business decisions at every moment of the day mean that millions of pounds are being lost as well as won, often on the basis of advice from accountants, consultants and lawyers. The catastrophic losses sustained by businesses and banks in the recent economic downturn are illustrations of the problem.

You will see when you study tort that in a series of cases the courts have decided that in certain limited circumstances, people who have lost money may indeed claim for compensation from their advisers. This has naturally generated a vast amount of interesting and challenging work for lawyers. It also means that advisers must insure against the possibility of being sued for negligent advice. For a firm of solicitors the cost of the insurance premium is high, and it is often one of the main expenses of running the business.

As well as these losses arising from careless mistakes, there are times when people intentionally cause economic loss to others. If a rival business deliberately opens up a competing shop next door, the established business will probably lose money. This would usually be viewed as legitimate competition which benefits the public by keeping down prices and encouraging efficiency. However, there are cases where the law may intervene. Businesses often headhunt and poach key employees from their rivals. A popular product may be expensive and relatively easy to copy. So a rival produces very similar goods and sells them at a lower price. There is, for instance, a *tort of passing off* which can protect a business if a rival tries to sell very similar-looking products.

REPUTATION

For many people, their reputation in the eyes of others is extremely important. For some people, their reputation in the eyes of others is essential to their ability to earn a living. In all human communities, including schools, universities and workplaces, and in the media reputations are built up and destroyed. So the law has always had to respond to the problem of one person damaging or destroying the reputation of another.

The tort which deals with this type of harm is *defamation*, which includes both slander and libel. Essentially, slander is defamation of a transient kind, such as spoken words, and libel is defamation in permanent form, such as in writing in a newspaper or in an e-mail. With the arrival of the Internet and social networking, the power to damage the reputation of another person has increased enormously. The law here has to answer a host of questions about how to protect reputation.

Nevertheless, we also place a very high value on the ability of every person to express their ideas and opinions as freely as possible. Freedom of speech is a fundamental aspect of a good, liberal democratic society. So this area provides a classic illustration of how the law tries to strike a fair balance between these rights, which is one of the key principles we considered in **Chapter 1**.

EXAMPLES

- A newspaper article claims that a politician has been taking bribes in exchange for voting for a particular cause.
- A celebrity magazine suggests that a rock star is hypocritically hiding the fact that he is gay.
- A sports journalist writes that an athlete takes illegal performance-enhancing drugs.

PRIVACY

An issue related to that of reputation is the extent to which the law should protect an individual's right to a private life. Most people believe that they have a right to be left alone and not to have their private life exposed in the media or watched over by the state. Once again, there are other factors to be weighed against the right to privacy. The media believe that they have the right to inform the public about the behaviour of people of public interest. The state believes that on occasions it has the right to investigate very intimate details of a person's life, for instance when intercepting private e-mails between people believed to be involved in a major terrorist plot or a serious criminal conspiracy.

In this area there are some fundamental human rights in apparent conflict: the claimant's right to respect for his private and family life on the one hand; and the defendant's right to freedom of expression and, on occasions, the public's 'right to know'.

Tort law is dynamic and developing. In the area of privacy, over the past few years a new tort has effectively been created. There is now a tort protecting the claimant from 'the misuse of private information' about the claimant. The new tort does not offer complete protection from all invasions of private life, but it does deter the mainstream press from unjustifiably publishing some types of private information. Of course this raises questions about what we mean by 'private' and in what circumstances is it justifiable to publish.

EXAMPLES

- A married premier league footballer has sex with a prostitute.
- A politician who belongs to a party opposed to private education decides to send her children to a fee-paying school.

Are these examples of 'private information'? Is it justifiable to publish this information in the press?

PEACEFUL ENJOYMENT OF LAND

We mostly believe that we should be able to enjoy our home without unreasonable interference from our neighbours. If my neighbours' behaviour damages or destroys my ability to enjoy my own home, should the law intervene to protect me by forcing the neighbours to change their ways? Sometimes neighbours have incompatible ways of life. It may not to easy for a piano teacher and a DIY enthusiast to live easily side by side. If you want to enjoy your garden at the weekend but happen to live beside a small cricket ground, then for hours in the afternoon there is a danger of a cricket ball landing in your garden and hitting people or breaking glass. This area of law is dealt with partly by statutes such as the Environmental Protection Act and partly by the rules of the *torts of private nuisance and public nuisance.*

When should a judge tell one neighbour to stop doing an activity which annoys another? The answer to this question raises intriguing issues about the sort of society in which we want to live.

This area of law illustrates one of the key principles of tort:

> The law must try to strike a balance between the interests of the claimant
> and the defendant.

OTHER TYPES OF HARM

How do we classify the harm that results when a child with serious dyslexia goes to an educational psychiatrist and is misdiagnosed? This may mean that the child has a much more difficult experience at school and fails to achieve good grades, which in turn means that his earning capacity is reduced. Is this a mixture of mental and economic harm? Successful claims have been made for this unusual type of loss.

There are some types of harm which do not have any protection in law. Recently some claims were made by people who had received the results of x-rays showing shadows on their lungs that might later develop into mesothelioma. The claimants were well at the moment but worried about a future disease. They tried to sue the employers who had exposed them to asbestos in the past. The court controversially decided that this type of harm was not yet sufficiently serious to deserve legal protection.

You are in a good position to see why the law has developed a range of different principles to deal with claimants who have suffered different kinds of harm. In the next chapter we look at the 'winners', ie those people who have been successful in making their claims.

CHAPTER 3

WINNERS

ACTING FOR THE CLAIMANT

How do you win a tort case?

As we saw in **Chapter 2**, there are many different types of harm. In this chapter we look at some of the answers to the questions raised by examining the rules in a bit more detail. Most importantly, you will learn how claimants win their cases.

First, though, it is important to understand that the law of tort has set up different rules depending on whether the defendant's behaviour is intentional or simply careless.

INTENTIONAL HARM

Battery

Occasionally someone deliberately injures another person. Clearly, the law should protect us from intentional physical attack. Here there is an overlap with criminal law. However, even if the violent person is convicted, this does not provide the victim with compensation. So the civil law of tort provides the victim with the additional right to sue for damages or for an injunction to stop the violent person from continuing his actions.

If a person intentionally strikes another, the victim may consider suing the assailant in the *tort of battery*. Battery is defined as 'an intentional direct act of applying unlawful force to the claimant'. To succeed, the claimant simply has to prove that each part of the definition is satisfied, and then he has to defeat any defences raised by the defendant (see below). However, some of the words in the definition raise some intriguing and tricky questions for lawyers, especially the word 'unlawful'.

Every legal system must have a way of coping with wrongful intentional physical contact. There are many areas of life where we certainly *do* want to make physical contact with other people: hand-shakes, sport, and of course making love are just three examples. Other types of contact are socially destructive, though. Gangs and individuals sometimes get into violent confrontation. Muggers and rapists obviously intentionally hurt other people. In a school fight or a pub brawl, punches may be thrown. Occasionally people simply lose their temper and lash out. Many people suffer violence in the home from abusive partners.

What makes such contact 'unlawful'?

It is not easy to come up with a definition of 'unlawful' which protects the claimant but does not open the door to an enormous number of trivial claims. The judges decided to define 'unlawful' as 'socially unacceptable' touching. However, this test is one of those flexible tests that can be hard to apply.

Is it 'socially acceptable' to kiss someone at an office party? Is it all right for a doctor to operate on an unconscious patient without anyone's consent? How can you differentiate between battery and everyday contact?

> **EXAMPLE**
>
> In the case of *Wilson v Pringle*, one schoolboy jumped on the back of another and pulled on his satchel. The victim suffered a serious hip injury. Was this 'socially unacceptable'?

Of course the defendant may raise defences such as consent or self-defence. Whenever there is a serious fight it will be difficult to work out the amount of force that is justifiable in self-defence. The law does try to distinguish between genuine self-defence and acts of vengeance.

> **EXAMPLE**
>
> In *Lane v Holloway*, an old man was staggering home from the pub. He had been drinking and was making a lot of noise. A young couple who lived in an upstairs flat were disturbed by his noise. The wife went to the window and told the old man to be quiet. He shouted back: 'Shut up you monkey-faced tart!'
>
> Her husband came to the window and continued rowing with the old man. Then he went down into the street and confronted him. The old man threw a feeble punch and the young man then beat him up severely, leaving him needing many stitches in his wounds.

Threats and assault

Sometimes people threaten rather than hit. Again, we have developed rules to protect people from such behaviour. The tort of assault is defined as 'an intentional act by the defendant that causes the claimant reasonably to apprehend the infliction of immediate unlawful force'.

Once more, the words create some difficulties for lawyers. In particular, it is not easy to decide when the threat becomes immediate. In violent relationships, one partner often uses threatening words. Sometimes the words are followed by violent deeds.

> **EXAMPLE**
>
> *Thomas v NUM* involved a miners' strike during which strike-breaking miners were bussed into the collieries. They had to run the gauntlet of passing through very hostile lines of picketing strikers. Serious threats were shouted at the strike-breakers. They sued for assault, but as the strike-breakers were being protected by lines of police, the court decided that the threats were not immediate.

The law in this area also tries to protect people from threats such as harassment and stalking.

UNINTENTIONAL HARM – NEGLIGENCE

Who can sue whom?

The vast majority of injuries are not inflicted deliberately. Most people are hurt by accident or by carelessness. One huge issue that any legal system has to address is whether people who are hurt by the careless behaviour of others should be able to sue those others and seek monetary compensation. This area of law is known generally as *negligence*.

To win the case the claimant must show three things:

(a)   That the defendant owed him a duty of care.

(b)   That the defendant breached that duty.

(c)   That the defendant's breach is the cause of the claimant's harm.

Duty of care

The first rule of the tort of negligence is that the claimant can sue only if the defendant owes him a 'duty of care'. The law sets limits by deciding who owes such a duty to whom. Many of these duties are well-established and have become common knowledge.

We know that if you are injured by a careless driver you can sue. We also know that if you are hurt by the carelessness of a doctor you can sue. Medical negligence claims mean that the NHS has to pay out billions of pounds each year. If employees are injured by the careless behaviour of their employers, we know that they can sue those employers. So in three areas – road traffic accidents, medical negligence and at work – there are thousands of tort claims every year.

What about other areas? We are all consumers of products from the moment we are born until the day we die. Manufacturers create the wealth of the world. Many people are injured by products. Drugs have side-effects; food sometimes contains dangerous elements; machines go wrong and break or explode. Sometimes these products are constructed carelessly or packaged badly, or the instructions are faulty.

Often the person injured by a product will have a contract with the retailer from which it was bought and may seek compensation because a term of the contract has been breached. However, thousands of people are injured by products that they have not bought themselves. So should we allow people injured by a product to sue the manufacturer?

Manufacturers

Occasionally a product is put into circulation which causes great damage. One of the worst ever examples of this was the drug thalidomide. This drug was particularly good at reducing morning sickness in pregnant women. Unfortunately, many thousands of babies were either born with devastating physical problems or still-born before the connection was made between the drug and the birth defects. This illustrates a major problem for any legal system. If a manufacturer puts into circulation a product such as a new drug or cure, and it proves to have disastrous side-effects, should the manufacturer be held liable? Naturally, lobbyists for the pharmaceutical industry argue that this would stifle innovation and restrict research and development. Of course safeguards are in place, but there is still a risk.

> **EXAMPLE – THE MULTIMILLION DOLLAR SNAIL**
>
> The facts of *Donoghue v Stevenson* were as follows. Mrs Donoghue and her friend went into a café. They ordered ice-cream floats. Mrs Donoghue's friend paid for the treats, so Mrs Donoghue had no contract with anyone. She poured some ginger-beer (which was in an opaque bottle) over her ice-cream and ate some. When she poured the rest of the ginger-beer over her ice-cream, the remains of a decomposing snail fell out of the bottle. Mrs Donoghue became ill and sued Stevenson, the manufacturer of the ginger-beer, in tort for negligence.

When this case came before the courts, the judges realised that the decision that they made was likely to be the most important that they would ever have to make. This is because it affected the legal relationship between consumers (everyone in the world) and manufacturers (who make all the wealth of the world). Should the judges decide that manufacturers owe a duty of care to people who consume their products, even when they have not bought those products? If manufacturers were able to be sued in tort by anyone then, for instance, drug companies would be at risk of being sued by everyone harmed by the unintended side-effect of a drug.

Back to first principles – foreseeability of harm

The judges deciding the case went back to first principles and asked fundamental questions about why we have law and what sort of legal world we should create. Hence this case became the leading case of all time regarding the tort of negligence. The lead judge, Lord Atkin, considered the fundamental questions of human relationships. Almost all religions and moralists agree that we should love our neighbour. However, it is probably not realistic to make this the rule of law. Instead, we base the law on a negative rule that you should not harm your neighbour. However, that rule needs to be looked at in more detail. When should you not do harm?

The judges decided that there are times when you can foresee that if you act carelessly, you are likely to do harm. Thus the judge said that a key principle was the *foreseeablity of harm.*

Proximity of relationship

The next concept the judge considered was proximity: which people are in sufficient proximity to the defendant that the defendant should be held legally responsible if those people are injured? As I drive my car or play contact sports, I know that if I drive carelessly or go carelessly into a tackle I could do serious harm. There are also certain people whom I should have in mind when I am acting in the world. Some people are much more likely to be affected than others. As I drive, I literally can see people who might be injured by my bad driving. If I manufacture a product, I cannot see the people who might be injured if that product is faulty, but I know that there will be consumers of my product and I should be aware that I might harm those persons.

Foreseeability and proximity

One part of Lord Atkin's leading judgment in *Donoghue v Stevenson* has became world famous and is often known as 'the neighbour principle'. He said:

> The rule that you are to love your neighbour becomes, in law, you must not injure your neighbour. You must take reasonable care to avoid acts or omissions which you can reasonably foresee would be likely to injure your neighbour. Who then, in law, is my neighbour? The answer seems to be persons who are so closely and directly affected by my act that I ought to have them in contemplation when directing my mind to the acts or omissions which are called in question.

Because the House of Lords decided that foreseeability and proximity were the essential components of a duty of care in the tort of negligence, for many decades people brought claims for all sorts of injury based on the idea that the harm was foreseeable and they were in a close relationship with the defendant. The floodgates were open. Millions of pounds have been paid out by manufacturers over the years because of the decision in *Donoghue v Stevenson*.

The third test – fair, just and reasonable

The judges are aware that their decisions on who owes a duty of care to whom may have enormous implications, especially when they do impose a duty and the floodgates open. Because of these difficulties, the judges have decided that they will impose a duty of care only when they consider that it is 'fair just and reasonable' to do so. Clearly this gives judges plenty of scope.

As we saw in **Chapter 2**, there were two particular types of harm which caused great controversy: economic loss and psychiatric harm. These may involve advisers and public authorities, as shown below.

Advisers and pure economic loss

If you do decide to become a lawyer, an accountant or an adviser to businesses, this is the area in which you are most conscious of being a possible defendant. The type of harm caused by advisers is 'pure economic loss'. Advisers are highly unlikely to cause physical injury or property damage, but bad advice from a solicitor, a tax adviser or a business consultant might easily cause an enormous amount of economic loss to a client.

Each day people make millions of decisions about how to use their money. The stock markets around the world are continually seeing investors move their funds from one business to another. Often such decisions are based on the advice of experts. If the expert gives careless bad advice, investors may lose all their money. So should it be possible for an investor who has been badly advised to sue the adviser?

The rules of law here are clearly of enormous importance to all sorts of people involved in the financial services industry, another multi-million part of the economy.

Clearly, if a financial adviser gives bad advice, it is foreseeable that the investor might lose his money. Equally clearly, the adviser and the investor may be in a close relationship. So the conditions of foreseeability and proximity are often satisfied. For this reason, the present law is that the investor may sue even if he has no contract with the adviser, and so another enormous floodgate of liability is opened up.

It is not surprising that the investor is able to sue his adviser when they have a contract and the adviser breaches the contract, but no contract is required when the investor sues in the tort of negligence.

Because of this, advisers such as lawyers have to insure against the possibility of being sued in negligence. Lawyers pay very substantial premiums on these insurance policies. All lawyers must be insured for at least £2 million of potential liability. City firms require much greater insurance cover.

Claims against public authorities

Sometimes it is not the type of harm but the type of defendant that creates controversy. For example, the House of Lords has had to consider whether the police owe a duty of care when investigating crime.

EXAMPLE – INVESTIGATING THE YORKSHIRE RIPPER

The police are hunting for a serial killer. They are fooled by a hoaxer who deceives them into wasting time and resources. As part of their investigation they interview the serial killer on three occasions without realising it. The killer murders again before finally being caught by chance. The family of the last victim want to sue the police for their incompetent handling of the investigation.

The example above is taken from a real case. The House of Lords decided that it would not be 'fair, just and reasonable' to impose a duty on the police, partly because their Lordships feared that this would open the floodgates to claims by all sorts of people who were the victims of crime.

Negligence – breach of duty of care

So the first hurdle for the claimant is to prove that there is a *duty of care* in law. Next the claimant must show that the defendant has breached the duty.

Who is responsible?

How do we decide who is really responsible for the injury?

Consider a car crash. Sometimes it is relatively easy to say who was to blame, for instance when a drunken driver veers across to the wrong side of the road. However, often the events leading up to the crash are complex and many different decisions contribute to the eventual collision. The law of tort has come up with a number of rules to work out who is to be held responsible in law for the harm done.

Fault

How do we decide whether a person's carelessness is such that he has to pay compensation? We all make mistakes. Children who break things often say: 'I didn't mean to!' In this area of law the claimant is not saying that the defendant has intentionally caused the harm, so the claimant is not arguing that the defendant is morally wrong. But what type of fault is required? Should we judge each person individually and expect each person to do his best? Or should we simply expect each person to try to be reasonably careful?

The court asks two questions:

*   How would a reasonable person have behaved in the same situation as the defendant?
*   Has the defendant's actual behaviour fallen below the standard of the reasonable person?

If the defendant falls below the standard, he is at fault. This means that legal liability may be very different from moral culpability. The defendant may be trying his best but is still not behaving as well as a reasonable person would.

The judge therefore has the tricky task of deciding what amounts to reasonable behaviour in any given situation. The lawyer also has the challenging forensic task of finding out exactly what happened. In this respect a lawyer is like a detective gathering evidence to build up an accurate picture of the precise sequence of events. Police accident reports and medical records may be vital sources of evidence.

So how does a judge decide how a reasonable person would act? To some extent the judge uses common sense. However, that is rather vague. Judges expect people to carry out a conscious or half-conscious on-going risk assessment as they go about their activities. Take someone driving a car. The driver knows that if he loses concentration even for a moment, someone might very easily be injured. The driver also knows that the injury could be extremely serious or even fatal. One moment of carelessness on a motorway and a family might be killed. The driver also knows that there are many relatively straightforward ways of reducing the chances of this happening. Nevertheless, thousands of people are killed and seriously injured on the roads each year. The court expects the drivers to drive with great care. The standard required of all drivers is high.

What about learner-drivers? What about a driver with the emergency services rushing to get to an incident?

> **EXAMPLE**
> *   A learner driver is having her third lesson in her own car with her driving instructor. There are no dual-controls. A few minutes into the lesson, the learner panics and her hand grips the steering-wheel tightly. She fails to steer correctly and the car mounts the pavement and smashes into a lamp-post. The instructor's leg is broken in the accident.

An ambulance driver hurrying towards the scene of a serious accident is justified in driving faster than a motorist on the way to work.

Negligence – causation

The defendant is liable to the claimant only if his actions have caused the harm suffered. How does the court decide who has caused any given incident?

When any event happens, numerous previous events may have played some part in causing it. Different academics have different ways of understanding the concept of causation. A scientist and an historian may both use the word 'cause' but in very different ways.

A judge has to make a decision between two sides arguing about a real event. The judge does not have the luxury of being able to take a purely theoretical or academic view. Judges accept that their view of causation may not satisfy a philosopher or a purist. Nevertheless, they have to give clear and consistent reasons for their decisions. So which is the legally relevant cause of an event? The law has come up with several tests of causation.

One idea that seems reasonable is to say that if the harm would have happened anyway, regardless of the defendant's behaviour, then the defendant's behaviour is not the cause of the event. This seems logical and sometimes produces a satisfactory workable rule.

Unfortunately, complications often arise in practice. It is not always easy to say what would have happened if you change one thing in the past. Also, when we do not know exactly how the injury occurred, the test may either become useless, or it may produce highly controversial results. Often it is not possible to say exactly what caused an injury.

The legal problem is best illustrated by the disease of mesothelioma. Each year several thousand people die from this type of cancer, which is triggered by exposure to asbestos. A single strand of asbestos can start the cancer. It may lie dormant for years. When the cancer develops it kills quickly and painfully. Many victims dying now were negligently exposed to asbestos by several of their former employers. It is not possible to find out which strand started the cancer. So you can never really know which of the employers caused it. Does this mean the claims should fail? The House of Lords decided to allow these claims even though, strictly speaking, it was impossible to prove causation on ordinary principles. The decision is an example of allowing some flexibility into the rules to produce justice for victims and their families.

Before any injury, there is a long chain of events leading up to the moment of harm. Sometimes, after the original breach of duty by the defendant, another event happens which plays a part in the story of how the victim gets hurt. If this new event is really significant, the original defendant may argue that the new event 'breaks the chain of causation' and that it is therefore wrong to say that the original defendant's fault caused the injury.

EXAMPLE

A car stops suddenly on a motorway and a van drives into the back of the car. The van is damaged but the van driver is not seriously hurt. A minute later, a lorry driving too fast crashes into the back of the van and kills the van driver. The lorry driver is clearly to blame for the van driver's death. However, is the car driver also responsible for the death of the van driver, or has the lorry driver's action 'broken the chain of causation'?

DEFENCES

In a tort claim the claimant has the burden of proof. The civil standard of proof is on the *balance of probabilities*. So effectively, the claimant argues his case first and the defendant needs to do nothing until the claim is made out.

If the claimant has established that all the relevant legal tests are satisfied, the defendant may raise defences. The most significant defence is one which occurs to everyone: if the claimant willingly consented to take the risk that resulted in the injury, surely the claim should fail. Indeed, this is basically the correct position in law. When footballers or rugby players tackle an opponent, to what extent should they take into account the risk of injuring their opponent?

However, it is not always easy to decide when a person has consented. Is it enough that they consent to taking part in a risky activity? Does the consent have to be given expressly, or might it be given by implication? What happens if the claimant is put under pressure to consent?

The law states that the consent must be 'real'. This means that it has to be shown that the claimant must have known the full extent of the risk, and that the claimant willingly took the risk and accepted that the defendant might behave carelessly.

> **EXAMPLE**
>
> You go on an adventure holiday run by a business and sign a form saying that you consent to the risks of climbing. Does that mean that you are agreeing not to sue the company if they organise the expedition carelessly and you fall and break your neck?

Often, even when the defendant is at fault, the victim is still partly to blame for his own injury. This is known as 'contributory negligence'. In these circumstances the amount of damages that the defendant has to pay is reduced by a percentage to reflect the victim's share of the responsibility for the injury. If someone who is not wearing a seat belt is injured in a car crash by a negligent driver, the damages are likely to be reduced because the victim's own carelessness has played a part in the injuries he suffered.

WHO ARE THE WINNERS?

The following types of claimant are most likely to sue successfully:

- Victims of car accidents.
- People hurt by others at work.
- People hurt by medical negligence.
- Visitors injured by the state of the premises they are visiting.

CHAPTER 4

WHO PAYS?

THE DEFENDANTS

In tort cases there are various groups of people who end up as defendants and who pay the vast amount of the damages that are awarded each year. Among these are:

- drivers
- employers
- public authorities
- health care professionals
- lawyers and accountants
- manufacturers.

The first four groups of defendants are examined in further detail below; the liability of lawyers, accountants and manufacturers was looked at in **Chapter 3** above when discussing negligence.

DRIVERS

We all know about the dangers on the road from early childhood. This is still the way in which a young person is most likely to be killed.

Each year about 3,000 people are killed on the roads in the UK and about 12,000 suffer serious injuries. Drivers must insure against their liability to people injured by their negligence. The insurance companies therefore end up paying for these injuries, and they in turn increase the premiums they require for insuring drivers.

Why do so many of these claims succeed? Having looked at the rules of negligence in the previous chapter, this should be clear.

First, it is well-established in common law that drivers owe a duty of care to all other road-users.

The victim must prove that the driver has breached his duty. The test is the same as usual: has the driver fallen below the standard of the reasonably competent driver in the circumstances. However, drivers are expected to be very careful.

As with all risk assessments, the courts will consider various questions, including:

- How likely is it that harm would occur if the defendant behaved carelessly? When driving carelessly on the road, it is very likely that harm would occur.

- How serious would the harm be? A driver of a car knows that he may easily kill as a result of a small error of judgement, so the driver is expected to be extremely careful.

In many road injuries there is no problem with causation. The first test is often easily satisfied as the victim would not have been hurt if the driver had driven more carefully. In complex cases, such as a motorway pile-up, there may be arguments about whether a new intervening act breaks the chain of causation. The types of harm involved are nearly always personal injury and property damage, both of which are foreseeable.

Sometimes the victim has behaved carelessly and loses some of the damages because of contributory negligence. For instance, a passenger who does not bother to wear a seat-belt and whose injuries are made worse as a result, may well lose up to 25% of the damages.

However, there are relatively few difficulties with bringing a claim once the facts have been established.

EMPLOYERS

After drivers, the next most common defendant in a negligence claim is the employer. Again, employers must insure against liability.

Physical injuries at work

Especially in the era following the Industrial Revolution, many injuries were suffered by people at work. Industrial machinery was often unsafe and not fenced-off. Factories not only could be noisy and hot, but were also full of physical dangers such as moving parts of machinery, burning furnaces and dust-filled air. Although there have been many improvements, some factories still have many dangers lurking. People also often fall from ladders or from scaffolding. Occasionally there are cave-ins at mines, or explosions at factories. In spite of there having been great improvements, thousands of people are still injured on building sites each year. Some jobs inevitably involve severe dangers: bomb-disposal is an obvious example. Many people working for the emergency services, such as the police, ambulance and fire services, are often at risk.

Nevertheless, today many of the injuries suffered at work are less immediately visible. Repetitive strain injury (RSI) and eye-damage may arise from people working on computers. Very serious harm may be caused when there is asbestos, or silica or coal dust in the air. It is not widely known that a form of cancer called mesothelioma kills almost as many people each year as road accidents. This form of cancer may be triggered by a person coming into contact with a tiny quantity of asbestos. The disease may lay dormant for decades before the victim becomes aware of the injury. Liability for mesothelioma has given rise to a series of complex, challenging legal cases in recent years.

The employer may be sued in common law negligence or for breach of a statutory duty; or the employer may be found 'vicariously liable' for the tort of an employee committed in the course of employment (see further 'Vicarious liability', below).

The employer owes a well-established duty of care to each employee. This duty means that the employer must take reasonable steps to ensure that the employee is kept reasonably safe. This includes several different obligations. The employer must provide safe fellow workers, a safe place of work and safe equipment, and a safe system of work which is properly supervised. If you look at building sites you will see many signs aiming to fulfil this duty. All well-run businesses carry out risk assessments and try to minimise the chances of being sued.

Psychiatric injury at work

At one time people were usually injured physically at work, when mines caved in or limbs got trapped in the machinery for example. Now that happens less often, but an intriguing new problem at work has been created by stress-induced psychiatric and psychosomatic injury.

The law has had to grapple with the tricky problem of whether someone who suffers a stress-induced injury at work should be able to sue the employer. There are many powerful arguments for and against.

Arguments for ability to sue

- The employer would be liable for physical injury, why not also for psychological harm?
- It is often more difficult to recover from a stress-induced breakdown than from some physical injuries.
- The employer will be liable only if he is in breach and his breach is proved to have caused the injury.
- Stress is a huge problem in the 21st century and we should not just ignore it.

Arguments against ability to sue

- People are often paid for the increased level of stress which goes with their jobs.
- It is very difficult to tell if the claimant is genuinely injured.
- It is very hard to tell the extent to which the pressure at work caused the injury compared with the stresses outside work.
- To impose liability would over-burden employers.

The present position is that an employee may sue an employer for stress-induced injury, provided that it was foreseeable that the individual was at risk from this type of harm.

EXAMPLE

A social worker has a very demanding case load dealing with the victims of child abuse. He has time off work with various psychosomatic injuries. He asks his employers to reduce his workload. They promise to do so but in fact they do not. He suffers a stress-induced breakdown and his anxiety is so great that he can no longer function at work.

At the moment only employers are liable for stress-induced injury. This raises numerous intriguing but difficult problems. Should it be possible to sue a hospital for causing stress-induced injury to patients, or to the families of patients? Should it be possible to sue a school for failing to prevent stress-induced injury caused by bullying?

Vicarious liability and liability without fault

We have seen that it is usually necessary to show that the defendant has been at fault, ie that he has breached his duty of care. However, there are areas where liability is imposed even though the defendant has done nothing wrong.

The idea of vicarious liability is that another defendant becomes automatically liable for a tort committed by the first defendant. The first defendant remains liable. This is most common in employment situations.

The employer is in law 'vicariously liable' for the torts of an employee *committed in the course of employment*. The employer is liable simply because he has employed someone who has committed a tort while going about his job. Why?

Some argue that as the employer benefits from the activities done by his employees, the employer should bear the cost of harm done by the employee. Others argue that the individual employee is unlikely to be rich enough to pay significant amounts of damages, and so the rule enables the victim to sue an insured defendant and thereby be relatively certain to receive compensation. For others the rule is completely unfair, but it has been accepted for so long that it has become socially convenient.

Since employers are vicariously liable for torts committed by their employees in the course of employment, they have a big incentive to show that the person who committed the tort was either not an 'employee' or not acting 'in the course of employment'.

There have been many problems with defining exactly what makes someone an employee as opposed to an independent contractor or someone working freelance.

(There are many other legal contexts where this distinction matters, eg for tax, social security and of course employment law purposes.) Some situations are clear-cut. A factory worker, a teacher and a nurse are all usually employees. However, there are grey areas, and the courts have ended up with quite complex tests for establishing whether or not any particular defendant comes within the definition of being an 'employee'.

There are even more difficulties with what amounts to acting 'in the course of employment'. Consider the following examples and decide whether or not you think the defendant was 'in the course of employment'.

> **EXAMPLES**
>
> A children's home employs a warden to look after the children at night. The home carries out all the correct checks to make sure that the warden is safe before employing him. Nevertheless years later it emerges that the warden has been abusing some of the children. He is arrested, convicted and imprisoned. The children try to get compensation by suing the owners of the home.
>
> At a semi-professional football match one player slides in to tackle another. He is competing aggressively and he mis-times the tackle. His boot and studs catch the opposing player just below the knee, breaking his leg.

Breach of statutory duty

Furthermore there are many statutes that impose additional obligations on employers. Over the years there has been a massive shift in power from employers to employees. If you have studied the Industrial Revolution you will know that factory workers had to endure horrific conditions; children worked as chimney-sweeps and mining disasters were frequent. Factory Acts and Health and Safety at Work Acts, supplemented by numerous directives, now regulate many aspects of the workplace.

PUBLIC AUTHORITIES

Public authorities often have to make decisions that affect people's lives. When these decisions are made carelessly, people may suffer. For example:

- A social worker fails to remove a child from an abusive and dangerous parent; a social worker wrongly removes a child from a good parent.
- An educational psychologist fails to diagnose that a student has dyslexia.
- The local authority fails to provide housing for a homeless person.
- The CPS fails to bring any evidence against someone held on remand for several weeks.
- The police sometimes fail to prevent crime.

In many cases people who suffer as a result of what they see as mistakes made by public authorities seek compensation using the law of tort. Sometimes they link these claims with allegations that their human rights have been violated.

Public authorities do have plenty of money. However, their funds come from taxes, so in one sense successful claims against public authorities are paid for by all of us as taxpayers.

In cases brought against public bodies the law has developed cautiously. Claimants here may seek other remedies, such as asking for judicial review of administrative decisions (see further **Public Law**). In general only a few claims have been successful. The CPS cannot be usually be sued. The police cannot be sued for the way in which they choose to investigate crime.

HEALTH CARE PROFESSIONALS

The amount paid out by the NHS in damages can be around £1 billion in a single year in compensation for people injured by medical negligence. Misdiagnosis and mistakes during operations and treatment may have devastating effects. Some claims in this context account for some of the highest awards of damages of all. If a young person's brain is damaged by medical negligence and he needs life-long care, it is not surprising that the damages awarded may run into millions of pounds.

> **EXAMPLE**
> • A woman is having a hard time in the process of delivering her baby. A doctor is called to help out. He decides to do a 'high forceps' delivery. The forceps have to close on the baby's head in the womb. The doctor using the forceps grips slightly too tight and pulls for slightly too long. The baby lives but is severely brain damaged.

CHAPTER 5

HOW MUCH?

You may have seen stories in the media about victims receiving apparently large payments. A successful claim in negligence might result in damages of a few hundred pounds or many millions. How is the figure reached?

Clients will be very keen to know how much the claim is worth. Claimants obviously need to know how much they might get; defendants need to know how much they might have to pay. In practice the tort lawyer spends much more time on working out the value of the claim than on issues of liability.

Many clients can afford to make a claim only if the lawyer will act on a conditional fee basis. This means that if the client loses, the lawyer will not be able to charge his client for the work done; but if the claim succeeds, the lawyer is able charge an increased rate. This means that it is vital for the lawyer to decide whether or not a claim is worth pursuing.

NEGOTIATED SETTLEMENTS

The vast majority of claims are settled by negotiation between the clients' lawyers. Both sets of lawyers need a full understanding of the rules so that they may reach a settlement that is reasonably acceptable to both parties – even if it is less than the claimant wants and more than the defendant hoped. A good negotiator is worth a huge amount of money to the client, as there may be big differences between possible settlement figures. Occasionally the lawyers cannot agree and the parties go to court for the judge to decide how much to award. The amount of the award is known as the 'quantum' of damages.

EXAMPLE

Lesley Ash, the actress, was injured when she fell out of bed. She went to hospital where she contracted a variant of MRSA (a so-called 'super bug') through the negligence of the hospital. She became very ill and for some time was confined to a wheelchair. She lost the chance to work on some valuable contracts. Her claim was settled for approximately £5 million.

THE GUIDING PRINCIPLE

The aim behind an award of money to a successful claimant in tort is to put the claimant back into the position he would have been in if the tort had not been committed.

This idea is strange but also familiar. It involves a bit of theoretical time-travelling. You go back to the moment the tort was committed and compare what has happened to the claimant as a result of the tort and what would have happened to him if the tort had not been committed.

Time travel and alternative universes

If you have seen the film Superman you will get the idea. In Superman, Lex Luther plants a nuclear bomb in the San Andreas Fault, California. Superman's girlfriend, Lois Lane, is killed when her car falls into the chasm. Superman is so heart-broken that he failed to arrive in time to save her, he flys faster than the speed of light backwards round the world, which – surprisingly! – has the effect of reversing time. The film rewinds and Lois emerges from the chasm, restored to life. Superman is doing just what tort damages are designed to do – taking Lois back to the position she was in before Lex Luther committed the dirty deed.

Of course this aim cannot be achieved in reality – we cannot reverse time. All that the law can do is order the defendant to pay money. This in itself is unsatisfactory, as money cannot raise the dead, heal a wound or restore a missing limb. Nevertheless, money can achieve a great deal for the injured claimant, and sometimes may go a long way towards providing a genuinely effective remedy.

Assessing damages and mitigation

The courts try to work out how a sum of money might best compensate the claimant, leaving him as well off as he would have been if he had not been injured by the defendant. The aim is not to reward or over-compensate the claimant, and not to punish the defendant. The idea is that the claimant should be fully compensated but no more. For this reason the claimant is not allowed to seek damages for losses that might easily have been avoided. The rule is that the claimant is expected to mitigate, or reduce, his own losses. As the claimant cannot claim for such avoidable losses, the defendant will often argue that the claimant should have done more to reduce the impact of the injury on his life.

So what can the successful personal injury claimant claim for?

PUTTING A MONETARY VALUE ON A CLAIM

It is, of course, very difficult to arrive at a figure that is fair to both parties. The law allows claims for a number of different categories of harm, known as *heads of damage*.

Pain and suffering

First the law attempts to provide compensation for unquantifiable things such as the 'pain and suffering' and the 'loss of amenity' experienced by the claimant.

For instance, if you consider a car crash in which the victim has broken some bones and been badly bruised, the claimant may have suffered pain at the moment of impact, and medical treatment and other subsequent activities may also be painful. The claimant may well no longer be able to carry out the activities that he or she used to enjoy before the incident. Injuries often stop people being able to play sports, or to enjoy the usual other pleasures of life.

How can losses such as 'pain and suffering' and 'loss of amenity' be translated into money? The truth is that any attempt to put a price on such lost experiences is likely to seem arbitrary. How do you quantify in financial terms the loss of the ability to play sport or make love? How do you compare the pain of breaking a leg with that of losing your sight?

As this is an impossible task, all that we do is to collect precedents (ie previous examples) of the value of claims which have already been settled or decided by a judge. These are recorded in practitioner works such as *Kemp & Kemp* and the decisions are summarised conveniently in the Judicial Studies Board Guidelines. Here you can look up previous cases which have dealt with every part of the body that might be injured. It is interesting to compare the sums awarded with your own guesses. How much do you think someone who loses their eyesight might be awarded? Is this likely to be more or less than the award made to someone who loses an arm?

When you look at the specific decisions in *Kemp & Kemp* you are often given the key details about the claimant, such as age, sex and lifestyle. For example:

(a) Tom, aged 21, an active sportsman.

(b) Y, aged 17, a female dancer.

For any new claim, you simply look up three or four of the nearest equivalents, which will give you a general idea of the amount of money that might be expected to be awarded under this head of damage.

For instance, the guidelines put figures on the possible amount awarded for 'pain, suffering and loss of amenity' for injury to different parts of the body. For example:

Very severe brain damage	£220,000
Total loss of sight	£125,000
Serious hand injury	up to £30,000
Broken nose	up to £12,000

Financial losses

The next category or head of damage that may be claimed is the financial expenses that have arisen because of the injury: medical bills, travel to the doctor's surgery and hospitals, and any necessary changes to the claimant's home.

Any earnings that have been lost as a result of the injury may also be recovered. In cases of serious injury, this may be a huge sum. If someone is brain-damaged in a car crash or as a result of medical negligence, their entire life's earnings may be lost.

It can sometimes be quite easy to work out how much has been lost up the date of the trial or settlement. If the claimant was in a steady job before the injury and has not worked since, the sums are relatively easy to do. If the claimant is self-employed or works in the type of job that pays occasional bonuses, this becomes more difficult.

However, the biggest problem comes when trying to calculate the figure for future lost earnings. We are now trying to estimate the difference between two unknowns: what they claimant will earn in future; and what he would have earned if he had not been injured.

What would the claimant have earned after the trial if he had not been injured? Call this X. How much will he now earn after the trial? Call this Y. To put him back into the position he should be in, the claimant is able to claim X – Y.

We would also have to consider for how long these losses will continue. Someone brain-damaged at the age of 30 has probably lost 35 years of potential earnings. So at first you calculate that that person should receive his net lost earnings per year multiplied by a figure of 35. However, if you award damages as one lump sum at the date of the trial, this would mean that the claimant receives the equivalent of his entire life's earnings at this time. The claimant could then invest the lump sum and earn far more than he would have earned had he not been injured. So a complex actuarial calculation is made to try to ensure that the amount awarded does not over-compensate the claimant. With a potentially high-earner, the award for lost future earnings can run into millions of pounds.

Deductions

The injured person will often receive money from a number of sources as a result of the injury: insurance pay-outs; social welfare benefits; possibly charitable pay-outs. These are not generally deducted, so the victim may receive not only damages from the defendant but also income from other sources. Although this might seem to over-compensate the claimant, if the rules were different it would be the negligent defendant who really benefitted because he would have to pay less.

Death

What happens when the claimant dies?

Many victims of negligence such as road accident victims die either instantly or soon after the incident. Sometimes victims of industrial diseases die within months or a few years of contracting the disease. It might be argued that their claims should cease with their death, but the law does not say that. Instead, there are two statutes which enable the claim to continue even after the victim has died.

The people who bring these claims are nearly always the personal representatives of the deceased. Usually these are the executors who are dealing with the deceased's affairs.

One statute (the Law Reform (Miscellaneous Provisions) Act 1934) enables a claim to be made for all the losses suffered by the deceased arising from the tort between the moment when the tort was committed and the death.

Another statute (the Fatal Accidents Act 1976) enables the deceased's dependants to make a claim against the defendant for the financial losses they have suffered since they no longer receive the financial benefits that the deceased would have provided. So, for instance, the deceased's spouse and children might claim for what the deceased would have spent on them if he had not been killed.

These rules can mean that sometimes the defendant has to pay hundreds of thousands of pounds in damages, and sometimes he need pay very little. If a negligent driver instantly kills an old man with no dependants, there will be minimal damages. However, a negligent driver who kills a young parent who had a highly-paid job would have to pay millions of pounds in damages.

CHAPTER SUMMARY

Conclusion

The law of tort plays an enormous part in the real world. Millions of pounds change hands each year because of these rules. Thousands of people who suffer harm receive compensation and are able to rebuild their lives. However, many of the rules which have emerged from the amazing variety of tragic incidents are highly controversial.

You will find this a fascinating area of law. It affects everybody by shaping the rules of the game of life.

Ten key principles of tort law

•   The law should generally offer people protection from harm.

•   However, the law must be realistic and set limits to the types of harm that are protected.

•   The law must try to strike a balance between the interests of the claimant and the defendant.

•   The law should encourage careful behaviour and discourage socially harmful behaviour.

•   The law should provide clear rules, but these rules should be sufficiently flexible to take into account a variety of circumstances.

•   The law should encourage an economically efficient way of allocating risk.

•   The law should distinguish between relevant factors which it will take into account and irrelevant factors which it will ignore.

•   The law should satisfy the claimant's grievance without unfairly punishing the defendant.

•   The defendant should be liable only for harm which was objectively foreseeable.

•   The law should strike a balance between the individual's rights and the public interest.

TRUSTS

CHAPTER 1

INTRODUCTION

Equity and trusts are often thought of as dry and dusty subjects, useful in an academic sense but not having much relevance to most people's real-world existence. This part of the book will seek to dispel this myth and attempt to show that the evolution of trust law contains more plot twists than an 'Eastenders' Christmas Special and a Stephen King novel put together.

On reflection that might be overstating the case fractionally; however, it is true that trusts and the operation of equitable principles are located at the centre of the everyday lives of each and every one of us.

It is for this reason that a broad understanding of their workings and influence is vital, not only for a proper appreciation of the subject within the context of this course, but also to aid a wider perspective when trying to gauge how commercial principles impact upon decisions, both in regard to the individual and in a wider context.

What the following pages will not represent, however, is anything even approaching a comprehensive textbook on the subject, or even a 'potted' guide to the essentials: rather, it is hoped that they will serve both to point out the nature of some of the major types of trust that may be encountered in the world and to flag up some of their more important functions, both to us as individuals and to wider society as a whole, and to elicit just a modicum of curiosity to find out a little more about these strange and exotic creatures that already exist amongst us, if we could but see them.

HISTORICAL BEGINNINGS

As mentioned above, this part of the book is not trying to set out a definitive story of the evolution of trusts, and therefore you just need to be aware, briefly, that the concept of equity evolved in the Middle Ages as a partially separate branch of law used to 'plug the gaps' both where the existing case law (or 'common law') did not cover a situation and in situations where the strict application of the common law rules would lead to an unjust (ie unfair) result.

One of many devices used by judges to arrive at a fair result included the concept of what we now would call a trust. The essence of this idea allowed for the separation into distinct parts of the legal ownership (or responsibility of ownership) from the actual enjoyment of the physical assets themselves.

CHAPTER 2

TRUSTS AND THE INDIVIDUAL

WHAT IS A TRUST AND WHAT USE IS IT?

As indicated above, a trust effectively allows us to break open the parcel that we generally refer to as 'ownership' into its constituent parts – responsibility and enjoyment. Often both these concepts are present in the same person at the same time; however, in many situations different people retain the legal responsibility for dealing with and caring for an asset ('administration'), while at the same time someone completely different may have the right to enjoy the asset. The former would be termed a *trustee*, and the latter is called a *beneficiary*.

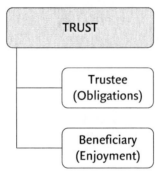

Figure 1: Interests under a trust

A trust cannot be created by accident – certain basic requirements must be met. This is important, as there are many substantial similarities between the requirements for a person to make a gift to someone as compared to a person setting up a trust.

GIFT OR TRUST?

Three certainties

Whether A intends to set up a trust in favour of B or whether he intends to make a simple gift to B, there must be clarity as to some core elements – known as the *three certainties*:

- intention;
- subject matter (ie the property concerned); and
- objects (ie the beneficiaries or people whom it is proposed to benefit),

together with an actual transfer.

Making a gift

The most obvious and important thing is that A must actually mean (ie intend) to make a gift – it cannot happen by accident or mistake.

Also there must be people who can receive the gift (a gift to a pet, at least from a legal point of view, is not possible – although my dog might try to dispute this). Further, the person or people receiving should be described clearly enough that they may be identified.

There should also, of course, be subject matter to the gift, and again that should be sufficiently well identified ('I'm giving you that thing of mine you like – you know …' obviously would not work here).

Further, there needs to be the appropriate element of transfer. This is usually dependent upon the nature of the property itself: certain types of asset require more formalities for their transfer than others; whereas with simple goods, the mere fact of handing them over – or 'delivery' – is enough.

Figure 2: Requirements for a valid gift

Creating a valid trust

By comparison with a gift, a basic private trust (ie not one which falls within the particular definition of a charity) must also meet certain formal requirements in order to be valid – the essence of these requirements being similar to those required for a gift (above).

Three certainties

Like a gift, a trust must fulfil the three certainties (intention, objects and subject matter – see above).

Intention

Certainty of intention is reasonably straightforward and, in the context of trusts, means that the person trying to create the trust ('the settlor') must show sufficient evidence that he means to create a trust (or impose obligations on someone (X) to deal with the asset – 'subject matter' – for the benefit of someone other than X), to make it clear that the transfer to X is on trust rather than a gift for X's own personal use.

This certainty of intention may also be referred to as 'certainty of words', and that is how certainty of intention is evidenced, ie in the words used accompanying the transfer. For example, if A hands B a cheque for £100,000, saying 'take this and use it for C's benefit', those words are likely to be sufficiently certain to evidence an intent to impose an obligation on B for the benefit of C, ie to impose a trust upon B. If, however, A said to B, 'Take this – I hope you will use some of it to look after C', here the wording is not strong enough to impose an obligation on B to do anything for C, and it is likely to be held as a straight gift to B. Words expressing a mere wish or hope that someone will do something are styled as 'precatory' and insufficient to impose trust obligations.

Objects

Additionally, a trust must be capable of being accurately described as directly benefitting real, identifiable people (as opposed to intangible ideals or moral concepts). This is known as the 'beneficiary principle' and reflects upon the requirement for *certainty of objects*. With trusts that name particular individuals and give them each a distinct share ('fixed trusts'), this does not usually present many problems. However, this level of certainty is not always present when settlors create trusts, especially when they are more concerned to benefit a *class* of people – sometimes allowing their trustees an element of discretion in identifying this class (eg a branch of the settlor's family or members of a distinct group) rather than nominating specific individuals. In such cases the words used to describe the proposed group or class intended to benefit must be sufficiently clear to identify them adequately. For example, it should be reasonably straightforward to ascertain the proposed beneficiaries from the words 'for the current teaching staff of the College of Law', but the words 'for my good friends' would be more problematic. How close a friend does the person have to be in order to benefit? This trust is likely to fail for lack of certainty of objects.

This beneficiary principle stems from the acceptance that the 'trust police', should anything go wrong in the administration of a trust, are the beneficiaries themselves, and it is these beneficiaries who will keep the trustees in order and pursue them through the courts if necessary. Therefore if the beneficiaries are not sufficiently clear, there will not be anyone capable of enforcing the trust as against the trustees.

Subject matter

The same considerations apply as are applicable to the making of a valid gift (see above), ie the asset concerned should be clearly identified and distinguished from similar property if necessary. For example, 'some of my paintings' would not be clear enough to distinguish one from another and so the trust (or gift) would fail for lack of certainty of subject matter.

Rules against perpetuity

Further, the trust must not breach the *'rules against perpetuity'*. In brief, this means that private trusts cannot go on forever and must be capable of being wound up within set, finite time periods.

The essence of the rules against perpetuity is that even though trusts try to create property rights not just in the present but in the future, these future rights cannot be allowed to drift for an unlimited length of time – especially where the rights offered can be claimed only if the beneficiary meets a particular condition or contingency (very often relating to surviving to a particular age). This aspect is known as *'remoteness of vesting'* of the beneficial interest, and a person attempting to use a trust to benefit, say, 'my great-great-great-great-great-great-great-great-great-great-great-grandchildren provided they reach the age of 76' would obviously be unsuccessful, as far too long a time would pass before anyone could take an interest under the trust.

There is also a bar where a trust would otherwise keep its subject matter 'locked' within it for too long a time (ie longer than the maximum 'perpetuity period' which is currently set by law at 125 years) – the rule 'against inalienability of capital'. This would arise in a situation where the subject matter of the trust was such that it could not all be spent within the perpetuity period (eg, if the words of trust allowed only for the interest from the capital to be used and not the underlying capital itself). The logic behind this is that otherwise, too much of the capital in the economy might be taken out of circulation, and therefore lead to a reduction in economic activity generally.

Formalities

Lastly, for the trust to be 'express' there must be a successful 'declaration of trust'. What this means is that all of the above requirements must be met, together with any further formalities which there may be with regard to particular types of asset – certain types of asset require more 'hoops to be jumped through' than others. Land often has the greatest administrative requirements, particularly as it is one of the most valuable and durable of assets (see **Figure 3** below).

DECLARATION OF TRUST
- Three certainties
- Beneficiary principle
- Perpetuities

+ TRANSFER = EXPRESS TRUST

Figure 3: Creation of an express trust

Basic structures of express trusts

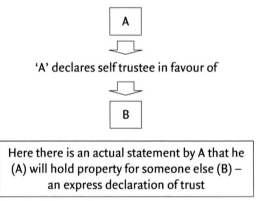

A

'A' declares self trustee in favour of

B

Here there is an actual statement by A that he (A) will hold property for someone else (B) – an express declaration of trust

Figure 4: Express declaration of self as trustee

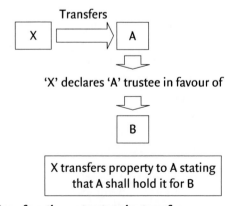

Transfers

X → A

'X' declares 'A' trustee in favour of

B

X transfers property to A stating that A shall hold it for B

Figure 5: Express declaration of another as trustee plus transfer

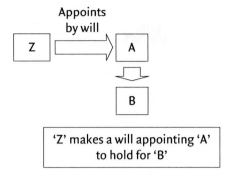

‘Z’ makes a will appointing ‘A’
to hold for ‘B’

Figure 6: Express trust by will

In each of **Figures 4** to **6** above there is a clear statement that a trust exists (declaration), but only in **Figure 5** is there any transfer of the property to a trustee.

This is because in the first example (**Figure 4**), A already owns the legal title to the property, so there is no need to transfer the legal title (responsibility, obligations) to anyone else; A can simply declare a trust over the beneficial interest (right to enjoyment, use) for B.

In **Figure 6**, because the appointment is made by a will, when Z dies his personal representative (A) effectively steps into Z's shoes and stands in for Z as his trustee until A transfers to B in accordance with the instructions in the will. There is no direct transfer by Z himself, but his death operates automatically to transfer Z's property into the trust as a 'holding' move, pending the carrying out of the terms of the will by the personal representative (or trustee), A.

CHAPTER 3

COMMON TYPES OF GENERAL EXPRESS TRUST

FIXED INTEREST TRUSTS

These are the more straightforward type of trust (see **Figures 4** and **5** in **Chapter 2** above), where both the identity of the beneficiaries and the shares which they are to take in the trust assets are clearly set out.

EXAMPLE

Nisha sets up (settles) a trust in which her brothers Mohammed and Syed are appointed trustees and the beneficiaries are named as being her two children, who are to take the trust assets in equal shares provided they each reach the age of 21 (see **Figure 1** below).

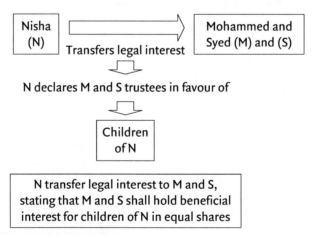

Figure 1: Creation of a fixed interest trust

SUCCESSIVE INTEREST TRUSTS

There is another type of fixed-interest trust, except here the aspect of the interest in enjoyment (or 'beneficial interest') is a little more involved, in that it is what we call 'postponed': some trusts allow for layers of beneficiaries, some to take different types of benefit from the asset. For example, some beneficiaries might take a benefit (or enjoyment) immediately; others might take a benefit only when the prior beneficiary has finished taking his enjoyment, very often upon that beneficiary's death.

This is known as a successive interest trust: the beneficiary with the immediate right to enjoyment (the 'life tenant') will have the right to take the income from the trust that the underlying capital produces (eg like the interest from the capital in a deposit account), but will not be allowed to use any of the capital itself. The next 'layer' of beneficiary (the 'remainderman') will then be entitled to take the underlying capital when the life tenant dies.

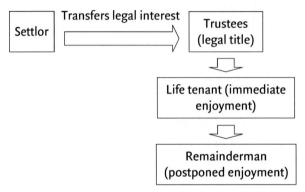

Figure 2: Successive interest trust

This is perhaps more easily understood if one imagines the various beneficiaries waiting at a bus stop. The person at the head of the queue is the beneficiary entitled to immediate enjoyment (also known as the 'beneficiary in possession'), whilst those behind him in the queue have their interests postponed until they, in their turn, are able to shuffle to the head of the queue.

DISCRETIONARY TRUSTS

Discretionary trusts, whilst still having trustees and beneficiaries, do not set out beneficial entitlements in any fixed way; rather, the question of who enjoys which trust property and in what shares is decided by the trustees, ie it is a matter for their discretion.

It therefore follows that the person making the trust (the settlor) should consider very carefully whom to choose as the trustees, as the settlor will be completely reliant on the trustees' judgement in order to put his wishes into effect.

Further, whilst the settlor may (and will have to) define a class or a type of people who might be chosen by the trustees to be beneficiaries (eg family members of the settlor), no one within such a class will have any right to benefit until they are in fact chosen by the trustees.

This is reminiscent of the National Lottery advertisement some years back, where a giant hand would appear from behind the clouds and descend to poke some unsuspecting member of the public on the nose to the accompaniment of a voice intoning, 'It could be you!'

CHAPTER 4

HOW DOES THE LAW REGULATE THE CREATION OF GIFTS AND TRUSTS?

We have seen that the regulation of the transfer of and creation of rights in valuable assets is generally thought to be a sensible precaution.

What sort of restrictions, then, are put in place on such activities? Naturally this is a somewhat open question, and therefore it is proposed to look at just a few, limited areas.

As mentioned above, certain assets are subject to a stronger requirement, or greater formalities, than others when it comes to their transfer, either in respect of making a gift or when creating a trust.

The three methods of correctly making (or 'completely constituting') a gift or an express trust during life are:

(a)   direct transfer to the beneficiary (gift);

(b)   transfer to a trustee for the beneficiary (trust);

(c)   declaration of trust with that person (settlor) as trustee (trust).

If a gift or trust is not correctly constituted, ie if the necessary formalities for that type of asset have not been complied with, then the attempted transfer or declaration of trust will not be effective.

It is not proposed to look at all the types of formality required for various assets. Suffice it to say that often, expressly stated words will be required as evidence of compliance with the necessary formalities, eg for a declaration of trust; and sometimes these words will need to be contained in a formal written and witnessed document (a 'deed'), at other times informal writing (eg a letter) will be sufficient and sometimes mere oral evidence will be enough.

This therefore has potentially serious consequences, as only someone who has paid or given some value will be allowed to enforce an incomplete 'gift' given to them by another.

Contrast that with the position of someone who has received a gift but given nothing in return; in this case if the formalities are incomplete, such a person (a 'volunteer') will not, generally, be allowed to enforce the gift in law.

As one might imagine, people generally might not be aware of these formal requirements and so errors may occur. If that does happen then the law will not allow the incorrectly performed (or constituted) gift to stand. However, the doctrine of equity, and its incorporation over time into the general law, means that to take account of these human frailties where there was no dishonest intention, the gift or trust might sometimes, in limited circumstances, be saved.

There are a number of such saving provisions, but two of the more prominent ones include:

(a)   cases where otherwise there would be an obvious and significant element of injustice (*unconscionability*); and

(b)   where the person making the gift or transfer has done everything possible to effect the gift and it has simply fallen down on administrative matters (eg for failure to register with the appropriate authority, such as Land Registry) – known as the '*every effort test*'.

CHAPTER 5

IMPLIED TRUSTS

INTRODUCTION

The methods examined in the preceding chapters represent the ways in which a person (the settlor) may choose to create a trust while he is still alive (an inter vivos settlement).

We have also seen, briefly, that a will may be used to make a gift or create a settlement upon a person's death.

Both of the above situations involve a clear (or 'express') statement as to the nature and terms of the proposed trust. Sometimes, however – and for a number of varying reasons – there may be no accompanying express words of trust to clarify the situation. It is in this rather limited area that we find *implied trusts*.

Implied trusts are just that – there are no express words to set out their terms and so the court has to imply the parties' intentions from the surrounding circumstances.

The situations that may give rise to an implied trust are quite tightly defined, and this has restricted the number of such trusts to two essential types: resulting trusts and constructive trusts.

RESULTING TRUSTS

A resulting trust is usually implied where there is some lack of information as to rightful beneficial ownership. For example, if a settlor creates a trust for a beneficiary but makes the benefit conditional ('contingent') upon that beneficiary surviving to, say, 21 years of age, and the beneficiary dies before satisfying the condition which would otherwise allow him to take the benefit absolutely (ie both the legal and beneficial interest), what happens?

If no further information is given (ie no details of any substitution in such an eventuality are set out) and the beneficiary dies before reaching the 'contingency' age, the trustees would be at a loss as to whom they should transfer the gift. In such a situation (or information gap) the only logical destination for the subject matter of the gift is to revert (or 'result') back to the estate of the original settlor (as if on a piece of elastic).

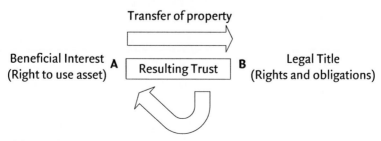

Figure 1: Resulting trust

As indicated above, a resulting trust may be implied in a situation where there is a lack of express information.

One such scenario which affects individuals is where money is provided by one party towards the purchase price of an asset which is then purchased in the name of another (ie the legal title). In the absence of express statements at the time as to how the money is to be regarded (ie whether a gift or a loan), the law is forced to fall back on certain presumptions, namely, of resulting trust and its competing alter ego *advancement* (ie gift). In such 'information gap' situations, then, one of these two presumptions will apply.

It should be emphasised that these presumptions apply only when there is nothing else upon which the court is able to base its decision (ie as to what was intended between the parties at the relevant time). As this is something of a 'last resort' position, it is easy to see that it may often work less than perfectly, although perhaps better than if there were no presumption at all (as the counter-argument would go).

The law as it stands currently decides which is the relevant presumption based on what might be described as patrician Victorian values if one were feeling generous, or outdated sexist nonsense if one were feeling less so. Recent legislation has attempted to make the operation of the presumptions more up-to-date but, at the time of writing, has not yet been implemented.

So how do the presumptions currently work? Essentially, if the provider ('donor') of the money is male and is providing the funds for someone to whom it might be supposed he owed some duty of maintenance (eg wife – not husband; female fiancée, not male fiancé; or dependent children) then a presumption of advancement would apply. This would mean that the donor would have no right to claim back the money provided; it would be treated as a gift to the recipient.

Contrast the above situation with the position where the donor is female and providing funds either to a male family member, or to her own children. In this case no moral imperative of maintenance or support is implied and the presumption is reversed, so that it is assumed a resulting trust was intended (ie that the money would be 'returned to sender'). Thus an accident of gender can impact upon property rights even today.

However, should any further information come to light, it may be used to remove (or 'rebut') the presumption.

Figure 2: Using a resulting trust to hide assets

This has further, interesting consequences, especially in cases where individuals have tried to hide their assets from the authorities or from their creditors by transferring the legal title to them into the name of a family member until the coast is clear (see **Figure 2**).

In such cases the donor would naturally wish to claim that he had not intended a gift but rather a resulting trust. However, to do so he would have to reveal evidence of his scheme (which, revealing an intent of illegality, the court would not ordinarily allow in evidence).

It has been established that, in the absence of express statements as to ultimate ownership, where the respective genders and surrounding circumstances gave rise to a presumption of resulting trust, the donor could recover her money despite the presence of a fraudulent motive for the transfer. This was based on the logical deduction by the court that because the presumption automatically worked in the donor's favour (ie due to accident of gender, etc), she did not have to give any further explanation for the transfer and therefore did not have to reveal formally to the court or otherwise rely upon her illegal motive. This therefore meant that she was allowed to reclaim the subject matter of the transfer as if it had been on a piece of elastic, brought about by the operation of the presumption of a resulting trust.

CONSTRUCTIVE TRUSTS

A constructive trust, unlike a resulting trust, is rooted more in elements of ideas of justice (or 'unconscionability'), such as when the legal owner of property tries to prevent (or deny) a claimant taking a seemingly justifiable equitable interest in it. For example, where the non legally-owning party has taken some action on behalf of the legal owner (eg paying part of the purchase price) as a result of being led to believe (by the party who has the legal interest) that he will obtain an interest (ie beneficial) in the property. This could lead to the court ordering that the legal owner holds the legal title on trust not just for himself, but for the other party in equity too.

However, it is important to note that constructive trusts are not ordered by a court solely because there has been perceived unconscionability – ie courts do not order constructive trusts 'out of thin air' – they arise by operation of law.

This means, first, that a constructive trust is imposed by the court as part of the operation of a set of rules or procedures (ie in accordance with established principles) and is not a creature of the judges' discretion. This procedural adherence is acknowledged in the classification of such trusts as being 'institutional'. Secondly, notwithstanding the above, the constructive trust is sometimes imposed in spite of (or at least regardless of) the intentions of the parties: however, what this actually means is that the court upholds the intentions of one of the parties against the other in situations where the formalities necessary to create an express trust are missing.

A constructive trust may therefore cover a number of different situations, including:

- trusts of family homes
- remedies against trustees who have made an unauthorised profit (which would include, at its most extreme, stealing from the trust)
- remedies against non-trustees (ie 'third parties' who are neither trustees nor beneficiaries) who have nevertheless either received trust property or assisted in its misuse.

CHAPTER 6

PRACTICAL USE OF TRUSTS AND CONTEXTS IN WHICH THEY COMMONLY OCCUR

Let us try to put this into context by looking at some common situations where people and trusts may come into contact (the micro-economic view).

DEATH AND TAXES

EXAMPLES

- Rob dies leaving a will in which he appoints the partners in the solicitors firm Sue, Grabbit & Run as his executors and trustees, and states that (after payment of debts and tax) he leaves everything to his wife, Ann (ie she is the sole beneficiary under his will). In this situation a trust exists in favour of Ann during the administration period of Rob's will (the period when all the debts, taxes and gifts are paid or distributed). When the executors/trustees eventually wind up the estate by making the final payment of what is left in Rob's estate to Ann, Ann will then have both the beneficial and legal titles, ie absolute ownership.

- If Rob had also included in his will a gift to his 8-year-old daughter, Hope, of the ring he had inherited from his own mother (ie goods or 'chattels'), a trust would also exist in Hope's favour – not just during the normal administration period but beyond. This extended period of trust would come about because Hope, being only 8 years of age, would not be old enough in the eyes of the law to enter into contracts generally, and flowing from that – and of particular relevance here – she would not be able legally to give a receipt for any money or assets handed to her by the executors. This is very important, because any executor would require a receipt from the person to whom he transferred assets as proof that they had been properly and fully paid out (ie to prevent the executor later being sued by a disgruntled or mischievous beneficiary who says she never received what she was due).

- If in his will Rob had left Hope a gift of land (ie including any buildings built on or fixed to it), this would represent a gift of realty (as opposed to personalty – the ring – in the example above); and again, the law does not allow those aged under 18 (minors) legally to own land, as the legal title involves responsibilities for carrying out obligations relating to the asset and a child could not be expected to undertake these properly. In such a situation, therefore, Rob's attempted outright gift of land to his minor child would be taken to be a declaration of trust over the land by Rob in favour of Hope, the trustees again being the executors named in Rob's will. The trustees would continue to hold the legal title to the land until Hope reached the age of 18, at which time she might demand the transfer of the legal title by its registration into her name.

- Meanwhile Fatma, a successful entrepreneur, decides that the substantial income she is making from her various business interests is taking her over the threshold for higher-rate income tax, and she is therefore suffering too much – in her view – 'unnecessary' tax. Fatma seeks tax-planning advice from her accountant, who advises her that this income could be 'shielded' by means of a trust. This would involve Fatma transferring the legal title to some of the income-producing assets (ie with all the responsibilities and control) to trustees; they, in turn, would hold the beneficial (or equitable) interest for Fatma's family members who, having a much lower initial income, would be likely to enjoy a lower rate of income tax, or possibly no tax at all. This would obviously mean that, overall, less tax would be payable, thus potentially freeing up greater net family income.

COHABITATION AND CO-OWNERSHIP

Whilst trusts have a significant role to play in the ownership of assets as between married couples and civil partners, there are also other particular rules that are used in conjunction that may sometimes alter the operation of the basic trust, especially when assets are divided upon divorce. For this reason, trusts will be considered in the context of unmarried cohabitees only for these purposes here.

Where cohabitees start out seemingly 'owning' land together, but with one person, whilst contributing to the purchase price (or being promised a share in the property somehow), not being officially registered as a legal owner, then trusts can be a very useful tool in order to decide the question of rightful beneficial entitlement (ie who gets to enjoy the assets/spend the money).

To the extent that there is no expressly agreed statement by the parties as to how the assets were intended to be owned (ie a declaration of an express trust) then, as we have seen previously, trusts may be taken by the courts to have been implied such that the legal owner will hold the beneficial interest in the land as trustee for the beneficiary.

If the non legally-owning party has made a direct contribution to the purchase price of the home then this might be sufficient to show a resulting trust (as considered above).

Alternatively, it might be possible for the court to infer a common intention constructive trust (if there is no express statement of the parties' intent) from the conduct of the parties. The law is not entirely clear as to everything that might be relied upon as giving rise to such a constructive common intent (ie the categories are still, to some degree, not yet conclusively decided); however, it is generally agreed that the strongest type of evidence is that of direct contributions to the purchase price, and it seems increasingly likely that indirect contributions, ie to household expenses, will suffice where they have had the effect of freeing up overall household income to enable the other party (ie the one in whose name the legal title is registered) to pay the mortgage. The trend is now to review the whole 'course of dealing' between the parties in order to decipher their common intention as to ownership, rather than narrowly focusing on direct contributions to the purchase price.

The actual amount (or share) awarded to the non legally-owning party will therefore depend upon the particular type of trust implied by the court.

CHAPTER 7

REGULATION OF THE ADMINISTRATION OF TRUSTS

Naturally, property ownership (in its wider layman's sense) and strict legal ownership need to be regulated both by the people directly involved (the individual parties) and by wider society as a whole. Without such regulation, the risk of inappropriate use or transfer of assets becomes significantly greater and might ultimately lead to a breakdown in business confidence and commerce in general.

For this reason society deems it necessary for the law to take an interest. This then gives rise to the further question, to what extent this is necessary or desirable (ie what law is required in the face of these potential risks).

Too little control may have no meaningful regulatory effect and might lead to market anxiety resulting from such uncertainty, whereas too much regulation may stifle (or even drive away) the market. Either extreme might, therefore, have a serious effect on the country's overall economy.

The law is able to assist, however, in terms of requiring trustees to meet certain obligations as regards the trust, and by providing remedies to aggrieved beneficiaries when they feel that a position of trust has been abused.

TRUSTEES' OBLIGATIONS

Trustees are under a number of established duties, both under common law and under statute. These range from investment duties and powers of delegation (ie passing their responsibilities on to an agent to act on their behalf – which are mainly statute-based) to more prosaic obligations (essentially common law-derived) such as keeping an eye on one another to make sure, say, that a potentially rogue trustee is not in a position to steal the trust fund.

REMEDIES AGAINST A TRUSTEE IN BREACH

If a trustee (or even someone not formally appointed as a trustee but who is nonetheless in a position of general financial responsibility, ie a fiduciary) should breach one or more of his duties, two principal categories of remedy are available:

(a)   a personal claim; or

(b)   a proprietary claim.

Personal remedies

These remedies are brought against the trustee personally, essentially hunting value (ie, merely requiring payment of the amount claimed without specific concern as to from which of the defendant's personal assets it is sourced). This may be contrasted with proprietary claims where the claimant is not seeking mere value but rather the recovery of his own property, whether it remains in its original form or has been converted into another type of asset. The advantage of a proprietary claim therefore lies in the claimant being able to say that the asset is his property rather than a debt owed to him (see below).

Personal remedies may be useful where the defendant (whether a trustee or someone not a party to the trust – a third party) has other assets of his own, sufficient to meet the claim, and:

(a)   the defendant, whilst owning these other assets personally, does not still hold any of the property subject to the trust (or any property which has been substituted for that original trust property);

(b)   the original trust property has fallen in value.

The main drawback to this personal type of claim is that if the trustee has very few assets of his own or is bankrupt, there is no value left to track down, thereby making it pointless to bring such a claim (ie 'throwing good money after bad').

A further drawback to a personal claim is that it may be subject to rules limiting the time period in which the claimant is allowed to bring a claim (these are known as rules of 'limitation', with the cut-off point usually being six years, unless the trustee was fraudulent or stole the asset, in which case there is no time limit).

Proprietary remedies

A proprietary remedy seeks to assert a trust in favour of the beneficiary, which has the effect of making the claim not a claim of value but rather a claim for the return of the beneficiary's own property (which has been subjected to a trust).

A proprietary claim is therefore potentially of greater use to a beneficiary where:

(a)   the defendant is bankrupt/insolvent;

(b)   the property has increased in value since it was taken (ie it allows the beneficiary to take a share of any profit or, alternatively, might allow the beneficiary to take a charge over the property, eg just as a mortgage lender takes a charge which it can enforce to protect the value of the loan it has provided);

(c)   the breach took place a long time ago, thus time-barring personal claims (proprietary claims not being subject to statutory limitation periods – see above).

In order to bring an equitable proprietary claim, ie for the beneficiary to claim back his own property, that property needs to be identified. This is often done by means of *tracing* rules (identifying the asset even though it has changed form, eg a picture which is sold and converted to cash and then that cash being used to buy a car).

Sometimes the property stolen from the trust may have been mixed in the bank account of the guilty trustee, or in the account of a third party, and various authorities are able to assist in allocating the money between the beneficiary and the owner of the mixed account.

Such rules depend upon the mind-set of that account-holder, ie whether he was innocent. Naturally, a trustee in breach of his duties will always be held accountable, but it may be that such a trustee has transferred the asset in question to a *third party*. The third party may actually be aware of the breach (or it may be held that in the circumstances he ought to have known of the wrongdoing, or at least ought to have been suspicious enough to have refused the gift). The third party will be treated similarly to a guilty-minded trustee and be deemed to be a *constructive trustee*.

Alternatively, the third-party recipient may have had no knowledge of any wrongdoing by the trustee transferring the asset, nor any reason to be suspicious. In this case, the third party is deemed to be an *innocent volunteer*, and therefore the rules applied in order to apportion ownership of the asset between the third party and the claimant are more generous to that third party in order to reflect his innocence.

CHAPTER 8

TRUSTS AND SOCIETY

Apart from enabling people to structure and rebalance their own individual financial positions, trusts also play an integral part both in the running of the national economy and in formal and informal social provision for the citizens of the state.

COMMERCE

Constructive trusts may be found in commercial settings, but they are much rarer there than they are in the setting of a family home.

In a commercial context the parties will usually demonstrate their mutually agreed intentions by entering into a formal and binding contract. Before this point is reached, each party is free to withdraw and thus 'pull the plug' if it cannot see a viable financial return, thereby keeping costs to a minimum. It is consequently rare for the courts to infer a constructive trust in this area before a contract is concluded, and it is therefore difficult to say at what point the courts will be prepared to find that a constructive trust has been implied by the parties' informal pre-contract arrangements.

However, a constructive trust may be more readily inferred where one party has acquired property in circumstances where it would be unfair ('inequitable') to allow that party to keep it. The most commonly accepted circumstance is that of a joint venture, where it has been informally agreed that one party will attempt to buy property whilst the other party will not act in the market but will hold back from competing, and in return that party will take a share of the property if the first party's bid is successful. Where that first party then ignores the 'deal', it may be found to be a constructive trustee in favour of the other in relation to any profits arising from the arrangement.

It is also possible for a resulting trust to occur, particularly where one party has made a loan to another for a particular purpose which is not then carried out. In those circumstances, one possible interpretation is that there is held to be a primary trust for the specified purpose; and when that fails, there is taken to be a secondary, resulting trust back to the lender. Another interpretation is that the lender always remains the beneficiary under the primary trust for the purpose, and so will be able to then go back and claim the unused money as its own property (ie a proprietary right). This proprietary remedy has the advantage of maintaining the lender's property as its own (beneficially) throughout, so that it is never at risk from the borrower's creditors (since it was never part of the borrower's own assets).

CHARITY

Look along the High Street of any town in the UK and you will see shops selling items to raise funds for a host of different charities, ranging from the alleviation of particular diseases to the protection of children and beyond. Indeed, these familiar charities represent only some of the vast range to which it is possible to contribute.

Why, you may wonder, are charities so popular? And indeed, when looking in some of their windows, how are some able to survive? The answer, as always, comes back to money – specifically tax.

An appropriately recognised charity will enjoy huge tax advantages, both at a national level (income/corporation tax) and also at the local level (business rates), especially when compared with the tax treatment of their commercial neighbours on the same High Street. Therefore, anyone who wishes to advance a cause close to their heart would be well-advised to see if their endeavour might be made to fit within the necessary charitable requirements.

Trusts for charitable purposes form a clearly distinct and separate part of the general law of trusts.

As mentioned above, such trusts may have considerable tax advantages, but they also enjoy further privileges as compared with private trusts. These include dispensations to do with the perpetuity rules, at least as far as not having to comply with the rule against inalienability of capital (the *remoteness of vesting rule* still applies).

Further, unlike private trusts, charities may take advantage of the *cy-près* doctrine, which effectively allows a failed charitable gift a 'second bite at the cherry'. When circumstances have made it impossible to carry out the purposes of the gift, eg where the original named charity has ceased to exist, where such purposes may be held to be broadly charitable then the subject matter of the gift may be reapplied for purposes as close as possible to the original one intended by the settlor (and could thus be applied for the benefit of a charity with similar aims which is still in existence). So, for example, if there had been a gift to the Motley Mutts Rescue Society, which has since ceased to exist, the gift might be applied for the benefit of the Dogs Trust, another charity that rescues homeless dogs. Contrast this with a failed private trust, where in such circumstances, the subject matter is taken to 'result' back to the settlor's estate.

You will also remember that when we looked at the fundamental requirements that need to be fulfilled for a private trust to exist, we saw that one of those crucial elements was the satisfaction of the beneficiary principle, ie that a trust must have distinct and clearly identifiable human beneficiaries, who are capable of enforcing its terms against the trustees should such terms not be adhered to or some other breach of duty or formality occur.

Charities, however, are not categorised as private but rather as public trusts, and for that reason they do not have beneficiaries in the sense mentioned above. They may therefore be framed so as to seek to satisfy an abstract purpose (eg for the welfare of animals), unlike non-charitable purpose trusts (see below).

In contrast, charitable trusts are enforced not by beneficiaries in the conventional sense but rather by the state (or 'Crown') via its senior law officer, the Attorney-General.

Flowing from this, charities, being categorised as public trusts, are required to meet a sufficient 'public benefit' requirement. The meaning of this phrase originally evolved from the case law, which effectively worked to define what would not amount to a public benefit: broadly, if there was a connection or link between the people who set up the charity and the people who were intended to benefit from it (unless the numbers of people likely to benefit, despite the connection, were so large so as to still be able to qualify as a section of the general public), a sufficient degree of public benefit would not be found.

The example of trusts for the advancement of animal welfare is a useful and intriguing signpost in determining the question of what amounts to *sufficient public benefit*.

It has been decided, in this context, that such gifts for the benefit and protection of animals:

> tend to promote and encourage kindness towards them, to discourage cruelty ... and thus to stimulate humane and generous sentiments in man towards the lower animals, and by these means promote feelings of humanity and morality generally, repress brutality and thus elevate the human race. (Re Wedgewood)

However, in another case (*Re Grove-Grady*), where the gift was to provide land to be a 'refuge for the preservation of all animals, birds or other creatures not human ... so as to ... be safe from molestation or destruction by man', it was held that there was insufficient public benefit because:

> [t]he one characteristic of the refuge is that it is free from the molestation of man, while all the fauna within it are free to molest and harry one another. Such a purpose does not ... afford any advantage to animals that are useful to mankind in particular, or any protection from cruelty to animals generally. It does not denote any elevating lesson to mankind.

It may be seen that this principle of public benefit is itself a relative concept and must be applied even where it leads to a contest between competing public benefits. It has been held (amongst other considerations) that a purported charitable gift in order to oppose the vivisection of animals should fail not because there is no public benefit in this, but rather because the public benefit of this 'kindness' to animals is outweighed in the circumstances by the competing public benefit that is provided by such medical research.

The old case law allowed for recognition of four broad categories of charitable trust:

- trusts for the relief of poverty
- trusts for the advancement of education
- trusts for the advancement of religion
- trusts for other purposes beneficial to the community.

It is this last category that has been replaced by a new statutory list of purposes in this regard, which has the effect of continuing to recognise as charitable purposes those previously so recognised under the old case law (whether or not expressly referred to in the new statutory list) whilst preventing new purposes being recognised unless they fall within one of the new 'approved' categories set out in the statute.

(Note that in the past, many private schools were set up on a charitable basis. There has been some discussion recently as to whether this traditional set-up has provided a sufficient benefit to the public at large for these schools to justify their privileged status. For this reason, many such institutions have sought to forge greater links with their local communities and local state schools, in order to ensure that they fulfil this somewhat nebulous concept.)

UNINCORPORATED ASSOCIATIONS AND TRUSTS FOR A PURPOSE

These form perhaps the most useful and prevalent example of a number of different categories of case in which, despite the fact that the beneficiary principle is not met, the courts will nevertheless allow enforcement of such trusts as 'concessions to human weakness and sentiment'. This list includes:

- trusts for the erection or maintenance of graves and monuments
- trusts for saying masses
- trusts for the maintenance and care of specific animals (eg for a loved pet once the owner has died)
- trusts for miscellaneous purposes
- trusts for the benefit of unincorporated associations.

It is not proposed to deal with any of the above apart from the last category, as this is of greatest general applicability.

Unincorporated associations

Again, as with the consideration of charities above, the beneficiary principle raises its ugly head. What is an unincorporated association? Essentially it is a club – a grouping of individuals who, whilst having common interests or ideals, have not gone so far as to organise themselves and register as a company. If they had gone that far, it would confer the advantage of giving the association a distinct and separate legal personality, meaning that assets could be held in the name of the company and that the association could sue (and be sued) in that company name.

This therefore highlights one of the potential problems with an unincorporated association – in a legal sense it does not exist, and therefore it cannot hold any assets (or, indeed, do anything) in the association's name. This means that if someone wants to make a gift to their favourite unincorporated association (eg their local naturist club), they will fall foul of the beneficiary principle (remember, gifts as well as trusts – charitable ones aside – must satisfy this requirement).

Nevertheless, clubs (unincorporated associations) do exist in the real world, and seem to be able both to receive and to spend money, so how is this circle squared? As with so much in life, it involves a little legal side-stepping.

As mentioned above, an unincorporated association is not itself a legal person and so cannot own property. Over the years (and most notably in *Re Recher*) the courts have come to interpret attempted gifts to such an association as being an indirect gift to the association's members (human beings) by way of increasing the association's funds, but also subject to the club's rules (the 'glue' which binds the people in the association together is the club rules or the contract between the members of the club). This would prevent an individual member from taking out his share of the gift and leaving.

Such gifts are also subject to the rules against perpetuity (discussed in **Chapter 2** above), specifically the rule against *inalienability*, ie that capital should not be tied up indefinitely otherwise the economy will eventually grind to a halt.

Re Recher gets around this potential problem of inalienability of capital, provided that the members of the club are allowed by their rules to end the association and divide its assets between them (note they do not actually have to do that, just be allowed to do it if they wish). That is, the contract between the members allows for the possibility of ending the association and making a final payment out to them so that the funds will not be 'doomed' to be locked up for eternity.

Trust for a purpose

Gifts on trust may also be made for a purpose generally. We have seen (above) that such trusts might satisfy the necessary requirements to achieve charitable status, but many purpose trusts do not meet such requirements and therefore are not classed as charitable. How are these treated?

These are collectively known as '*Denley*' trusts after the leading case on them, and are applicable where there is an express declaration of a trust for a purpose. In such cases the courts look to see whether the purpose will provide a 'direct and tangible' or real benefit to identifiable people who would themselves be capable of enforcing the trust, thereby satisfying the beneficiary principle.

This is particularly useful where, for example, the trust might otherwise satisfy the requirements of a charitable trust but falls down on the 'sufficient public benefit' requirement. The *Denley* construction (as set out above), although criticised in some quarters for its then radical approach, has been followed subsequently, notably in *Re Lipinski*. This case further allows for a 'twin-track' approach, allowing for a *Re Recher* contractual interpretation (see above) to be considered as an alternative to *Re Denley*. Indeed, one possible advantage to the *Re Recher* interpretation is that if a gift is made to an association and stated to be for a purpose, the stated purpose is taken to be a mere motive for the gift and is not held to be binding. This therefore allows the members to spend the amount of the gift as they wish (within their association's rules), whereas under a *Re Denley* interpretation such a purpose is held to be binding.

Further, there might be a gift made on trust for a non-charitable association/club for a non-charitable purpose which does *not* benefit the members (eg a gift on trust to the naturist club for the purpose of furthering and promoting the fashion industry). This involves a purpose which benefits people, but the benefit might be said to be too intangible or remote to give them standing or allow them to go to court to enforce the trust. This would therefore not succeed.

BANKING AND FINANCE

On a macro-economic scale, a key factor in banks' decisions whether or not to lend to businesses (or generally) is the level of risk attached, ie the chance that the bank will get its money back (it is hoped with some profit too). In assessing this risk, banks wish to retain as much control over the lending situation as they possibly can.

Naturally one of the safest ways (relatively) for a bank to lend is for the amount which it advances on loan to be secured (ie 'mortgaged' or 'charged') against a valuable asset of the borrower – usually the asset (often land) which the borrower intends to purchase with the proceeds of the loan. This means that should the borrower not meet the repayment terms of the loan, the lending bank is entitled to force a sale of the ('mortgaged') asset on which the loan is secured, and keep sufficient of the sale proceeds to pay itself back before giving any money left over to the original borrower.

However, in business it is not always practical, or desirable, for a mortgage or charge to be taken over an asset. In practical terms, if an asset is subject to such a charge then the permission of the charge-holding lender (ie 'chargee' or 'mortgagee') will be required before the borrowing business is able to sell or otherwise deal with that asset. This may have a serious effect on business efficiency when deals need to be put together and completed quickly. If this were the general situation then commerce would slow down, and this would therefore adversely affect the economy.

For this reason, banks recognise that not all of their lending will be of the secured (or 'mortgaged') type; and indeed they partly welcome this, as it enables them to charge a higher interest rate due to the greater risk of their possibly not getting their money back. However, as mentioned above, banks are (usually) naturally 'risk-averse', and therefore try to retain as much control as possible over their lending.

One of the main ways of exerting this control is through the lending contract made between the bank and the borrower. In this contract the lender will be in a position of relative economic strength and can set out the terms of the deal – 'take it or leave it'. If the borrower wants the money, he will have to accept these terms in order to be able to proceed with the loan. One of the most common and crucial of these terms (to the bank) is that any money advanced should be used by the borrower only for the purpose previously declared to the bank in the loan documentation (ie a purpose which the bank has 'vetted' and upon which it has assessed the risks).

Remember that here we are talking about a non-secured loan, so that if the borrower defaults there is no particular asset the bank can sell in order to recover the amount it has loaned. If the borrower defaults on the repayments, the bank will have to sue him in court (on the basis of the lending contract between them) and obtain a 'judgment debt'.

This type of claim is known as a *personal claim*, where the claimant is merely seeking value from the defendant to the amount of the debt due. In this case the claimant is not concerned about the source of the money in satisfaction of the debt, just as long as the debt is satisfied.

This, although inconvenient, is still not a big problem for the bank where the borrower has enough other assets overall that he can sell enough of them to pay back the bank. The real problem occurs when the borrower's total assets are less than the value of his total debts – this describes (very broadly) an insolvency (businesses) or bankruptcy (individuals) situation.

In this situation, the law does not allow one lender to 'muscle-in' to recover all the value of its own debt ahead of anyone else, as this would be unfair to all of the other lenders (or 'creditors') of the borrower. Instead, the law applies strict rules regarding which creditors come first in the queue when it comes to dividing up what few assets the borrower does have. Secured creditors (such as mortgagees – see above) are in a strong position because they are allowed to sell the asset over which they have taken security (the mortgage or charge) in order to recover the amount owed to them, with any surplus this time not going directly back to the borrower but rather back into the pot, for distribution amongst the other creditors by the person appointed for this process (either a *receiver* or *trustee in bankruptcy*).

The remaining *unsecured* creditors would be left to fight over what was left, except that the law sets out the order of priority for repayment:

- 'Preferred creditors' are first in the queue, These include, amongst others, the Government, in the shape of the taxman (HMRC), as well as the receiver itself.
- The remaining creditors rank equally with one another. Thus, if the borrower owed, say, £10,000 in total to all the remaining creditors together, but had only £1,000 of assets remaining for distribution (after the costs of this process had been deducted), each of the remaining unsecured creditors would get back only 10% of the amount it had been owed originally by the borrower.

As you can see, an unsecured lender could end up in this free-for-all scramble for the crumbs left over from the borrower's total assets, and naturally such a risk might deter banks from undertaking this type of lending (which we have seen is a very helpful way of keeping the wheels of the economy 'oiled'). One of the ways around this (which has the effect of giving greater protection to banks and lenders generally) involves the use of trusts: where in the unsecured lending contract it is stipulated that the loan must be used only for a particular purpose (ie the one already disclosed to the lender and approved by it as a safe risk), the borrower is taken to be a trustee (ie acting in an administrative capacity) for the lender rather than having the beneficial rights of enjoyment to spend as he wants.

If the borrower does not use the loan for the appropriate purpose then the lender may bring a *proprietary claim* (not personal this time) in which it asserts that the asset held by the borrower is not in fact the borrower's but is held by him as trustee for the lender, ie the lender 'traces' the money into whoever's hands it has gone and claims that money back as its own money.

Alternatively, it might be said that the fact that the money was originally loaned on trust for a particular purpose means that if that purpose is not carried out, that trust will fall away but will be replaced by a secondary trust – ie a resulting trust, see **Chapter 5** – which has the effect of 'pinging' the beneficial interest back to the lender.

There is a very important distinction which flows from the use of a trust here; it means that when the borrower misapplies the loan, the money he is misapplying is not held to be his own but rather – beneficially (or in equity) – still that of the lender. This therefore means, on the insolvency or bankruptcy of the borrower, that the amount of the loan is not taken to be part of the borrower's general assets for distribution to his unsecured creditors, and thus the lender is protected (to a certain degree) from the free-for-all scramble described above.

PENSIONS

Over the last 25 years or more, greater emphasis has been placed by successive governments on a move away from reliance by citizens on the state retirement pension towards a privately-funded, individually-tailored alternative.

It has become evident in the last few years that we, as a nation, can no longer afford to provide the same level of state pension provision as was offered before (in real terms, ie as to what could be bought with it, the supposed golden age being the 1970s and 1980s).

How, you might ask, is it not possible for the state to provide adequate pensions when private pension schemes are said to be a solution? Surely a pension is a pension?

The answer lies in the method of funding. In the UK, since the inception of the state retirement pension under Lloyd George's Liberal Government 100 years ago, payments to pensioners have been (and still are) funded out of current tax receipts year on year – there is no underlying capital pot (or 'endowed fund') to produce income to use for this purpose.

This means that the workers of today pay for the pensions of today's pensioners (who had themselves paid for the pensions of pensioners when they were working, and so on). If the economy is doing well then more money (in terms of tax receipts) is available to pay pensions (as well as all the other commitments of government spending). When the economy is doing less well (or there are significant changes in the make-up of the working population) then there is less money available to go towards paying pensions or anything else.

A private pension is funded differently. It is essentially a personal investment product solely for the ultimate enjoyment of the individual paying into it, and is funded largely by the income produced from the capital fund which builds up over the years as the individual pays into his own pot. Therefore, the longer the period over which deposits are made (and the larger the deposits), generally (subject to sensible investment decisions) the larger the pension payments on retirement.

There is a hybrid of the two known as a company's or industry's *final-salary pension scheme*, which used to be offered both by local and central governments to their employees and also by larger businesses. These schemes effectively involved workers (after completing a minimum number of years' service with the organisation) being guaranteed a pension based on a percentage of their final salary at retirement, such percentage being linked to the number of years worked in that organisation. The funding of this would depend upon the organisation, but might involve a certain requirement for contribution by the individual together with a further top-up by the company itself. The idea was that there would be no individual pot but the underlying total fund would produce income to pay for current pensions. However, as tax concessions have reduced, businesses have found this to be an increasingly expensive means of providing for their employees' retirement (indeed some large firms have seen their profits eroded by billions of pounds in trying to make up a shortfall where pension investments have fallen) and there are now very few such schemes available to new members.

With the last two pension types – private pensions and final-salary pension schemes – a trust is the medium by which the individual payments are accumulated and held over time, with trustees being legally responsible for the proper administration of the trust (although, interestingly, not *necessarily* responsible for losses suffered to the trust fund capital investments). The great advantage here is that the legal ownership of the trust fund is taken out of the hands of the company, so if the company becomes insolvent or otherwise ceases to trade then the pension funds should (theoretically) be safeguarded for the beneficiaries, ie the current and future pensioners.

INVESTMENTS

Trusts also have a large part to play in terms of investment in the economy. It has, of course, always been open to investors to put their money into individual investments, eg company shares, and to spread their money around between different commercial enterprises in order to spread the risk, so that if one investment does badly they will not necessarily lose all their wealth. Since the early 20th century, more and more people have been looking to invest their surplus cash not just in deposit accounts but in the stock market too, the latter having usually, over the medium to long term, outperformed (on average) the returns offered by banks and building societies. However, if a person has only a small sum to invest then this process of spreading the risk (or diversification) is more difficult, as many investments require a minimum level of financial commitment.

Since the 1930s the unit trust has been available as a financial product. Such trusts are legally owned by trustees, with a fund manager who will invest the capital for the benefit of the beneficiaries (ie the holders of the individual unit trusts). This has allowed small investors to avoid 'putting all their eggs in one basket' by operating in one or more different trust funds with different objectives (eg capital growth, income growth or a balance of the two), different levels of risk and in different market sectors or types of company. This has allowed people to spread the risk of investment with even relatively small sums of capital.

Such trusts have also been utilised by large investment vehicles (such as pension funds – see above) as a means for them to diversify their investments in particular markets more cheaply (and trustees are under various duties to ensure diversification of their fund investments). One of the consequences of such large investors becoming involved is that it tends to amplify (and sometimes distort) underlying market trends. For example, many institutional investors utilise computer programs which will automatically sell out of a share or other investment when a particular price is reached, or when that investment falls into the bottom, say, 10% of its projected market range (eg the FTSE 100 Share Index). When this happens the initial movement in the share price is then further magnified by the various investment houses automatically piling out of that share or other investment which, in a demand-driven market, will force the price down still further.

It is the lack of an immediate human presence (or common sense if you prefer) that has contributed to the severity of market crashes in recent years. Indeed, this has come to be recognised by the major global stock exchanges, which have nearly all introduced various forms of 'circuit-breaker' or 'cooling-off' periods should such circumstances of likely extreme negative volatility be detected. These systems act to prevent the market being forced to further extreme lows by any market panic.

SUMMARY OF USES OF TRUSTS IN SOCIETY TO PROTECT AND PRESERVE THE RIGHTS AND ASSETS OF INDIVIDUALS

As has been seen above, trusts are used in society in a number of different ways which we all encounter in one form or another every day.

Commerce

Resulting and constructive trusts (and proprietary estoppel – a close relation to constructive trusts, being founded upon the notion of righting *unconscionability*) attempt to protect investors when commercial ventures fail.

Charitable purpose trusts

These seek to perpetuate such particular types of 'good works' as are recognised under the current law. Whilst they enjoy particular advantages, ie as to tax treatment and the fact that they do not need to satisfy the beneficiary principle or the perpetuity rule against the inalienability of capital, they must display sufficient public benefit, which can be problematic.

Unincorporated associations and trusts for a purpose

Often found in the context of sports or 'social clubs', these both attempt creatively to circumvent the need to satisfy the beneficiary principle, or at least to demonstrate that such principle has been satisfied in novel ways (eg, unincorporated associations may use contract law to overcome some of the inherent difficulties with the strict application of the pre-existing trust law).

Banking and finance

Trust-based proprietary claims are used to protect a lender's assets on the insolvency/ bankruptcy of the borrower.

Pensions

The very existence of such vital institutions of both the welfare state and of private welfare provision would be impossible without the availability of the trust.

Investments

Again, trusts are fundamental to the smooth operation of the capitalist system, not only in terms of allowing small investors to have access to the means to spread their risk more effectively, but also in the basic nature of share dealing. Any instruction to a stockbroker to purchase or sell shares on the investor's account which would give rise to the stockbroker holding those shares (for however short a time) on behalf of a client as his nominee (ie so that the investor would be legally entitled to direct the stockbroker as to where to transfer the legal title), would give rise to a trust situation.

Conclusion

It is therefore hoped that these brief chapters have demonstrated the fundamental nature of trusts in our daily functioning both as individual citizens and as part of society as a whole.

Index